MUSICOLOGY AND PERFORMANCE

From left: Arthur Rubinstein and Paul Henry Lang.

Musicology and Performance

PAUL HENRY LANG

Edited by

Alfred Mann and George J. Buelow

Yale University Press

New Haven & London

Designed by James J. Johnson and set in Electra Roman type by The Composing Room of Michigan, Inc.
Printed in the United States of America by BookCrafters, Inc., Chelsea, Michigan.

Library of Congress Cataloging-in-Publication Data

Lang, Paul Henry, 1901–1991
    Musicology and performance / Paul Henry Lang ; edited by Alfred Mann and George J. Buelow.
        p.   cm.
    Consists of published and unpublished essays.
    Contents: On musicology — New thoughts on old music — Music in twentieth-century civilization — On performance practice.
    ISBN 0-300-06805-0 (alk. paper)

    1. Music—History and criticism. 2. Musicology.   3. Performance practice (Music).   I. Mann, Alfred, 1917–   II. Buelow, George J.
ML60.L2362   1997
780—dc21   96-39636

A catalog record for this book is available from the British Library.

The paper in this book meets the guidelines for permanence and durability of the Committee on Production Guidelines for Book Longevity of the Council on Library Resources.

10   9   8   7   6   5   4   3   2   1

Contents

Contents

Music in Twentieth-Century Civilization

On Performance Practice

Foreword

It is a great pleasure, indeed a high honor for me, to provide some preliminary remarks to this collection of essays by Paul Henry Lang. As the one who occupied from 1970 to 1976—very much in respectful awe—Professor Lang's office and chair upon his retirement from academic duties at Columbia University, I feel particularly close to the befitting and timely project undertaken by Alfred Mann and George J. Buelow. But it is not so much my recollection of the Dodge Hall office, consecrated by eternal cigar smoke, but rather my continuing personal exchange with this unforgettable mentor and fatherly friend, for well over two decades and until the final months of his life, that allows me to sense in this volume of collected essays a genuine memorial.

On the occasion of his eightieth birthday, Paul Henry Lang received a *Festschrift* of contributions by his students, colleagues, and friends. Its title, *Music and Civilization* (New York, 1984), refers to his imposing first book, *Music in Western Civilization* (New York, 1941), which left a lasting mark on American musicology and helped—at least to some extent, even if without proper recognition—to pave the way for what is nowadays often heralded as "the new musicology," musical scholarship paying uncompromisingly close attention to contextual matters of all kinds, be it direct, indirect, implied, or hypothetical. Lang, who abhorred narrow-minded specialization, did not merely tolerate a pluralism of methods, approaches, and thematic orientation; he provoked and demanded it. Though he could hardly have predicted the wide spectrum of American musicological discourse that has emerged in recent decades, he welcomed and applauded it. Moreover, he was intensely aware of, and happy about, the fact that he had been able to contribute to shaping the scene.

As the essays in this volume demonstrate, Paul Henry Lang wielded a pen that liked broad strokes; he had very little patience for footnotes and had a clear leaning towards contemporary issues, themes of general interest, even current affairs. As a musicologist-critic, he felt inclined and obliged to address a general audience. He was among the very few music historians who liked and never lost the larger public. For quite some time the most influential advocate of musicology, he almost single-handedly kept the discipline in the public eye, not minding in the least when he seemed to lose touch with some of those from the deeper trenches of musicological research.

Festschriften in honor of prominent colleagues, as well as collections of essays by eminent scholars published during their lifetime, have become common fare. It happens much more rarely that the selected writings of a renowned musicologist are deemed deserving of a posthumous edition. Lang's fascinating, brilliantly formulated and often argumentative essays, no matter whether dealing with musical scholarship as such, great composers, modern music and musical phenomena, or controversial stands on performance practice, present a deliberate antithesis to musicological research papers. Hence, their primary value lies much less in the scholarly detail than in the blend of a formidable musical and cultural-historical knowledge with the articulation of a boundless passion for individual musicological style. As of late, subjective and even opinionated voices seem to be gaining more ground in matters concerning musicology and contemporary musical culture, Paul Henry Lang's lifelong endeavor. Yet, with its literary elegance, his musicological prose will surely remain a challenging model for the discipline.

CHRISTOPH WOLFF, *Harvard University*

Introduction

Paul Henry Lang (1901–1991) was the first scholar to be called to an American university in order to establish a formal curriculum in musicology. Throughout his distinguished career he regarded this fact with modesty, recalling the pioneer labors of Oscar Sonneck and the other founding fathers of American music scholarship. But no one before him had held the titular appointment, and not until it was under his guidance did musicology come of age in the United States.

The young Hungarian who came to this country on a Rockefeller Foundation Fellowship in 1928 had studied in Budapest with Kodály, in Heidelberg with Kroyer, and in Paris with Pirrò. An experienced orchestral bassoonist, he had served as assistant conductor of the Budapest Opera and, during his studies for a literature degree at the Sorbonne, as assistant editor of the *Revue musicale*. While holding his early American appointments at Vassar and Wells College, he completed his doctorate at Cornell. But it was characteristic of the prevailing situation that his American mentor, Otto Kinkeldey, still represented a generation of specialists who initially had to go to Europe for a musicological career, and that Kinkeldey's principal appointment at Cornell was that of university librarian.

The very term *musicology* met with bewilderment and even suspicion in those days. During Paul Henry Lang's long tenure at Columbia, it rose to distinction. It finally became an indispensable household word on the American scene, but it continued to change its connotations. Until his last year, which was his ninetieth, Paul Henry Lang remained its guardian. In one of his last letters he said that he wondered whether he had become what Hindemith once called the learned Music Curator of the Metropolitan Museum—"ein Museumstück." But his vast historical command had kept him and his devotion to scholarship young.

The young generation, too, remained a major part of his audience. This is a fact that reflects the immense vitality and freshness of his thought, his ever-readiness to address new issues, and his remarkable dexterity in applying historical perspective to the complexities of a modern world. He relished rather than suspected them. He was at home in changing circumstances, no matter how seemingly confusing the innovations were.

Lang had set aside for his waning years a major project that would present a summary view of musicology. It would be marked, he said, by a revolutionary approach: it would begin and end with *music*—he wanted to be sure that the reader knew "how to approach a work of art before worrying about the Pythagorean comma." He worked on it with unflagging spirit under the duress of failing eyesight; but when he arrived at the section on performance practice, he recognized the greater need—the chapter began to grow into a book in itself, and he decided to revise his plan.

Performance practice had become musicology's greatest liability. The discipline experienced a totally new popularity, impelled by newly won skills in instrument making and the persuasive thrust of the recording industry. What at the turn of the nineteenth century had been a quest of rediscovery born of the Romantic spirit saw a new rediscovery in the mid-twentieth century. It seemed to involve everything but the cautionary voice, and Lang sensed an obligation that was truly his.

The stand he took is not easily appreciated in its full meaning. At the height of his career, the preeminent American musicologist, a founding member of the American Musicological Society, President of the International Musicological Society, and long-time editor of *The Musical Quarterly* had also become the chief music critic of the *New York Herald Tribune*—a move that must be viewed not so much from the perspective of American as from that of European journalistic tradition. The example of such scholars as Edward Dent and Alfred Einstein comes to mind. Communication with the audience of a more widely educated and greatly enlarged musical public, presented from the vantage point of authoritative scholarship, had become an issue in mid-century America.

Thus it was in his role as the country's leading music critic that he took on the discussion of performance practice, and though he dealt with the events of the day, there is nothing ephemeral in his writing. He spoke with a command of subject matter and from a background that no one else could muster. Yet what had grown into a plan for a book was destined to remain a torso. The new chapters on performance practice were to be his last, written in almost complete blindness, and he left a final letter addressed to the editors of this volume in which he himself formulated the design of his collected essays, a book in which his unpublished work could appear in print.

The editorial task, which in past months and years had had the benefit of extended exchanges with the author, was as gratifying as it was humbling. An outline structure for the choice of essays offered itself readily; formed by the story of the book originally intended, it moves from the broader concepts of the musicologist's calling to their detailed application in informed performance. It was the direct impression of performance that again and again sparked the scholar's new thoughts on old music—the title for this volume's second part is taken from one of his journal articles—for Lang, equally at home in all phases of music history, was forever involved in the current musical scene. His all-embracing historical perspective is evident from the very title of *Music in Western Civilization*, the book that made his name famous. The heading for the third part, therefore, makes conscious reference to Lang's chef-d'oeuvre. The historian was equally committed to music present and past, but he never failed to engender a larger context. Asked on one occasion to speak on the subject "Music and the Humanities," he gave the disarming answer: "But music *is* one of the humanities."

Nevertheless, this basic structure represented entirely different aspects of the author's work and greatly varied challenges of editorial procedure. Throughout his life, Lang treated musicology as a branch of the art of letters, and he safeguarded the integrity of scholarship as much as the principle of impeccable scholarly prose. The grace of his literary style stands as a paradigm for the profession. But the journalistic assignment—which he relished—demanded an orientation of its own.

In his old age, the domains of the man of letters and of the critic of current events began to merge, and the resulting changes in style rendered the problem of editorial review the more intense the more the author became isolated in the tragic situation in which he could no longer read his own writing.

It goes without saying that the essays in this book which were taken from printed sources called for a presentation that strictly followed the given text (with the exception of adjustments whose slight nature would render detailed accounting pedantic). It would, in fact, have meant tampering with the nature of Lang's work to assume a critical attitude toward his well-known habit of quoting from memory. With gusto he used to relate the almost panic-stricken reaction of an editor to whom he had delivered his copy for a requested article—"Wo sind die Fussnoten?" It was not the bibliographical detail that mattered to him, but a summary of ideas which was apt to suggest to the reader a broad literary perspective. Conversely, his essays on performance practice contained topical references and names that to the present-day reader are no longer of primary significance and whose inclusion would merely have obscured the exposition of principles.

It was generally more difficult, however, to deal with the posthumous publication of these last manuscripts. When Lang decided to change his plan for a book on musicology to one on performance practice, he began with a preface that he later rewrote and expanded to the extent that it tended to overlap with the other portions. One of the subsequent versions bears his annotation "Preface or End," but both this and another form of the text remained incomplete, and it becomes clear that he was finally no longer sure what he had already put on paper. The editorial task here was to collate and reapportion. Yet at the time he wrote the original preface, he also drafted an outline for the complete work, documented on the inscriptions of folders that contained individual sections. A number of them were evidently rejected by him and intentionally left incomplete. In others, it was time that overtook the author's labors, but he himself expressed the view that what he might have to leave as a fragment would reflect a unified concept.

There is a special caveat of whose message we are ever aware in Paul Henry Lang's work. He was once called upon to take on a task similar to ours, the edition of Alfred Einstein's *Essays on Music* issued by W. W. Norton in 1962, and in deep respect and affection we borrow these words from his introduction:

> There is among laymen a rather widespread notion that the scholar's thoughts are cold in contrast to the artist's warmth of feeling, and for that reason inferior. But they forget that the scholar's thoughts likewise spring from his experience, from his brushes with the world and with himself. These essays are the fruit of their author's inner life, of his mind and heart together.

ALFRED MANN, *The Eastman School of Music,*
University of Rochester
GEORGE J. BUELOW, *Indiana University*

On Musicology

Musicology and Musical Letters

he gradual expansion of the field of musical knowledge has proceeded at an accelerated pace during the twentieth century, and the time is already past when one-man histories of music of the traditional type could attempt to bring the reader into contact with the prime essentials of all phases of music history. It is not surprising, therefore, that those who nurture the hope of making such studies popular in the honorable sense of the term should have turned their attention to forms of summarization which are from the outset deliberately eclectic in design and limited in scope. Still, this enforced methodological alteration has not simplified the task but aggravated its difficulties. There is less than the usual measure of agreement as to which parts of the whole can be regarded as essential, which subsidiary. It is not the conquests of scholarship that are obscure; rather, it is that confused and active battlefront along which knowledge is advancing and from which the smoke of conflict has not yet cleared. The intellectual interests of our time demand an immediate report on what is going forward in that disturbed area.

From *Musik und Verlag: Karl Vötterle zum 65. Geburtstag*, ed. Richard Baum and Wolfgang Rehm (Kassel: Bärenreiter, 1968)

To give us the latest news from the front, special interpreters have become necessary, and the popularization of knowledge, in this sense, has become a new profession.

A respectable place in literature has long been held by certain books written to arouse and satisfy the interest of the general public in the natural sciences. Their authors had firsthand acquaintance with the intricacies of their subjects while understanding the working of untrained minds. They have often been masters of a literary style, of simplicity and restraint befitting their high theme. On the other hand, many men of learning are convinced that the results of their investigations can never penetrate the mind of that singularly obtuse person, the "general reader." The very attempt to make scholarly findings intelligible to the professionally untrained savors of the charlatan to some of those who dwell on the Olympian heights of scholarly research. It is allowed that *l'oeuvre de vulgarisation* was not despised by some of the giants of former days—Galilei, Buffon, Faraday, to name only a few—but it is claimed that the world of scholarship, within which musicology is included, is now so specialized that such an approach is no longer possible. It is a corollary to the subdividing of scholarship that the exponent of one discipline becomes a "general reader" for his colleagues in another department. On the other hand, scholars who have strikingly distinguished themselves in one field often believe that their knowledge extends to all others. Regrettably, music is a frequent victim; philosophers, physicists, psychologists, even economists, and others like to invade its territory, and before they know it, they are engaged in the fundamental *artistic* questions of music.

But everything is relative, of course. No Nobel laureate scientist can outdo the Tasmanian aborigine as a naturalist, for the latter knows the way of every living thing about him from the standpoint of the practicing naturalist in search of a dinner. The physicist's measuring instruments, no matter how accurate, cannot equal the *artistic* ear of a good musician. If musicologists intent on their researches leave undone the interpretative part of their work, they must not be surprised when others less fully equipped attempt it. Until the scholar dares to give a lead, the masses of material collected by him and his confreres must either be a dead weight of neglected scholarship or dangerous material in the hands of the unskilled. If those savants are right who assume as inevitable their own unintelligibility to a public all too ready to accept their dicta, then our intellectual outlook is gloomy indeed. As knowledge advances and becomes more specialized, it will be accessible only to an ever-narrowing circle. In the end each investigator will be understandable only to himself; he will leave no scholarly heir, and the whole system of knowledge must collapse. Fortunately, such an eventuality is based on a fantastic fallacy.

Between "pure" and "applied" scholarship the arbitrary distinction that still exists in many minds can hardly continue to be maintained. For one thing, the practical application of the findings of musical scholarship has made possible in our musical life changes so radical and so numerous as to have profoundly affected the mode and substance of that life. Old and long-departed instruments have been resuscitated and are enjoying a growing vogue. The performance practices of music antedating the Romantic era are studied by artists, and the anachronisms that only a couple of decades ago were the rule in public concerts are now seldom encountered. A growing acquaintance with "old" music has markedly enriched the repertory—who would have thought thirty years ago that Telemann and Vivaldi would have become popular composers? But in writing about music for the public we have failed; we have not even approached the excellence that has been exhibited in the sciences, the visual arts, and literature. The application of musicology to the practical ends of our musical life has brought us to a crisis, in which we have embroiled the devoted lover of music. True, the processes of music are not easy to understand; the pursuit must be strenuous. The only way we can examine a composition is to take it to pieces. This is the difficulty that besets every writer on music: he must analyze, and in so doing he realizes that he is diverting attention from the wholeness of the work which is its life. Yet the perception of the facts has much to do with the vital experience of the wholeness of music. Listening to music is an exercise in sensitivity, for "listening" is much more than "hearing"; yet many laymen and artists still believe that music should not be contaminated by even a semblance of learning; and though with the best of intentions, they are incessantly at work to deform and degrade the content of art, forcing the innocent reader to ask himself how far it is wise for him to risk spoiling his enthusiasm by disturbing his ignorance. In the end, however, most people have the inclination to learn something about what they like; yet, instead of providing them with reliable guidance, we abandon them to writers who pride themselves on the achievement of a method which need seldom stoop to observation and study.

The historian is not dealing with today, which, however variously it is valued, is still fresh in the mind. He is dealing with yesterday, the recollection of which is always vague. The historian of the arts has an even more difficult task, because he must defend, applaud, and explain creative artists not one hundred but possibly one thousand years before him as lucidly as if they were his contemporaries. This is the first major stumbling block to our cause, because modern man acquainted with science and technology is accustomed to think in terms of "progress." In the natural or social sciences he would consider any idea or concept a hundred years old as completely antiquated. Most popular literature reduces "old" music to a skeleton, even to a sack of bones; one hears them rattling. It is our duty not only to charm the interested reader into listening to this music, but to make the dry, disconnected bones live. But how is this done?

No art is understandable from history alone; it must be understood from the experience, from the style, which is like a splinter that penetrates the flesh: at first one hardly notices it, but gradually it causes pain. Hardly less unmistakable is historical continuity, and again it is not so much the historical facts and the historical connections that are important. The minute we attempt to explore the historical connections we are entering the area where the idea is to be found, and idea, no matter how relative, means style. This is understood and appreciated, yet many a younger musicologist today is not, strictly speaking, a historian but an antiquarian, for whom, moreover, one piece of antiquity is as good as another. He shows accuracy and thoroughness to the neglect of interpretation; he considers the accumulation of facts more important than the eliciting of the general idea which gives the facts their significance. This absorption to the intensive investigation of single aspects of problems may blind the scholar to the living articulation of history. An absence of discrimination and the lack of a sense of proportion are no longer crimes; the only mortal sin is ignorance of details. In addition, many music scholars are inclined to think good writing style a meretricious ornament upon thought. The young musicologist believes that he must avoid narration and supplant character by data. Music and musicians as units can be made to fit statistics almost as well as white mice or vitamins, and hence handled by the computer. This makes the historian a pure spectator, an uninvolved witness. The computer can be a most helpful servant, an excellent clerk; but statistics ignore psychology as well as spiritual values and therefore do not end and cannot tell the whole story.

The bits of music that can be put in test tubes or beneath microscopic lenses are remarkably unlike music itself. It is high time that we realize what the laboratory scientists have long since discovered, that their sciences are concerned with abstractions, with single aspects of things, not with things themselves; with tools rather than with wisdom. So long as that truth is borne in mind, musical philology is worthy of all the honor that we accord it. Yet, insofar as man's and the creative artist's purposes extend beyond these abstractions, the scientific method alone is inadequate for dealing with the subtle problems of art and human existence. The most serious events in history are often accompanied by ridiculous side occurrences, and even if these do not in themselves constitute history, they add much to the telling of the story. Above all, in analyzing a work of art, the scientific principle of ruthless fidelity to the original is not enough; the work may disintegrate into a mere mass of materials. The mystery of poetic imagination defies scientific analysis and can but be elucidated in ways that may be condemned as aesthetic and oracular. This approach is often criticized as fantastic and unscientific, but it is often strikingly fruitful, humanly moving, and intellectually stimulating.

At the opposite pole from the antiquarian is the musicologist who examines the materials consistently and logically but is concerned only with the forms and styles the artist used, not with the reasons why he chose them or with what he has made them into. And yet the work of both types is indispensable and invaluable—provided that the quest does not stop in the archives or in the seminar room. Research, like money, is a good servant though a bad master, and it is one of the misfortunes of our time that the conditions of academic life tend strongly to encourage subservience to it. It has caused all manner of misunderstandings, and some of the anti-musicologists, especially in the United States, certainly luxuriate in their revulsion to it. The public—and the practicing musician—may ridicule the dust-ridden disciples of pure archival scholarship, but it is the work of those students that furnishes the reliable pediment on which to build a particular subject, and no one in his right mind could take exception to the fabulous spadework accomplished by modern musicology. They say that the odor of the library hangs over too many of these writings. Well, quite a few people like the aroma, but there is no question that more vitality is called for.

The scholar must be able to translate into written words the zest he has in his own work. It is also his business to take the work of art from the sleep into which our conventional familiarity has thrown it, to restore to it the intensity of life with which it burned in the spirit of its creation. In so doing, detail must illuminate, not distract, and thought must be concrete—that is, adequate both to its subject and to its purpose. It must also recognize that circumstances are continually changing. History, whatever the field, must be tense and closely knit, like drama. It should be a living stream that runs swiftly; the backwaters of digression are often filled with sunken dangers. The historian must not invent; but the reader may, if he likes, and he will derive great pleasure from his effort. But the historian, in order to enable his readers to invent, must carry them into that blissful state. There are instances when new conceptions destroy time-honored realities, as well as some that were anything but useful.

7

Musicology is often regarded as a body of knowledge. Reflection, however, will lead to the conclusion that this cannot be its true nature. History has repeatedly shown that a body of scholarly knowledge that ceases to develop soon ceases to be scholarly at all. The scholarship of one age has often become the nonsense of the next. No matter how willing and liberal the publisher may be, he is powerless if he cannot find the authors to submit writings that offer the general reader a worthy counterpart to the great scholarly essays. The popularizer, who takes on this task because the professional musicologist is unable or unwilling to assume it, blinded by the immediate realities and unaware of the great strides and changes made by special research, endeavors to comprehend his subject from secondhand data alone and is thus compelled to wander on the outer fringes of scholarship. But he is not altogether to be blamed; a good deal of the responsibility rests on the scholar's shoulders.

Research, though toilsome, is easy; imaginative interpretation, though pleasant, is difficult. For the critical exercise of imagination excludes all that is irrelevant in research; it is the irrelevant part of research that is easy, and it is easy because it is irrelevant. It is at this point that the popularizer enters, taking the irrelevant as his jumping-off point. The scholar, unlike the popularizer, has always more or less understood the limits of propriety: when to be intuitive and inductive, when to be logical and deductive. The scholar with intellectual imagination must try to use words which mean precisely what he says and only what he says, whereas the amateur musicologists often uses words to circumnavigate the problems. Thus the latter ends with islets of facts sprinkled along the stream of fiction, and in his hands music history and appreciation turn into a form of higher gossipry. Not a few who call themselves scholars take the position that there is no nonsense that may not be attributed to a composer of bygone days and confidently upheld as intentional.

The tendency to turn composers into symbolical figures has grown during the last hundred years, until all reality is lost. To this must be added the many pitfalls caused by the writing about and personifying of nationality. For this situation both camps—the popularizers and scholars—are responsible. Some figures in world music or literature are either not appreciated in their home, or placed too high. Vivaldi is far more admired abroad than in Italy; Pfitzner and Reger, well regarded in Germany, are all but ignored elsewhere; and to this day Byron is held in more esteem in the world at large than in England. Then there are the vacillations that often surround some popular composers, *vide* Franck or Sibelius. One recalls with a painful smile the prophecy of Cecil Gray, who claimed a mere generation ago that the future of music in the twentieth century would be determined by the influence of Berlioz, Sibelius, and van

Dieren! All these difficulties and uncertainties show up most embarrassingly in the biographies of musicians, the favorite genre for the "general reader." Today it is fashionable to put biographies in the form of fiction, which in a way is more honest than to call a book a biography when it is in fact full of imaginary conversations and conjectural sentiments. A biography which lacks the facts is merely fiction, and a biography which is nothing but facts is merely source material. Though in biography the frontier line between ascertained fact and sympathetic imagination must be precisely drawn, it should not form a wall of separation.

The real problem faced by the popularizer is to get used to a way of thinking which is very unlike his own. Since he lacks the equipment and the patient study of the true scholar, who knows how to weigh what is relevant and what is irrelevant, he will not notice when he crosses the frontier from the Land of Substance to the Land of Shades. With this we have arrived at the genre which is eagerly sought by the general reader: the analytical guide to masterpieces. Here again we, the professional musical scholars, bear heavy responsibility for our intemperate indulgence in musical hermeneutics. Though these excesses were far more attractive to our elders than to us, nevertheless, the ideas of Schweitzer or Kretzschmar and some of their disciples, that a spiritual allusion may be lurking behind every note, have been adopted with a vengeance by the authors of guidebooks and program notes. Today most of us realize that these accounts of hermeneutical content must be handled with extreme care; it is a valid approach, but one must never forget that it is to a considerable extent an artificial reconstruction after the event. In the popular (and regrettably also in the professional) literature, one encounters farfetched and unqualified comparisons between things extremely unlike each other. Some of these things may have occurred in the private universe of the composer's mind, as purely personal images. But the reader or the student of the score is expected not only to perceive them, but also to make his own mind work in the same way, and to think unerringly of, say, candlelight when he hears a certain arrangement of notes which do not, indeed cannot, refer to it.

This brief essay cannot begin to do justice to the vast subject indicated in its title. Its aim had to be restricted to calling attention to the wide gulf that exists between musical letters for the professional and those for the cultivated general reader. There is a continuity in the history of the art of music, a continuity of delicate but powerful forces, which preserves unity amid difference and which prevents events on the one hand from becoming a mere casual sequence of happenings and on the other from revealing themselves as the rigid consequence of a mechanical formula. Historical study, however, is rarely static. Specialists' contributions make steady additions to knowledge, and the pulling together of the results of research into a narrative is a task that needs to be done at intervals. The remarkable scholars of the heroic period of modern musicology, such as Spitta or Chrysander or Riemann, hewed their own stones from the vast quarry, laid their own foundations, and went far in building the walls. The facts and fictions they bequeathed to us are indispensable, but we do not turn to these pioneers for a comprehensive picture. We could not trace it without them, but they could not trace it for us; new materials and new knowledge of all sorts have stirred a host of new questions and set many old problems in a new light.

Jahn's and Abert's works on Mozart are an excellent example of this periodic comprehensive summary, while pathbreaking essays, such as Schering's on the oratorio or Rolland's on early opera, have not yet been subjected to revision. There are, of course, many, many more such valuable writings, but all of them are now in need of revaluation and reinterpretation. We know many things not available to these great scholars of the past; what we need is their all-encompassing view and their ability to create a synthesis. This is our task, and we should not leave it to amateurs. There is, too, the impulse that every age has for an expression of its own peculiar relationship to the past. It sometimes burns its incense to false gods or substitutes ridicule for veneration, whitewashes rogues or denigrates good men. History is written from historical data, and the justification for writing new histories is either to adjust verdicts in the light of new evidence or to present old verdicts in a different but undistorted form. Every generation, therefore, can work within these limits, but none has the right to tamper with the two essential ingredients of historical writing: accuracy and impartiality. In the last resort, "taste," response born of and limited by the writer's innate sensibility, must be the arbiter; only within its circle can his other faculties be exercised.

Musicology and Related
Disciplines

embers of the university community naturally represent considerable variety in individuality, beliefs, and principles; these differences are fruitful when they are related to, when they have reference to, a mutual center. And although the disciplines taught under the heading of the liberal arts do separate us, we can see, even within the framework of the different themes, the kindred nature of our research and the shaping of this research into communicable wisdom.

Culture is the sum total of our heritage in its historical development: religion, science, the arts, the social order, the forms of life. Literature is not simply the sum total of writings, and art is not the aggregate of artistic objects, because culture is more than the piling up of individual objectivations—it is a spirit pervading and linking them together. A scholar who, like a Hindu ascetic immersed in self-contemplation, confines himself to his narrow field of specialization loses the larger view. The first requirement for the musicologist is to

From *Perspectives in Musicology: The Inaugural Lectures of the Ph.D. Program in Music at the City University of New York*, ed. Barry S. Brook, Edward O. D. Downes, and Sherman Van Solkema (New York: W. W. Norton, 1972)

realize that the choice of studying other disciplines is governed not by his tastes and desires alone, but by sheer necessity. Further, he must not only absorb the content of other disciplines, but—and this is much more difficult—put each to constructive use in his own field. This is equally true of the technical means as of the final visions. The technique of research can be carried to a point where it embarks upon an independent existence, almost without reference to the material under investigation. On the other hand, it may and should lead to the uncovering of the inner regions of the spirit that lie beyond technique.

The second requirement may be called that of continuity. Once more, one may proceed on parallel courses—that of technique and that of idea. It seems to be an undeviating law that the continuity of the idea slackens sooner than that of the handling of the material. Consequently, what was meaningful in the enthusiasm and élan of the initiators may become changed, even meaningless, under the hands of their successors, who develop the original idea by manipulating its materials. To mention an example, the Baroque started out as an expression of the *Ecclesia militans* of the Counter-Reformation, but as it spread from the Latin-Catholic South to the German-Protestant North, the original motive gave way to a different set of ideas. Yet musicology persists in dealing with Baroque music in elaborate isolation, expecting to explain it by pure stylistic research and elucidation, but producing only a good picture of formal and technical developments without accounting for the underlying meaning. This is no longer the history of ideas; stylistic research has become independent of culture. The history of ideas needs this competent stylistic analysis, but the musico-technical research should not be a golem. The researchers busy with Baroque music picked up the original idea and explored all the possibilities, which at its inception had a palpable cultural meaning; but by restricting themselves to chronology, paleography, morphology, typology, and general *Fachlehre*, they lost sight of the idea and missed its mutation.

This leads us to the third point. We are capable of contemplating and enjoying such music even though we are far removed from its original cultural meaning and associations. It can give us aesthetic experience even though it is the product of a culture distant and strange to us. But make no mistake, this is an inadequate viewing and an inadequate experience—and I am afraid that much of our musicology is built upon a system of inadequate viewing. This situation is not altogether graceless, because with our techniques and stylistic analyses we provide invaluable contributions; it is only regrettable that the admirable ability of the researcher is cultivated so exclusively.

In every branch of culture the historical development reaches a point where an estrangement begins. This becomes perceptible to the individual when new experiences move him and he becomes aware of his alienation from the old content and old forms. There is then an attempt at reconstruction, and there enter the historians, the scholars. It is extremely important that these exegetes of changing events should see clearly the varying mentalities and purposes that predominate in the different periods. When humanity is concerned with primordial facts, when what occupies the creative artist is the inscrutable yet ever present soul, we are dealing with a religious culture. Then there are periods that feel, though not consciously and not theoretically, the inner laws of form, and the creative artist's work is concentrated on the optimum shaping of the material. Such a time is one of marked artistic development. The third orientation or state of mind becomes actual when the feeling of alienation comes to the fore, and the discrepancy of form and content becomes increasingly evident. When this point is reached, the laws underlying the shaping of the material, of form, which the previous generation created by obeying their pure creative instincts, become conscious; now it is theory that can grasp what to the creative artist has become more or less strange. In such a period critical research, logic, aesthetics, and history thrive. It seems to me that we are living in such a period; the great accomplishments of musicology during the last thirty years or so clearly indicate it.

The practitioners of any of the disciplines constituting the history of ideas are charged with the task of bringing to the surface the specific facts and qualities of their respective cultural domain and of examining how its development is regulated by internal laws. It becomes evident to the attentive student that these domains show essential differences, and that while the several manifestations of culture cannot be segregated from one another, neither can they be simply compared. Whether philosophy or poetry or music or physics, every manifestation of the objectivation of the spirit possesses a different construction, which is due to the medium through which it comes to expression. Thus the construction of each of the cultural objectivations, their respective yet mutual autonomy, is the proper subject of scholarship.

Today we know more about the technique of archival research than did our predecessors, and our command of the tools and means for the processing of the gathered material is impressive; but we lag behind in our ability to cast what we have gathered into interpretative syntheses. Knowledge of the métier and of the mechanics of music is essential to the understanding of the work of art, and the young student of musicology must acquire these tools and practice with them for long hours. It is essential, however, that he not stop there; he must look around him, for knowledge has a very sly way of accumulating in odd places where it is with difficulty perceived. Specialization is inevitable and necessary, for it is only the expert who can deal with the subtleties of any given subject; but specialization should not be encouraged at the start of a musicological career. It goes without saying that no single person can master more than a fraction of his own discipline, let alone the related disciplines essential for the exploration of music in all its manifestations. We recall the bon mot coined by a historian, that the last twenty minutes of the Renaissance would be too vast a subject for any one man to know adequately. It used to be the fashion among musicians to smile indulgently upon those writers who expended a lifetime of assiduous work and anxious archaeology compiling the music history of one city or one monastery. But we have come to see the inestimable value of this humble spadework, and we cannot withhold admiration from these men who delve deeply into their own little corners of music history, uncovering the great along with the insignificant. This kind of research is indispensable, although it usually offers only raw materials for the use of others. Such studies are not the historiography which becomes part of culture, for that historiography is at once a record of civilization and a contribution to it, and becomes so by virtue of its imaginative penetration and interpretation. Those whom we may call musical philologists often are not really aware of the difference between what is dead and what is alive; they want knowledge as a means of establishing a comfortable order. Their measures are quantitative, and everything available to them is equally worthy of attention. Their implicit or explicit thesis is that everything can be researched, everything can become object, for before scholarship, everything has equal rights. So to them this is the meaning of life. But overgrowth of material, be it factual or spiritual, and overgrowth of means, be they technical, scientific, or artistic, restrict the power of choice and lead to the impoverishment of the humane.

The Greeks already had two schools of musical thought: Aristoxenus was a pragmatist, interested in music as an art, whereas the Pythagoreans considered it a science, a department of mathematics. The Aristoxenian school relied on the musical ear, the Pythagorean on numbers. Neither the scientific nor the artistic mind is by any means homogeneous, however; under these generic names have been subsumed many distinct types throughout the centuries. Some of the greatest scientists have been men of a concrete imagination; abstraction was alien to them. Within the field of art, literary, or music scholarship a kindred variety apparently exists, and possibly there is some direct affinity between the various types of scientific and mathematical minds and those that reveal themselves in the appreciation of arts and letters. But there is also a weighty difference between the scientist and the humanist, a difference that the musicologist who wants to make his discipline an exact science tends to overlook: the exact sciences are largely nonhistorical. In physics or chemistry the facts are preexistent; it is only that we discover them one by one. Unlike the laws of invertible counterpoint, the laws of thermo-dynamics have always been here and always will be, and therefore a physicist or chemist can make quite precise predictions, whereas the historian of the arts cannot, not even imprecisely. A work of art is the result of a particular history, and every one of the histories is original, individual, and nonduplicable. Nevertheless, we have qualities that we share with the scientists, which indeed are shared by all scholars, the most important being the organization of think-ing, which in the scholar's world occupies the same place as does composition in art. Behind each there is a view which can be just as sensory as it is intellectual, whether in physics or the arts. Only we must beware of the eternal danger of immediately freezing it into a system.

I spoke of the specialist and of his important role, but before the physicist becomes a specialist, he has acquired a scientific view, an overall attitude and awareness of the extent and nature of physics as a science and as a part of our cultural makeup. This awareness he carries over into his specialized studies. And of course the surgeon, too, begins his specialized career only after he has studied medicine in all its concepts, observed facts, and attitudes. In the sciences this indoctrination begins in the college in a serious scholarly fashion; in music, regrettably, our young students are often taught to be like the romantic tourists who, guidebook in hand, are always ready to pounce upon the celebrated place to make it yield the proper and prescribed sensations.

We are all agreed that musicology needs the assistance not only of the humanities but of the natural and social sciences as well, despite the fact that right now there is less than the usual agreement as to what can properly be re-garded as essential, what subordinate. The finished composition is, of course, an entity in itself, which can be detached from its cultural environment and examined purely on its own terms of construction. But music is a man-made art, despite its physical foundations, and in the end we must trace the work of art to its creator, who is subject to many other than musical stimuli and influences; if we stop with the music, therefore, we have investigated but half the story. (On the other hand, if we investigate only the man, as Ernest Newman did in his massive four-volume biography of Wagner, without one paragraph devoted to the music, we tell even less than half the story, because we leave out the work of art which should have been our point of departure.) This belief, that we can examine the product of human imagination completely divorced from its creator, is not true even in the sciences.

Sir Josiah Stamp's view, that economic tendencies are altered by the very fact that we study them, is applicable to music. This paradox is, indeed, the core of the case against laissez-faire both in economics and in scholarship in the arts; but before we can embark on our study of music, we run up against some serious obstacles. We must acknowledge the incontrovertible fact that neither the composition nor the enjoyment of music presupposes any scientific knowledge. Mozart and Schubert did not know the first thing about the laws of acoustics, the physiology of hearing, or the psychology of perception. Nor did either of them know anything about the principles of the social organization of their world beyond the fact that it was cruel to them. Yet both Mozart and Schubert managed to manipulate the physical phenomena underlying the art of music into supreme masterpieces. So all is serene and pleasurable in the world of music until the musicologist appears and disturbs the peace of this innocent enjoyment by asking questions, challenging the performing artists' conceptions, and establishing entirely new sets of values as well as the historical outlook. Until fairly recently—and, in not a few places, still—musicians, the public, the press, even university administrations, considered the music scholar an unwelcome intruder, an anomaly that threatened the orderly pursuit and enjoyment of music. Yet the end not only for music but for literary and scientific investigations is so evident that it deserves the high rank of platitude. We cannot solve problems by ignoring them, and we must insist that art is structured by reason and not solely by the waywardness of feeling and inspiration. The concept that the universe is a rational system working by discoverable laws is the essential foundation for all the activities which a university comprises. Without the life of reason conditioned by that concept of the world, there could be no university discipline in arts, letters, and sciences. And while the laws of the workings of the universe are stressed more by the exponents of the sciences, consciousness of these laws is no less implicit in the other departments of learning. In musicology we speak of the auxiliary or subsidiary disciplines that have relevance to our work; they may be subsidiary to art itself, but they are nevertheless the ones that mediate between the rational system of the world and the arts. Thus acoustics, psychology, and physiology are, or should be, part of a musicologist's equipment; but it is a great mistake to begin musicological studies with the associated and auxiliary disciplines. Regrettably, all introductory textbooks on musicology begin with acoustics and the physiology of hearing, even before the student knows anything about his musical tasks. Musicology deals with an art, not with an exact science. The young scholar should be taught pride in the unique quality of the arts; he should learn that the poetic idea as an abstract formulation of the power of the imagination is totally independent of all science and physically indestructible. Once it is planted in the world, it is its own value that preserves it. Nevertheless, a scholar wishing to gain a comprehensive view of his field simply must have at least a nodding acquaintance with these scientific underpinnings. Besides, they are interesting. The musicologist is not expected to match the acoustician, the psychologist, and the physiologist on their own ground, but he should have some knowledge of the important processes whereby the physical phenomenon called sound is produced, perceived, and converted. There are excellent summaries available, like Geldard's *The Human Senses*, but those prepared by musicologists for musicologists should be shunned. Anything beyond that becomes an interdisciplinary matter carried out by collaboration. The musicologist should not attempt basic research in these areas unless he is willing to go through the mill and make it his speciality, which, of course, is entirely legitimate but calls for full devotion to the task.

Goethe declared that the literature of a nation can be neither recognized nor appreciated unless at the same time the whole content of its existence is taken into account. Substitute "music" for "literature" and we have arrived at the group of disciplines which are not only closest to the musicologist but without which he cannot properly function as a respectable scholar: religion, philosophy, literature, history, sociology, and the other arts. Since it would be impossible to deal with all of them within a brief essay, I shall single out history and sociology, two disciplines that are always present in our everyday work.

If we grant that the development of the several branches of culture is marked by a steady distancing from an original point of departure, then the retrospective view of posterity—that is, history—is of paramount importance to us. If we add that even within a generation this distancing may be apparent, if we realize that already to the Athens of Pericles the Homeric world appeared as a very distant mythus, it becomes clear what an immensely difficult undertaking it is to interpret the cultural accomplishments of past generations. Put in the simplest terms, when the musicologist ascertains that the composer he is investigating lived and worked in a particular place at a particular time, he accepts the implication that the events surrounding this musician to a considerable part constituted his experience. Thus the question of style is also a sociological question: What does life give to the creative artist, and what does it withhold from him? This is not useful "background" stuff, as one critic who wanted to say at least a few kind words about a recent book on Handel saw it, but the essential point of departure for the historian; for in certain periods only certain concepts of life are possible, and others are excluded. The external social determinant is the effect whose causes are the more social the deeper they are. But the history of this effect immediately involves cultural psychology too, because we must find out what was pleasing in a given age, what influences predominated, and what made certain genres more acceptable than others. New levels in creative consciousness are achieved and manifested in the various periods of civilization, each expressing a characteristic principle. The historian must always seek the determining political-social blueprint; the causes, influences, and effects need close attention if an understanding—even a superficial understanding—of the history of music is to be obtained. Indeed, we must enlarge our horizon by investigating why a manifestation of culture such as music does have social relations, why in many respects art is all but determined by the social order within which it is realized.

Learning is never more industrious nor less helpful than when it accumulates facts without affirming their true relevance, without probing into how the sequential events are related to one another. History is not mere chronicling, nor is it a digest of events. We must always strive for the critical referent, and we must check and judge even old and traditionally accepted labels and catchwords, because they may be the residue of a once living force and truth. We peel back the layers of events one by one, from the outermost to the innermost, until we arrive at the beating heart. It is true of course that to the historian nothing is alien, not even the amorous vagaries of kings and composers, but a constant critical vigilance is imperative. It may happen to any man of genius that his most trivial compositions, notes, or letters are preserved along with his important papers. But it assuredly does not follow that all trivia are worth studying and printing; yet we see it happen almost every month in one or the other of the professional journals devoted to musicology. The discovery of a harmless little minuet by the young Mozart or Haydn can send certain musicologists into transports of scholarly passion; they have visions of upsetting the whole Köchel apple cart, perhaps of documenting a hitherto unreported spelling of forte and piano, and the paper may bear a watermark linking this with another equally insignificant piece. The discovery, complete with a ten-page *Revisionsbericht*, is duly published—and where does it get us? This is hand-to-mouth musicology, which we must guard against, lest it become a habit. The mere bones of history will not do, for our task is not the collection and cult of relics, but to find out what is still living and thus part of the present. The real meaning of history to the music scholar is to see where the highest possibilities were realities once upon a time; all his other activities, including the lost and found minuets, are only necessary preambles.

So far so good. We learn the modus operandi of the historian, and it helps us enormously; we know that the various manifestations of culture are connected, and that this connection is their vital force. Still, we must never forget that we are historians of an art, and despite all our scientific equipment, to us the work of art really has no past, only different degrees of eternity; to us the great ones are great because of their never-fading newness, not because of their age, not because hundreds of years ago they were, but because after hundreds of years they are. The musicologists of the nineteenth century were the great pioneers of our discipline, and their merits were outstanding, but they made mistakes, and it is extremely difficult to sponge out a picture imprinted upon the mind. They sifted out and put together the composers of every country in "schools" and left us with our musical masterpieces neatly arranged, grouped, and pigeonholed. Each one of the schools had its exclusive heroes handed down, bright from incessant polishing, and one marvels how quickly the human image dissolves into the mythical image. The consequence of this classificatory zeal was that the nineteenth century bequeathed to us, together with its industriously amassed facts, many misleading deductions and prejudices, as well as a large dose of national bias, all of which it is our business fundamentally to reconsider. Before continuing, perhaps it would be useful to illustrate the traps the musicologist can fall into if he fails to examine the inherited facts and conclusions and proceeds without sufficient critical historical preparation. Let us take first a case in which the entire musical culture of great musical nations was affected by historical events; and second, a small but very annoying misconception of performance practice that persists because of insufficient acquaintance with contemporary economic history.

Our textbooks deal with the Reformation as a general movement that exerted a weighty influence on the history of music. This is true, but only half the truth. The Protestant Reformation was a revolt against papal theocracy, clerical privilege, and the hereditary "paganism" of the Mediterranean races. Our first great mistake is to regard the Reformation as one unified movement, whereas, broadly speaking, the first of the reasons for the revolt moved Luther, the second Henry VIII, and the third Calvin. But Luther, with his formalized thought which found expression in the ninety-five theses, his boisterous tongue which rolled off phrases rich and elemental, managed to tame his romantic emotions to disciplined issue in music—he is the typical German.

Similarly, Henry is English—so English that he summoned Parliament to assist him in his conflict with the Holy See; while Calvin's cool, methodical, and uncompromising mind is impregnated with logic of the French genus. As a consequence, we find not one common manifestation of European Protestantism, but three separate and altogether different movements, one German, one English, and the third prevalent among peoples whose emotional makeup leaned toward that strict conduct which only French thought can devise.

Faced with these facts, how can a music historian continue to deal with the Reformation as a whole? Only one of the three movements produced great music and, what is more, a great musical culture: the German. The others hampered, if they did not virtually destroy, musical creativity where they prevailed. Now what are the answers, what are the explanations? The scores themselves will not explain why it is that, as early as the beginning of the seventeenth century, a pamphleteer in England ruefully says that "more musicians are out of order than their instruments."

The other example I should like to cite shows in one small detail how deeply economic forces can influence musical style and practice itself; it concerns the large choral-orchestral works of the late Classic era. The conditions of public music making changed after the Baroque, and so did the hierarchy of musical genres. The old professional church choir was too expensive to maintain; on the other hand, the gradual but positive displacement of vocal by instrumental music and the increasing practice of public concerts called into existence professional orchestras that could earn their keep. The oratorios and other similar works reflect the reality of the socioeconomic conditions: instead of the professional chorus and the ad hoc orchestra of the previous era, Haydn wrote for a professional orchestra and an ad hoc chorus. A good deal of nonsense has been written about Haydn's last great choral works, especially the oratorios, with their highly developed symphonic orchestral parts and their relatively simple choruses; but the fundamental regrouping of the constituent musical forces, the socioeconomic as well as the artistic reasons for them, are ignored. Because of this ignorance, neither conductor nor musicologist can account for certain anomalies, which they blithely perpetuate. Take Mozart's Requiem, every performance of which is blighted and falsified by the incessant *colla parte* playing of trombones. Why should they play with the voices? Is it not difficult enough to get clarity from a chorus, so why should the lovely choral sound be overlaid by these insistent brasses? Yes, the trombones are marked in the score, but it was not Mozart who put them there, nor did Süssmayr really want them blowing from beginning to end, but he was compelled to do so. It is the musicologist's duty to enlighten the conscientious conductor who cannot be expected to study church history in Vienna and go over the imperial household records; the documents are all there, and they tell a story that cannot be gained from a purely musical study of the score. The Empress, a shrewd and thrifty housewife, decided that the three music establishments maintained by the court consumed too much money, so she summoned the imperial kapellmeister, Gregorius Werner, and told him that henceforth he must operate within a fixed budget, and it was up to him how to apportion this money. Werner could not very well make economies at the court opera, for that was the showcase; but at Saint Stephen's he could fall back on the practice followed by ordinary churches: first of all, reduce the chorus. The employment of trombones as replacement choristers was the customary solution, since each one of the stentorian instruments was worth half a dozen human lungs. (Incidentally, things got so bad that at times Saint Stephen's did not even have an organist.) When Süssmayr completed the Requiem, he put in the trombones because Count Walsegg, for whom it was composed, had a musical establishment as modest as the usual church ensemble: an orchestra that was reasonably complete and a handful of singers. We are faced with an ancient emergency practice that does not apply to the contemporary scene; yet we let the trombones pointlessly trot along with the vocal parts all the time for want of a little knowledge of history.

Now let us turn to the youngest branch of our discipline, formerly known as comparative musicology, but today labeled ethnomusicology. It is rapidly growing—indeed, so rapidly that its devotees already manifest the symptoms of the movement colonial regimes end with: they want independence, independence from the parent country, musicology; they want a discipline of their very own. How they intend to use this independence, I do not know, because the demand is being voiced just when it becomes ever clearer that ethnomusicology has an organic and generic connection with universal music history. (Incidentally, the so-called theorists are also clamoring for a republic of their own, complete with customs guards at the frontiers. But unless theory stands for figured-bass realization, which is Fachlehre, or for what you can read in *Die Reihe*, which is surrealist metaphysics, I do not see how theory can be removed from the very center of historical musicology.)

How far can ethnomusicology be said to have justification and meaning, what degree of scientific value? If we were to judge by the way it is practiced in many institutions of learning, it would seem no more than a pseudo-intellectual tool for that vague interracial brotherhood that any decent person would naturally espouse, and for the sake of which foundations are happy to support anyone with a tape recorder who is willing to go to Tibet or Kenya. Again, we are dealing with a nineteenth-century inheritance that was neither digested nor correctly interpreted. The problem of folk art was first discovered by the Romantic era—that is, at that stage of cultural development when the alienation from form first became a conscious experience. It is for this reason that there began to be an interest in foreign cultures; and folk art, even their own, appeared to the Romantics as such a foreign culture. Ever since, the sentimental attachment to folk art has remained strong, and it has great appeal to the layman. But ethnomusicology is not for the dilettante, not for the musician who suddenly takes a liking to it; the subject is of great importance to all of us and requires vast training and expert knowledge. Primitive culture is our own contemporary, but there is a likelihood that this primitive culture may reflect certain aspects of earlier stages of the higher cultures, so that in it we can read some of our own past where other documents fail, and it thus becomes a link in our general history. And yet non-Western musical styles are better understood by us with reference to the art of the West. This is vaguely realized, yet the way the idea is put to work is altogether dilettantish. To transplant Japanese or Indonesian music wholesale and expect it to flourish in an alien culture is mere *chinoiserie*, which ignores the first principles of mental cultivation. An example of the sad results is that the Hindu sitar, now mass-produced in this country, is used by noble savages in discotheques to play Western junk. It is precisely because the sociological background of folk and primitive music differs vastly from our own and represents an alien culture that we must proceed with the utmost care. The scrappy collection of random observations here and there throughout the world that usually makes up the content of college courses on non-Western music is worthless, misleading, and basically unscientific. Any structure based on surface observations of fleeting travelers, or on brief sojourns, often without the slightest linguistic and other preparation, is good only for a travelogue. Primitive cultures are necessarily self-centered and attached to an inherited body of customary practices and associated beliefs. The only approach to such groups is through a sympathetic acquaintance with all phases of their lore, which in turn calls for elaborate preparation and studies. There is, happily, an undeniable improvement in the quality of ethnomusicological work, for we now have a number of genuine scholars working in the field who realize that a thorough training in plain musicology, social and cultural anthropology, linguistics, history, and other related disciplines is indispensable to honest scholarly results.

The concerns of ethnomusicology are really identical with our own; they go to show that every culture has its own recognizable roots from which the complicated branches of its development have grown. Society as a growing organization, a quasi-biological organism, is differentiated into more and more homogeneous form, and art, being a social phenomenon, supplying society's aesthetic needs, can similarly be considered a quasi-biological organism that grows from the unorganized to the organized. But even if we connect all loose ends and relate all individual factions, we still get only the contours of historical sequence unless we learn to view comprehensively. At this particular juncture there is a danger that we may overestimate the range of applicability of the scientific mind and underestimate the value of accumulated wisdom. The computer, which some hold will revolutionize not only our economic life but also our aesthetics, our morals, and our arts, can be a trusted and invaluable helper. But permit it to become the master, and the scholar is reduced to mere spectator. Neither the height of the mountains nor the depth of the seas can be measured in millimeters—such precision is feasible only to the unpoetic. The musicologist should always remember that the true function of the scholar is the illumination of the particular in terms of the universal. And if he bogs down in his work and cannot seem to find his way out, he should be mindful of the paradox that, uniquely in the arts, ideas can transform facts.

Music and History

It is entirely owing to our ways of learning and teaching music that there are relatively few who clearly perceive what music means within the history of civilization, and thus what it means to the nation and its culture. In a fog in which all contours of thought are lost, the figures of the past other than the principal heroes of recent times sink to the status of mere means by which the music historian satisfies his desire for a play with aesthetics, forms, and techniques. We might call this sort of art history— to use a terminology much in vogue these days—a mere historical eroticism, for it eschews the essence of the scholarly procedure: objectivity and rigorous regard for the truth. Historiography, even in the arts, cannot be legitimized on grounds of beauty alone.

The most common approach to music history is, of course, the time-honored biographical or "personal history" method. We might call this the method of idealization by isolation. But the detached single individual, even if he becomes a typical representative of a historical epoch, cannot always be grasped as such; in fact, in many instances he appears as a strange, not readily understandable phenomenon that refuses to be reconciled with the milieu.

The Eleventh Kenyon Lecture, Vassar College, 21 November, 1952

Perhaps the best-known—and least understood—of these strange phenomena is Bach, who simply evades all attempts at classification, even though he is considered the embodiment of the High Baroque.

Even when we deal with music history on a plane considerably higher than hero worship, what we examine and teach is not the history of music as an integral part of the history of ideas, but the history of a craft or métier. Now while the craft of music is of the utmost importance, it should not occupy the forefront in musical historiography. Every one of us has had the experience of listening to a fine musician performing with a flawless technique, yet the music rising from the strings or from the throat was dead, because the mere technician was confused by precisely that which is served by his technique. This concept that equates the evolution of the métier with history has led to a most regrettable attitude in viewing music history, one which has actually tended to ruin our appreciation of music, of a legion of fine composers, and of a library full of great music.

I am referring to the prevalence of the honored institution of "forerunner." A few examples will help. When listening to Weber's *Euryanthe*, one of his forgotten works precisely on account of its experimental and forward-looking nature, the listener cannot suppress his suspicion of plagiarism—from *Lohengrin*. This may seem a chronological paradox, which turns the real facts upside down, yet given our conditioning, the earlier work becomes mediated by the later one; it tends to lose rather than gain in standing. According to this conception, new, shall we say, "inventions" in music lose all their interest, and their original freshness cannot be recaptured and enjoyed. The idea is of no importance, since a later composer embodied it in a seemingly fuller measure. However, if the innovation is of a technical nature, the first employment of an instrument or of a chord, the record stands to the credit of the bold craftsman. It is no use pointing out that the direct forerunner principle seldom works satisfactorily, even if we tacitly accept this method which demotes great composers to the status of mere yeomen. Take the senior Bach, to choose this paragon of musical virtue acceptable to all factions. He certainly depended on older music—not, however, for technical features of the métier but for sheer musical thought. As he grew older, he quite obviously turned away from the musical current of his time, from the suave and sensuous style of the Neapolitans, to commune with the earlier composers, not the often-cited forerunners, but the forerunners of the forerunners, the long-buried Netherlanders and old Italians. Another such was Brahms, who consciously shunned the world of his contemporaries, Wagner and Liszt, to return to his North German ancestors and to the glories of the Classic era.

Thus it comes about that veritable monstrosities of historical judgment are calmly dished out to the student of music and no one loses a heartbeat over them, whereas similar ineptitudes in the field of fine arts or literature would make life unattractive to their perpetrators. Let me quote a typical instance of this queer philosophy of history. There is scarcely a book on the appreciation of music that does not qualify the first two symphonies of Beethoven as being still "just like Haydn or Mozart." This, we must bear in mind, is a judgment of value which, of course, immediately trims the two great Classic composers of whatever merit they may have had in the previous chapter of the book, before they became forerunners. It is clear that this shallow sort of historical procedure, which searches for similarities upon which to establish the continuity of evolution, only to dismiss the originator in favor of the exploiter, is not worthy of serious consideration. It rejects what was living in each period, of which the people of that period partook. It is no wonder, then, that until recent times the men of classical antiquity, the Middle Ages, and even the sixteenth and seventeenth centuries, appeared as deaf and dumb; and it was only in the days of Watteau and Hogarth and Tiepolo—that is, at the time when the sister art of painting was rather well established—that an obscure Protestant cantor emerges from the centuries of preparation to establish music as an art worthy of the other Muses.

An equally unsound approach professes to derive all facets of music from purely sociological circumstances. Again, the sociological is a most important factor in historiography, but its application to the history of art must be carefully balanced by other elements. There can be no question that society, the Church, musical establishments at the courts, or the middle-class music associations cannot be separated from the music written for and practised by these institutions; still, it is not possible to distinguish what is essentially Haydnesque in Haydn from his role as a servant in the Esterházy household.

Surely it is not enough to know more or less about the historical data to understand a historical phenomenon, for what this phenomenon signifies can be learned not so much from the phenomenon itself as from a general historical contemplation which poses the question whether there is a meaning behind that historical event and what this meaning is. In order to arrive at this understanding, we must temporarily abandon the facts and avoid concentration on the objects nearest to the eye and must widen our glance to a view. In fact, we must remove ourselves from our subject to such an extent that we shall ask ourselves, what altogether does the history of music mean in human history? We may then discover that in the shuffle of details we have forgotten that the central theme of music history is man. We are accustomed to see in literature or painting man as the center of art, but we fail to realize that music is not only the expression of man—but that it is a representation of man too. It offers a picture of man under the point of view of the always prevailing human ideal. Now what is this human ideal?

The dictionary explains the term "humanity" as "man's consciousness of himself as human in kind and as distinguished from the external and the superhuman world." The lexicographer gives the Latin *humanitas* as the term from which the English word descended but fails to convey the full, or rather extended, meaning of humanitas; for the latter does not only signify the existence of such consciousness, it also embraces the will and desire for it, which gives the notion of humanity a much wider meaning. The historian knows that this desire for human consciousness is the more telling of the constituent parts of humanity. It certainly gave art its most important impetus. However, neither the existence of, nor the will for, human consciousness discloses a palpable content until the stream of history flows through it and endows it with life and color. And now we can say that the history of music, and of course of art in general, is in its most profound sense the expression of the metamorphoses of humanity and of its ideals.

The notion of humanity originated in antiquity. Not in Greece, as one would think, but in Rome—more precisely, in the Rome of Cicero, who must be considered its creator. It did not originate in ancient Greece because the Greeks lived the life of the Greek man, whereas the Ciceronian Romans, who ruefully felt themselves inferior to that life, considered the Grecian as the human ideal and made a cult of it. Thus humanity was the ideal of that cultivated world which the less cultivated Romans saw in Hellas. Cicero systematized this ideal and analyzed it in detail. In so doing, he gave an answer to the Roman who aspired to rise to higher spheres, to become a man in the noblest sense of the world. Cicero's philosophy goes much beyond the immediate aims of the Roman world, for it implies what man should be in order to fulfill the high idea of man.

There are two characteristics which give the Christian ideal of humanity its particular content and cause it to differ diametrically from that of classical antiquity: a metaphysical basic tenet and the ascetic attitude, the fleeing from the world that naturally grew out from the first. The tremendous new idea with which Christianity eventually vanquished spiritually Greco-Roman antiquity is this: the meaning of life was shifted from the present to a metaphysical beyond. According to this new doctrine, which would have been incomprehensible to the man of antiquity, the purpose of all life on earth is to overcome this very life. As the radiant world of Hellas gave way to the somber world of

Christianity, two indivisible doctrines came to the fore that gave to the humanitas of antiquity its *coup de grâce*: the tendency of fallen nature to evil and the
complementary necessity of seeking salvation through supernatural forces.
Theologically speaking, this is the notion of original sin and of grace. It stands
to reason that this new humanity was strange, not only to the man of dying
antiquity but also to the unenlightened and unlettered barbarian of the West.
The Middle Ages cannot be appreciated unless we understand that it exem-
plifies and represents the struggle of the former barbarians against a conception
of life that was fundamentally alien to them. It was a struggle, but one that took
the noblest and most profound form that a spiritual contest can assume—
conquest from within. The West did not deny Christianity; rather, it experienced it creatively, the Germanic lands ultimately finding their own version of
it in the Reformed faiths.

The music of these Middle Ages has interested the historian, and reams
have been written about it. A very distinguished American monograph on the
subject is evidence that we too have contributed our share to its exploration.
Yet, earlier medieval music, especially that of the Gothic era, seldom leaves
the scholar's bookshelves. We should admit that there is a seemingly unbridgeable gulf between this music and ourselves, and although we can decipher it
and even explain its compositional features, we are unable to abandon ourselves to its charms, for we cannot discern them. Yet another century, and as
soon as the first rays of the Renaissance touch this art of the West, we have little
trouble in *experiencing* the music of the time. What can it be that makes this
music so forbidding? All contemporary documents speak of the esteem and
admiration tendered to the master musicians of the Gothic; what did their own
age see and hear in them that we cannot conjure up? Let us be faithful to the
premises we started from and forget for the moment the great organa and
motets of the Gothic and look at the circumstances under which they were
composed.

When probing into the music of the Middle Ages, the first thing that
strikes the student is the absence of folk and popular music. Until about 1300
such music is not even mentioned in any known document, and we must
advance well into the fourteenth century before we encounter more than
traces of it. Curiously enough, the appearance of this folk art coincides with
the rise of secular art music. Thus, on the one hand we have an elaborate
literature of sacred music, the work of learned masters most of whom were
clerics; on the other, the virtual absence of any other kind. It surely is not
possible that the naive naturalism of the people which is the root of all artistic
culture did not find an expression in the Middle Ages, for since the dawn of

history such folk art, whether music or painting, has always been present. Folk song is, to quote the poet, the interpretation of our happiness and sorrow, the confession of individual existence. Here is where our musical territory par excellence begins. The point of view of the people is naturalistic-mythical, and its art can rise only to the point where nature and human imagination are still in rapport. This naturalism the people defended tooth and nail against all outside influence. The European peoples submitted to Christian theology, but beneath its veneer they clung to their naturalism, thus creating that twin outlook always characteristic of their practical thought, and it was this that created the dialectic development of the West which rests on the constant struggle of the two poles. The naturalistic instincts of the pre-Christian West were instantly aroused when it made contact with Mediterranean meta-physics. Likewise, their naive conception of space and time, probably not clearly formulated, became articulate as soon as they were offered the eternity of time and the spaceless heaven. Much that in the first centuries had been proscribed by the Church now began to flourish following the absorption of the barbarians. That secular music did flourish, even though every trace of it has been erased, is clear from the many ecclesiastical censures against musicians other than the *magistri* of the church choir. This music had to be suppressed and proscribed because it ran completely counter to the dictates of the Church.

According to that aspect of Christian theology based on chiliasm, the millennium of the theocratic kingdom, there is neither space nor time, for the reality of the world is God, who is a unity without time or space. Obviously there can be no ideological compromise between the theological and the popular conception, but an empirical compromise was of course necessary and feasible. This was much more readily achieved in architecture than in music. It is characteristic of Gothic architecture that its formal principle does not follow natural and even division of weight, that instead of a practical and logical arrangement like that of the Renaissance, it strove for the fantastic and the supernatural. Its whole vertical, heaven-bound direction is opposed to the law of gravity, and the equilibrium of Gothic structures would be threatened were it not secured by buttresses and other elaborate auxiliaries. But these buttresses are on the *outside*, and their function is hidden; they take no appar-ent part in the formation of the inner space or the frontal, principal picture. This is in harmony with the view expressed early in the Middle Ages that earthly stability is a necessary evil. So much for space.

The same is true, and now we come closer to music, of the conception of time, or rather timelessness. The old painters whom we so condescendingly call "the primitives" had a very definite view in this regard. They followed the realistic popular concept of successive action, yet were trying to condense it into simultaneity. All this is relatively easy to explain, for the plastic arts, dependent on seeing, reach the external, and the external world is general. Even subjectivity is realized in collective signs, whereas in music even collectivism gains expression through subjectivity. Or more specifically, in the fine arts even the most individual is conveyed through the general, whereas in music even the most universal appears through the individual. Therefore medieval art, embracing architecture, sculpture, and painting, may be somewhat strange to us, but, unlike music, is it never forbidding, even to the layman.

The musical counterpart of this Gothic art is indeed frightening to behold. Let us take the principal and highest art form, the motet. At the outset we must realize that, according to every utterance from those times, whether by a theoretical writer or by a philosopher, the spatial conception of the fine arts weighs heavily on the subjectivistic nature of the lyric arts, causing the temporal quality of medieval polyphony to be a prisoner of a collective-universal spatial philosophy. The spirit of the motet makes the musical form timeless by mixing melodies of opposing nature and character in a manner that prevents their melting together; they remain separate entities. The sounding together of these several tunes does not result in a true polyphony, it is only an enhanced sort of heterophony. The listener can direct his full attention to only one part at a time, because the other melodies do not attach themselves to the first one; they merely coincide with one another in a sort of deliberate accident. The more we try to take in the motet as a whole, the more the melodies disturb one another; thus we either jump from place to place or follow one melody and let the others remain in the background. The whole of the form—and an infinitely chiseled and incredibly complicated form it is—is nevertheless nothing but a document, the document of the superhuman force of the verb. This conclusion is inevitable if we take the motet in all its seriousness as it should be taken. The often expressed opinion that music was still in its experimental stage, that the motet, and medieval music in general, constitute a mere groping for elementary effects, is only a sign of ignorance of historical developments. If this type of construction is not the result of the most serious philosophical and theological conceptions, it can only be humorous, like the many amusing pieces composed in later centuries under the name of *quodlibet*. However, it is hard to believe that the earnest and most learned masters of the Gothic era wanted to play a game of hide and seek with their musical melodies.

We can now contrast the spirit of medieval church music with the contemporary folk art. The insurmountable wall between them is not formed by their opposing qualities, by a metaphysical-religious and a naturalistic-secular tendency; church music always had in it secular-popular elements. The unbridgeable gap is created by the philosophical orientation which underlies Christian liturgical music, an orientation which turns against nature, whereas the fount of folk music is naturalism. The collectivism of ecclesiastical metaphysics oppresses the subjective, relegating it to the background; whereas folk music, even when nourished by metaphysical elements, seeks to reconcile the subjective with the universal. Church thought clings to the principle of timelessness and makes concessions to time to the minimal extent required by practical necessities, whereas the secular spirit of folk music regards time as the purest reality—hence the polar antithesis of the two which is apparent in every formal manifestation of their respective music.

But there are still other capital differences between the two. Liturgical music of the Middle Ages is almost always declamatory—that is, it favors the text—while folk music is mostly purely "musical," endeavoring to render the poetic form through musical form. The text of ecclesiastical music is mainly in prose, whereas folk music is always in verse. In ecclesiastical music rhythmic structure and text are related only by the sense of the words, while in folk music the mood of the poem is so fully absorbed by the music that rhythm even rules over the details of the poem. Medieval church music is denaturalized, and therefore its spirit is, strictly speaking, amusical; whereas folk music is music of the flesh, its texts are mostly amorous, its teacher is nature, and it rises from bodily motions and from sensual impulses. In ecclesiastical recitation the cadence is a logical close as represented in the *finalis*. There is no rhythmic ratio between *repercussio* and finalis, only a logical relationship. In folk music, leaning from the earliest date towards the major–minor system, the ratio of functional relationship between tonic, dominant, and subdominant is an autonomous musical phenomenon and is largely independent of the text.

Gothic music is, then, intellectual in its formal manifestations, while folk music is purely aesthetic. In the final analysis, it was the will for timelessness that created medieval ecclesiastical polyphony. There can be no question that a popular polyphony existed centuries before the ecclesiastical variety; nor can there be any question that it was from this foundation that the ecclesiastical variety grew. But since the most primitive functional harmony uses cadences for delineation of formal proportions, such naturalistic-primitive and subjective music had to be opposed by the Church; it was therefore against the secularism of popular metrics that the magistri opposed their philosophical convictions. Far from strengthening functional logic, far from promoting even time proportions or the clear rhythmic accentuation of drums and cymbals, they wanted to efface everything that would detract from the contourless mystery of religion.

The reverence we accord to the *ars antiqua* is, of course, fully justified. The tone material itself is of secondary importance, just as the man whose soul it represents is of secondary importance. The artistic form itself represents is of secondary importance. The artistic form itself represents a value only insofar as it is liturgical, because, according to St. Augustine, while all art originates from humanity, man is not able to represent the divine perfectly. The master of the ars antiqua was more a theologian-philosopher than a musician, and music, unlike architecture but very much like philosophy, is merely *ancilla theologiae*, the symbol of timelessness. Nevertheless, the aesthetic pleasure the medieval artist derived from the arrangement, symmetry, and logic of abstract proportions was a very real one.

As you can readily see, the métier which we so diligently explore is dwarfed by the tremendous issues raised by life and human ideals. Restricting ourselves to the technical aspects, we may miss the meaning of it altogether. Some might say: "Well, in the Middle Ages this may hold true, but as soon as we can exercise our native musical instinct we are on firm ground." All right, let us advance then on to this *terra firma*.

When the Renaissance produced the great movement known as humanism, the Ciceronian ideal of humanity was reborn. Yet, aside from superficial resemblances, the humanity of Cicero's time and that of the Renaissance are, viewed both historically and psychologically, two very different phenomena. The symbol reappeared but could not be the same, for, since Cicero, the world had greatly changed. The reborn symbol had to face the Christian ideal before it could assert itself. The great reckoning took place, and the new ideal of humanity, while not denying the next world as a theological doctrine, in practice put emphasis upon this life on earth. This new humanitas could not believe that the purpose of life should be its own denial; on the contrary, it stood for the cultivation of ever higher forms of life. The new humanity is, then, a conscious or unconscious protest against the Christian ideal of man the powerless; it again enthrones man as the measure of all things, and man becomes the meaning of history. Humanism is the conception of life from the point of view of man.

Music faithfully reflects the great upheaval that is implicit in the rise of this new aspect of life. The small garden of secular music grows into a vast nursery of flowers. Frottola, villanella, madrigal, chanson, occupy the composers, and the output spills over the old boundaries to inundate the entire domain of music.

With the easing of the theological pressure, as scholasticism was displaced, a pantheistic conception of nature creeps into the world of the Renaissance. Painter and sculptor embrace realism, and the architect emphasizes naturalness in static arrangements. With the use of perspective the visual arts reach a milestone of demarcation, yet they still conceive of space as nonexistent. Of course, in the representation of miracles, naturalistic space is by the nature of the subject negated; but more revealing is the fact that such pictures do seek to convey the impression of abstract or ideal space—the artificial space of the studio or the unreal and seemingly weightless expanse of the cupola.

This situation is paralleled in music. We have spoken of the two poles that are in constant opposition: theological philosophy and naturalism. In music, the lower pole encompasses folk song and folk dance, from which grew the general type of Western song and dance. This folk music is, of course, the result of a popular, naive-naturalistic conception of time and likes to build on a pulsating group-rhythm. Being the product of an essentially subjective conception, it can and does lead to the richest and most characteristic territories of music. But it could not achieve these higher art forms by its own resources, because popular art follows nature in seeking everywhere the simplest basic patterns, which it defends stubbornly against encroachment. It is for this reason that this art never proceeds on its own beyond an elementary dynamism, that the higher dynamism which reflects the struggle of universal forces is missing in the art forms of the people. The monochrome of its world outlook restricts folk art to the narrow region of artistic forms which is characterized by an even distribution of the collective and subjective elements on the plane of the naive-universal.

But the immense attraction exerted by this music on the learned composer of the rising Renaissance was the functional tonality embodied in folk song, especially since this functional tonality was not restricted to the major–minor modes but was tied to the subjectivity and to the naturalistic sense of time which accompanies the former. Thus, such functional relationship can exist even within the ecclesiastical modes if the cadencing is not dependent on a rhetorical order but is autonomously musical. The fundamental difference between church and folk music is therefore not to be sought in the scales upon which they are built but in the application of the time element. The same scale can have two meanings. If it follows the logic and sense of the prose text, it will be governed by its finalis; if it organizes autonomously musical proportions, it becomes functional. In one case the cadence represents the end of sections in asymmetric proportions; in the other it signifies the end of relatively evenly proportioned segments and conveys a definitely functional feeling. Thus, contrary to a widespread belief, functional architecture is not the sole property of the major–minor system, but a general characteristic of autonomous musical thought.

The procedure whereby these life-giving elements of folk music gained first slow and then rapid acceptance in art music is quite similar to the just-mentioned procedures in architecture. Popular polyphony, from which grew our Western art music, was originally essentially variation. Bourdon and round, in which the melody, so to speak, plays with itself, intensify themselves by strengthening, widening, constricting, or projecting the line. But it is lacking in such spiritual traits as would deepen its significance. We might say that popular polyphony is the result of an effort to amplify an already existing form in all its details. Popular polyphony, therefore, is really a mere variant of the monophonic presented simultaneously. This polyphony is a playful, hedonistic enjoyment of sound patterns. Against this stands ecclesiastical art music with anything but playful intentions; for while popular polyphony represents the intensification of such independent musical forms as need no intensification, to which polyphony brings not an essential but only a quantitative addition, ecclesiastical polyphony implies a multiplicity of moods, a metaphysical deepening. Therefore this music, which interprets a sacred text, will always have a mystical background in which hides a residue that cannot be brought to the surface.

It was in this ecclesiastical polyphony, as suffused by the elements of popular-secular music, that the most characteristic trait of Occidental music was born: the searching, penetrating, probing quality we feel so intensely in more recent music, but which was nonetheless present in earlier music. But let us make no mistake about one thing: this music of the Renaissance is no longer the work of the composer schooled in Augustinian thought, to whom time and space did not exist. While still clinging to a good many of the old tenets, he now composes music that can stand on its own as music. In the measure that popular music made itself felt in the course of the historical development of contrapuntal forms, the rhythmic and tonal construction demands a voice in musical architecture. And the optimum is reached when popular elements, notably dance forms, are completely assimilated and stylized, while at the same time the tendency of polyphony to profundity is retained but is dependent on a musical logic.

This music, from Dufay to Josquin, is fairly well known; but curiously enough, it is again the métier that is extolled, the unquestionably fantastic contrapuntal ability of these composers, while the idea, as usual, is ignored. And yet what important (and at times embarrassing) conclusions can be gained by studying history as a development of ideas and not techniques! First of all, ever since Dufay, musicians have declared, first timidly, then emphatically, the oneness of music—that is, that there is no essential difference between sacred and secular music: everything depends in art on the purpose and mode of expression. This is the great contribution of the Renaissance humanitas in the field of music. That subsequently, as in the wake of the Reformation, or during the Palestrina revival, the essential oneness of music was again questioned, even hotly denied, should not mislead us; any intelligent study of the history of church music shows that the stream of music could never again be deflected by extramusical powers; the old fundamental division between sacred and secular music, *qua music*, is gone forever.

Noble attempts have been made to return to the old medieval concept. The master of the Sainte-Chapelle, the earnest Flemish composer Ockeghem, tried to return to the contourless mystery of the Gothic, and his appearance must be considered a sort of neo-Gothic revival. At his death the French poets bewailed his passing in words accorded to princes, and indeed Ockeghem was called *princeps musicae*; his thirty-six-part motet is mentioned as one of the world's wonders, and his contrapuntal technique, canonic and imitative writing, were held unsurpassable. But this coldly glowing genius eagerly summoned his immense musical wizardry in order to cool his fever, to erect barriers for his passions. For this man is the last of the possessed in whom the eternal soaring, the mystery, the endless melody and endless counterpoint, the heaven-reaching architecture of the musical cathedrals of the Gothic once more raise their voice against the new humanity of the Renaissance. This art could not be continued by anyone else, and those who attempted it produced nothing but mannerism.

It was no longer possible to compose music for the Church that would be *fundamentally* different from secular music. It is true that Mass and motet took their departure from premises that were different from those of madrigal and chanson; but the chanson melodies intruded into the Mass and motet, and now the chanson tune came to have equal rights with the Gregorian chant as the material upon which a sacred work can be built. Some of the most exalted sacred liturgical works were composed upon popular Franco-Flemish dance tunes, amorous songs, or bantering ditties. The listeners, unlike their nineteenth-century brethren who thought such a procedure almost sacrilegious, were not scandalized, because they were children of the new humanity, to

whom a good melody was a noble melody, perfectly proper under any auspices. Much has been made of the presence of these chanson tunes in liturgical music, but all the conjectures and censures advanced in historically unin-
formed books are false. What mattered was the good tune, which remained
good in or out of church, and the original connotations were simply forgotten
when "La belle se sied" was turned into "Deus pater omnipotens." In its turn,
the chanson showed influences emanating from motet and Mass, for together
with the happy melodic sallies there are tears and sighs scarcely hidden behind
the courtly exterior, or, as the chanson itself says, "Triste plaisir et douloureuse
joie." How unjustly the world has judged this great music and these great
musicians, every inch the equal of their much more famous confreres in the
other arts. It has granted them respect, but mainly on account of their redoubtable craft of composition. Well, their compositional style eventually became
antiquated, but not their melodies, those wonderful, everlasting melodies that
have lived on for centuries. But it is no longer permissible to praise a church
musician for his melodies; he should not choose melodies for their sheer
beauty, and he should not be too happy about them either. Ever since the
nineteenth-century Romantic movement and the essentially super-Romantic
Palestrina revival, church music stands for unmitigated gloom, relieved only
by a plentiful and sanctimonious use of dominant seventh chords.

Let us examine one more metamorphosis of humanitas, one much closer
to us in time. I am referring to the so-called Classic era, the last third of the
eighteenth century, and extending through the first quarter of the nineteenth.
The word has become ambiguous in these days, when the record manufacturers advertise not only the "Classics" but also the "Semi-Classics," a definition that would stump a bevy of philologists. However, the philologists do not
have to worry, because our authors and critics simplify their task considerably.
These worthies equate Classicism with formalism, and every one of you must
have come across the statement that for the Classic composer form was the
primary concern; content was secondary if not negligible. According to this
opinion, amiable and rather playful composers such as Haydn and Mozart,
compass and ruler in hand, created nicely designed formal schemes which
they then proceeded to fill in with some pretty music. This idyllic and a bit
irresponsible music making came to an end only with the advent of Beethoven,
who, to quote the title of an incredible book that not too long ago had great
currency, was "the man who freed music." What did he free it from? The
pseudo-historians are ready with the answer: from the fetters of objectivity.
This may sound humorous to those who know the music of the Classic era, but

unfortunately it was meant in earnest. What is this formalism, this objectivity that allegedly circumscribes the work of the Classic composer, apparently preventing him from projecting his true feelings in his music?

First of all, we must remember that what we call the Classic era was preceded by a period that goes under the name of *Sturm und Drang*, Storm and Stress. The poets and composers of the Storm and Stress represent a human type that has been known for a long time yet always appears as new. They are the dissatisfied and the rebellious, the iconoclasts and the destroyers of form, the ones who always start and seldom finish things. They live dangerously and dynamically, they are forever excited and addicted to excesses; they want to widen the world, and in so doing form and measure drop from their hands. In a word, they are the revolutionaries who time and again return in Western art, who are both its embers and its bellows. They are the eternal Romanticists. Their role is the same whether in the North or in the South: they rip apart and unravel the fabric of music in order to liberate the magic hidden in the threads. There is a direct line leading from these eighteenth-century Romanticists to their more grandiose and durable brethren of the nineteenth century; but before Romanticism became the artistic faith of an entire century, it paused for an entr'acte which we call the Classic era. Indeed, we must begin to realize that in the few decades of the Classic era we are dealing not with a style period that follows and is followed in an orderly fashion by others, but, as I have just said, with an interlude, around which the previous stylistic current merely parts as around an island, only to reunite at the other end. That the epoch-making synthesis that is eighteenth-century Classicism blinds us to the current that flows around it is perhaps understandable, though not pardonable. As a teacher of a good many years' experience, I defy any student to name the names of the Romantic composers, many of them well worth knowing, who refused to go along with the sonata ideal which was the quintessence of Classic musical thought, who in fact rebelled against it. And yet they were there, before Schubert and Weber, even before Beethoven reached his peak.

Viewed from this perspective, we will understand that from the subjectivism of the Sturm und Drang there arose a new phase of humanity which, judged by its tendency, could be called nothing else but objective. But this new objectivity did not aim at displacing the subjectivity of the Storm and Stress movement, only at taming its amorphous excesses. And the remarkable fact is that this sobering up of the movement or, if you please, this new objectivity did not come from without, but began in the souls of the very men who were once buffeted by the tempest. They changed because they discovered that their boundless subjectivism did not lead to a heightening of life, but rather to a debasement of it, which found its poetic symbol in the suicide of Werther.

The music of Vienna did, once more, gather and elevate, achieve the miracle of synthesis, and this after Baroque weight, Rococo lightness, and pre-Romantic excitement. Once more every extreme is reconciled in the noblest equilibrium, to become the ultimate harmony of Europe's music, its looming tower, and its third and perhaps final crowning—a harvest that can come only after the most bountiful summer. This Classic synthesis offers a new, intimate yet spacious, peaceful, and warming home to humanity, a home whither it can always return and where it will always be on well-loved ground. This home and this security appear as a new idea and a new discovery after the rootless wanderings of early Romanticism. The world has found out that sunshine is preferable to eerie moonlight pierced by lightning, that the sky is more beautiful than the clouds, and sobriety better than eternal intoxication. But above all, it found out that only arrival gives sense to travel. The aged Haydn proudly declared that his London symphonies are understood by the whole world. Indeed, by the end of the century we no longer speak of German music, for this music became the musical language of the world, as in the two previous supreme syntheses the musical language of the Franco-Flemish composers and later of the Neapolitans became the language of the world. For in these symphonies of Haydn, as in the works of Mozart and of the other masters of the era, there speaks a musicianship that is universal, timeless, and valid under all circumstances. This music is not one solution or one aspect, nor is it a personal matter; it speaks to all peoples.

But Classicism does not stand for Olympian calm, cold reserve, haughty isolation from all that is disturbing or dissonant. On the contrary, the mature Classic style shows interest in every tributary stream, because its principal aim, and its very nature, is to contain the whole in every detail.

And now, returning to the lamented formalism of the Classic era, I should like to use a comparison from architecture, always felicitously related to music. The post-Baroque composers, the stragglers, the fugue-writers, who were clinging to contrapuntal structures when the world around them was more interested in decoration than in architecture, had lost the feeling for the life-giving substance that animated the true Baroque. What remained from the Baroque were the bare walls which stood there somberly, even menacingly, defying the new spirit that was pouring in from the South. The musical architects of that post-Baroque era were at heart fortress engineers, not church and palace builders, and they constructed bastions instead of colonnades. The Austrians, hemmed in by their northern and southern neighbors, Germans and Italians, were destined to reconcile the two musical cultures and in so doing to create a synthesis that was to conquer the world of music. They drove the hollow gloom from their edifices, and they tore down the bastions and in their stead built graceful spires. But let us make no mistake: the silly comparisons with Watteau and the *fêtes galantes* can only be ascribed to ignorance of history as well as music. For while the bastions were torn down, the massive foundations were kept, and the spires, although graceful and airy, had their own strength and majesty. This was still constructive architecture, not interior decoration.

The modern listener, used to the opulence of the Wagner–Strauss–Sibelius orchestral world, may be a bit disappointed when he enters the world of the Classic sonata, which includes everything from string quartet to Mass. He will find the interior of these works on a smaller scale and will look around somewhat embarrassed. He will find things apparently so well organized that every little stone has its formal and ordained spot that denies the flight of fancy. This disappointment accompanies every centrally constructed edifice, especially if the portals through which the beholder enters do not prepare and inform him about the underlying plan. What is the portal, the principal opening subject of a Classical symphony? Compared to the ample melody of a late Romantic symphony, it is indeed frugal and lapidary; but unlike the Romantic symphony, which exists right from the beginning and then endeavors to maintain this existence, the Classical symphony grows, grows like a centrally planned structure. And the more harmonious the interior of a building, the smaller the immediate dynamic effect it creates. No one would guess the actual vastness of St. Peter's in Rome unless he paces the nave. Only when we become oriented, when our eyes—or in this instance our ears—get used to the proportions, when we begin to measure without pacing, will the phenomenon grow and become understandable.

I have endeavored to single out three periods from the more than two thousand years of recorded music history to demonstrate that philosophical ideas, changing as the style periods themselves do, always profoundly influence the very concept of music. Penetration into the inner dynamics, tension, and rhythm of events—that is, into history—and into the interplay of being and value is the first prerequisite of the study of the growth of an art. This leads to more than an understanding of the past and the present; it also offers an anticipatory interpretation of the future.

From an Editorial

$\mathbb{O}$ur readers may have wondered why *The Musical Quarterly*, devoted to the publication of what we consider valuable additions to our knowledge of music, assigned two of its most eminent contributors to the task of reviewing some recent publications which they dealt with in unmistakable terms of indignation and censure. Presently, the Editor will take the liberty of adding still another publication, a musical encyclopedia,* if it can be called that, to this already fragrant bouquet.

The old Latin proverb, "to err is human," is a familiar cliché as well as a profound truth; another of more recent origin, that "even the sage trips over the truth seven times a week," is less known, although equally true. These adages warn us to be charitable; moreover, the critics must constantly bear in mind that an honest error or hypothesis often leads to brilliant correction, leaving us actually indebted to the man whose tentative ideas led to more positive and productive thinking. A case in point is the Runge–Aubry–Beck controversy on the music of the troubadours and trouvères. These were earnest and promi-

From *The Musical Quarterly*, vol. 40 (1954)
*Milton Cross's Encyclopedia of the Great Composers and Their Music (Garden City, NY: Doubleday, 1953).

nent scholars, groping for the truth, and even their mistakes were the result of serious scholarly endeavor. But demi-science that is served up as a corrective for the arduous labors of generations of dedicated scholars, ignorance that is paraded as information, and plain literary buccaneering—as well as publishing—to capture the mass market are different matters. Far from shrugging them off as beneath contempt, we should thrust them into the arena of professional musicography, and it is our duty to warn, expose, and indict, to guard the dignity of the profession and protect the unwary.

There is quite a difference between ignorance of history, lack of accuracy, or even downright misrepresentation as reflected in a work of art and the same errors in art history and criticism. The history of art and of *belles lettres* is a storehouse of anachronisms and of gentle 180-degree distortions of facts. He who would take it upon himself to correct these blunders would be guilty of the most barbarous destruction. Did not Virgil make Aeneas a contemporary of Dido, and did not Raphael paint the likeness of a great Renaissance Pope in a picture dealing with an early medieval scene? But if the artist's "mistakes" are accompanied by inspiration, he does not have to be accurate. The creative artist may very well counter our objection that it was not so by saying that it should have been so, and who is there to contradict him? The critic and historian have vastly different responsibilities. They are, to cite another inevitable cliché, seeking not beauty but truth. They are certainly entitled to present hypotheses, but these must be buttressed by solid arguments based on thorough historical research in which nothing should be lifted out of context.

Systemic research in arts and letters always flows over into historiography, and the overwhelming number of such essays are of a historical nature. But history is not exhausted by the random use of documents, nor should a purely genetic method of procedure be used. In the immense multitude of facts, the selective principle of history writing considers the degree of effect and influence of such facts. This is undoubtedly a relative measure, depending on the size of the picture that the historian paints and its amount of detail. A great many unessential facts demand inclusion in a thoroughgoing monograph, and it is here that the scholar's creative force and discrimination come into play; he must have a sense for values and proportions. In a way everything that has influence is history. In contradistinction, no phenomenon that is in some relationship to cultural life, no matter how tenuous, can be called unessential from the point of view of history; but its utilization depends on the scholar's mental rule.

A music scholar must be a musical philologist who knows the grammar, syntax, etymology, and morphology of his language, music, as his colleague the literary historian knows linguistics. *Philology* has both a narrow and a wider meaning. In the first case, philology is concerned with the critical restoration of the texts that are the subject of historical investigation, which is then proceeds to interpret. This is formal philology. In the second sense, philology, going beyond the formal aspects, endeavors to understand the restored texts from the cultural conditions of which they are documents. But this is already hardly distinguishable from historiography itself, indicating that philology and history are sister disciplines that support one another. Lack of one hobbles the other; hence it is that there are few if any true historians unwilling to assume the role of philologist, while there are equally few philologists who would be satisfied with the examination of the texts without investigating their contents.

The third work we alluded to above takes us out of the realm of even shadowy scholarship and ordinary incompetence, for it is falsehood and collusion, a hoax perpetrated on a "captive" public. This sort of thing would not be worth the space the invectives it calls for consumes on paper, but it is offered as a reference work and thus will find its way not only onto the shelves of schools and public libraries, where a wide public can consult it.

The author is a radio announcer. Now his is a perfectly respectable occupation and undoubtedly more lucrative than just ordinary music scholarship. However, one can understand why there is no record of a member of his profession turning, at the height of his annunciatory career, to lexicography— the latter occupation calls for mental rather than psittacistic exertion.

A search in the music reference works was fruitless; his name is nowhere listed. Then we realized that this is the wrong approach, for he is not so much a name as an institution, an American institution known to millions as the cultural embassy of the oil industry, established in a glass cage at the Metropolitan Opera House in New York. Therefore the proper work in which to search for him is *Who's Who in America*. We found him there at the first try, but the entry contains only three relevant facts, the first of which, "earned gold medal in diction," does not come as a surprise, while the other two, that he is a Republican and a Presbyterian, still do not explain how he turned, so late in life, to lexicography. Well, amiable reader, the riddle is solved as soon as you open the book: for inside there appears a co-author, who undoubtedly took a considerable hand in performing this chore.

If at a wedding party the bridal music from *Lohengrin* is played, no one notices it because it is a tradition and carries no other significance. If, however, at the end of the service someone should announce to the festive gathering that they were to be treated to some superbly original music, only to hear the strains of the same old march, everyone would be very much annoyed. This is approximately what authors and publishers are doing in this encyclopedia, thus calling attention to the trivialities, clichés, canards, and misinformation that are traditional in this trade. In any other field but music, such a thing would be tarred and feathered; but in ours the publishers have the audacity to present such a miserable compilation as the last word in up-to-date scholarly accuracy—"the most valuable work of its kind ever published." The publishers severely remind the reader that special permission is required to quote "more than five hundred words" from this work. Since almost every page contains something worthwhile—to the reviewer—this precaution is commendable. Being too bashful to seek permission, we shall restrict ourselves to a mere thirty words from the introduction, but trust that they are so meaningful that any further quotation or comment will be superfluous.

> There were eminent composers before Bach's day who wrote much distinguished music. They are not included in this volume because both the composers and their music are now somewhat esoteric.

The publishers bear considerable responsibility in the undertaking discussed above. Patently, they used the name of an author known to millions of radio listeners who, willy-nilly, have to submit to his gold-medal eloquence if they want to hear operas. Having placed his name on the *outside* of the book, they entrusted the inside to one of our notorious *Vielschreiber* who are ready to write a book, any book, at the drop of a hat. This is deceit and rates unmitigated condemnation.

Music Past and Present:
An Epilogue

The output of international music scholarship has reached staggering proportions. To find one's way through this ever-thickening forest on even a single topic becomes a steadily more disconcerting venture. We are inevitably moving toward greater reliance on the computer, for there is no question that the machines can perform in a few minutes some of the most laborious operations, such as the compilation of concordances or bibliographies, that otherwise can require months of drudgery. However, we must still master the traditional way of finding facts and attempting their interpretation by hand and brains; pen and paper are not in danger of being altogether replaced by punchcards. In the making of *Die Musik in Geschichte und Gegenwart* (MGG), a thousand brains and pens have been engaged, and one cannot but be consumed with admiration for all the industry, the burrowing investigation, the tenacity, the leaving of no stone unturned, that characterize this giant undertaking.

Much of the contents of an encyclopedia of music must needs be straight, workable musicological reportage, but this one contains many sizable essays

From *Die Musik in Geschichte und Gegenwart*, vol. 16 (1979)

remarkable for their wide-ranging coverage of important subjects, and there is also a good deal of new and little-known material. Manifold skeins of history and culture had to be kept in hand, countless details of numerous and variegated lives sorted out. Then there was the monumental chore of clarifying "influences," of deciding who originated what and when, who received proper credit, who did not.

The great are seen reaching their hands toward one another across the centuries, but visibility had also to be given to those lesser talents whom the world has overlooked. Some able composers have been misunderstood and undervalued; some had perhaps too much fame, then critical deflation, and subtle hostility from subsequent biographers. There is also the special case of the marginal composers who nevertheless were able to transcend their marginality. All the while the contributors to *MGG* had to remove musicians and their works from a time vault where they had been preserved, and they had to recover, through the generational conduit, the conditions that charged and shaped them. In these large, densely packed volumes, adorned with countless illustrations and musical examples, a confident track winds through musical thought and history. With its geographical breadth—all continents are represented—and its temporal scope—millennia are traversed—its achievement is simply formidable. The research is thorough and for the most part imaginative, the observations are pertinent and persuasive; this work does not presume to solve all the reader's problems, but only perhaps to add to his awareness of them, and it has the virtue of permitting the reader to use his own judgment. Withal, it is a reliable guide for the learner but also for the learned.

As Friedrich Blume, whom Karl Vötterle, the publisher, secured as editor, remarked in the preface to the first fascicle of *MGG*, the aim of the undertaking is "completeness of content and treatment at the highest level of present day scholarship." This in itself is the manifesto one expects from a scholar of his standing, but he adds something that is new: "*MGG* will not be a manual, not even a lexicon, but a genuine encyclopedia." This was written in 1949, and to many it seemed utopian to attempt an undertaking governed by such lofty principles and of such vast proportions. Where is Utopia? The Greek word means "nowhere"; this ideal would always emerge on the horizon then sink again. Did Blume and Bärenreiter Verlag reach it this time before it vanished?

The task that editor and publisher set for themselves was a truly cosmic one. The dictionaries of music are usually less guides to the examined life of music than operator's manuals; they attempt to compress all facets of music, its history and theory, into a relatively few, brief, and often cursory articles.

Though even some of these can bristle with intelligence, a good deal of this old method of putting together a reference manual is lexicography rampant, with scarcely a spark of imagination in the whole clay clump. Recognizing that this narrow concept now seemed to have run its course, MGG deliberately choose a new path. Sober factual presentation no longer suffices in the latter twentieth century. Today we expect that an article in a dictionary will leave the reader with a satisfying sense of gain: new information acquired, an enlarged historical appreciation, a stimulating critical perception widening his horizon. We have discovered that when we try to contemplate music and its history without placing it within a spacious landscape, we inevitably fall into circularity and cataloguing; the time has come to ask the hard questions. We have progressed from the times when music history, drawing much of its rationale from natural science, laid a disproportionate emphasis upon simple causality, without regard for critical significance.

While the learned journals often print articles which are content to pinpoint a source and let it go at that, good source study is nowadays governed by the principle that origins must be made relevant by criticism which illuminates meaning and thus deepens our understanding, as it does when it rises to the dignity of an independent act of critical inquiry into the composer's mind and art. We now realize that we must approach and examine a piece of music both in relation to its own time and as it existed in history, as it submits to one kind of perception in one age and another kind of perception in another age, as it exerts in each age a different kind of power. Modern scholarship tries to enlarge the perspective it enjoys within the framework of its own historical era by viewing both the work of art and its matrix epoch from greater distances of time. We now reach for the connections between the musical evidence and the pressing questions about the human conditions in society which are at the heart of social theory. This is a serious approach and must be treated seriously.

Humanistic scholarship moves within two worlds at once: the world of the scientific method and the world of creative art. Our challenging duty is to conform to the challenging stipulations of each, without impinging on those of the other. Many of us tend to see and follow the method only and at times forget the end; the fascination of the means distracts us from the object for which they are employed. This "end" toward which we are working is interpretation of the art of music. The application of historical knowledge to music scholarship ranges from the minute to the panoramic, its variety is endless; but its essence, demonstrated on the thousands of pages of MGG, is to reveal in bold outline the patterns of art and thought that were hitherto obscure or buried under the weight of detail.

It is undeniable, however, that the focal point in historical musicology is gradually shifting from style criticism, which was the great new departure inaugurated by Guido Adler and the other grand old men who pioneered modern musicology at the turn of the century, toward a social-critical orientation, and that the role of music's scientific components as represented by systematic musicology, notably acoustics and psychology, is moving into the foreground. Also, we often find that a problem heretofore considered purely musical may very well be more cultural than artistic. The planners of *MGG* were duly aware of both the advantages and the pitfalls of this new orientation, and took steps to meet its requirements without jeopardizing the humanistic traditions. They were also aware that this is an era in which it is fashionable to flirt with the extremes represented by Freudism, Marxism, Existentialism, and all the other "isms." The stream of history has been contaminated from many sources, and we must call on our critical intelligence as the disinfectant that will make the water potable by counteracting the variety of misinformation that lurks in the data that come our way. Once a mistake is set adrift, it proliferates. One compelling reason why a myth becomes persuasive and increasingly difficult to discredit, despite exposure, is that it is often so much more picturesque than the prosaic truth, vide the tenacious legend of Palestrina as the "savior of church music." A good anecdote, however doubtful its credentials, appeals to the romantic in us. The famous story of the keyboard duel between Mozart and Clementi was enacted on many occasions in several countries with several different casts.

It may not be amiss to examine some of the exercises in reality and unreality that are the lot of the editor-in-chief attempting to guide such an enterprise as *MGG*. First of all, he must contend with things as concrete as sources. As an illustration of the snares he encounters, I shall quote a few examples. We may call it axiomatic that no edition of letters published before the 1920s, at the earliest, can be relied upon. Among the notorious cases of this are the pettyfogging of Mozart's inelegancies and the censoring of Nietzsche's letters. Memoirs are usually idealized and embroidered by the desire for self-justification. Adrianus Petit Coclico's stories would do honor to Baron von Münchhausen, while Berlioz's boundless enthusiasms are matched by his implacable hatreds. The Commandment's injunction against worshipping false gods says nothing about man worshipping himself. Moreover, at times (Stravinsky comes to mind) the autobiographies are written by ghost writers. Composers also have a way of tossing garlands to one another, though not without a concealed thorn here and there, while others sound like a sparrow patronizing a nightingale. Then there are the piratical publishers who discovered the advantages of the "big name" long before modern times; forgeries and imitations have a long history, and they bedevil the work of the most careful scholars. In general, even the primary evidence must be critically weighed, and some errors will never be detected.

The really exasperating problem for an editor is the extreme variety in the training, attitude, and ability of contributors. All large reference works compiled by a considerable number of writers are bound to be uneven and to some extent inconsistent, despite the greatest editorial skill and care, for each author has his personal standards of pertinence and importance, each responds to the problems and challenges according to his lights and temperament. As is well known, the greater the dilettante, the wider he opens the window when he plays. There are those who discharge a thousand volts of charm, while others, notably those laboring under repressive and dogmatic impositions that reduce experience and thought to accord with pre-defined political objectives, offer a landscape that is gray and flat. The neon-lighted nationalism of some is now no more acceptable than the benumbing sobriety of the old-line German, as well as the modern American, lexicographer.

However, there are far more grievous faults than dilettantism, and they must be met, head on, by the editor. The façade of an article may be noble and its dimensions imposing, but closer inspection may reveal serious defects. One is a tendency to irrelevance, another the failure to ask the important historical questions, or the intrusion of suppositional detail that the author could not possibly have verified; we should remember that doughty François-Joseph Fétis, whose many invented data are still being run down and found spurious. Some authors have a tendency to go off on tangents whenever they get a chance, while others struggle from one page to the next, hardly knowing where they are going until they get there. Certain types have a taste for apocalyptic rhetoric, some like to berate a cow for not being a horse, and there are those mystics who touch the unseen and unreasonably insist that we share their experience. Many biographers believe that they are custodians of their subject's posthumous reputation, which makes them dismiss any criticism as ignorance, and there is the not infrequent antipathy of one biographer toward another.

Nothing can devitalize a topic more effectively than the manner in which it is discussed. It is possible to hold forth on music with the seriousness it deserves and yet not be grim or heavy-footed; we need not don suits of solemn black. Nuances in meaning are as important in learned writing as they are in poetry; a touch of wit in a serious article is no more reprehensible than a bon mot in a lecture, yet it is a thousand times less common. Even a bibliographical article under the right auspices can entertain as it informs. One witty sentence can instantly characterize a whole age, as when Michelet, the great French historian, sums up one facet of the history of civilization: "Personne n'a pas pris un bain en Europe pendant mille ans." The style of many influential modern scholars and critics, heavily tinted with borrowings from the vocabulary and ponderous mannerisms of sociologists, psychologists, and anthropologists, ultimately enters into our own bloodstream. There should be no difference between a good scholarly style and a good literary style addressed to the intelligent layman; standards of scholarship can be maintained no matter how large the audience.

On any chart of values, MGG largely succeeded in holding this litany of impediments to a minimum. Even this encyclopedia inevitably has its share of what we may call "clinical scholars," who spend the space allotted to them in checking minor details, remote from intuition, emotion, and conception; but MGG is characterized by soundness of reasoning, clear exposition of the topics' significance, unaffected, terse, and lucid presentation. The contributors are alert to the shoals of over-generalization, and they do not compel the reader to steer his own way; they probe into the relationships between artifice and reality, into the cultural mutations that changed the course of music history, and their skill in running down a particular phenomenon is matched by their ability to analyze it. Above all, most contributors never leave the reader uncertain as to their own as well as the reader's destination, and one is aware of a sustained and sensitive respect for the great venture.

It is quite obvious that someone must be credited for this remarkable unanimity of purpose and execution that surmounted massive egos, scholarly narcissism, and all that is obsolete in lexicography. He managed to avoid acute incompatibility to topic and author, and prevented intelligence or intellectual passion from being wrongly applied or misdirected. The success or failure of such a tremendous undertaking depends on the editor who is at the heart of all things. Aside from scholarly and organizational competence, he must be a negotiator, diplomat, and peacemaker, able to adjust his own sights; for in editing it is necessary to acknowledge that truth is as much a matter of perception as of cold facts. Indeed, the editor must function as an omniscient director of a many-sided stage, manipulating the characters, setting the pace of the action, and, so to speak, introducing all the characters to one another. He must have ideas, a will, a purpose, a store of knowledge, an instant grasp of what is workable, and he must always try for the attainable and resist surrendering to the vast, swollen, teeming irrelevance of "too much of everything", judging the expendable element is a prime duty. The editor must know how to

49

harness the positive qualities of fussy minds, deal with obsolete sensibilities, watch for subtleties that might be eroded in transition, and prevent recalcitrant materials from taking their own wayward course. He should know that prestige can sometimes sway any judge, that a problem defined is only the beginning of a problem solved, that taking on a great subject is not the same as finding a fresh way to see it, and he must use discrimination through choice toward an end. Still more, though a scholarly editor proceeds in a manner not unlike that of a lawyer interrogating witnesses, a great editor of a work dealing with the arts is also required to be an artist of sorts, a believer in the power of an invented world. Finally, on top of everything, he is responsible for the important requirements concerning the technical niceties that make a text homogeneous.

In reviewing the work of a great departed scholar, it is difficult for an admirer to keep the obituarist's hyperbole in check; still, it is an unquestioned and unquestionable fact that in Friedrich Blume (1893–1975) MGG found the editor who answered all the specifications described above. He was a man of ideas to whom ideas were his environment, a man who took pride in piercing through procedure to substance, careful to separate fact from conjecture, but not afraid to speculate if evidence was unavailable. His was a keen sensibility, a discerning intelligence, selecting, heightening, reshaping, a lucid writer able to make his meaning plain. His command of German prose style was admirable, with a remarkable economy of words and matter, and frequently in a brilliant phrase he will flash a beam illuminating some dark corner of history. One quickly comes to trust his learning, judgment, and critical honesty, and the pleasure he takes in discussing Bach or Mozart or Bruckner is a pleasure to share. His own writing as well as his judgment of the other contributions, which it was his duty to supervise, was obviously nourished at every step by the rigors and rewards of exacting work well outside the musical orbit. He could always see another point of view, but was also properly wary of national bias in either thought or style, none of which he permitted to appear on the pages of MGG. He certainly did not follow the examples of Samuel Johnson, who, when annoyed by an unappetizing piece of writing, "would rather praise it than read it"—every contribution to MGG was read and scrutinized. Blume knew the old German proverb "Eine Rede ist keine Schreibe," and was familiar with the chronic inability of some writers to be precise, as well as with the chaos of even clear ideas when too much experience is swept into one package; nor was he oblivious to the dangers of unleashed statistics. Prudence and the recognition of limits were always important to him, and he refused to overturn permanent conclusions because of momentary doubts.

Yet Blume was far from a neutral observer. While as an editor he was impartial and respected his colleagues' views, when a conflict arose, he favored surgery over homeopathy. He held firm opinions about what scholars should and should not do, and he had strong commitments to certain values and was never less than steadfast in his attachment to them. What authors wrote about, even how they saw things, would not have been quite the same without Blume's firm but sensitive hands. One of the editor's many laudable policies was the exclusion of the kind of intemperate criticism that was frequent in Riemann's day. Differences of opinion there will always be, but such painful altercations as the famous exchange, liberally sprinkled with invectives, be- *(Adler &* tween two distinguished scholars about whether Vienna was a mere suburb of *Riemann)* Mannheim, or vice versa, are not to be found. Here the encyclopedia has established an ethical standard.

How Blume's commanding personality and his plans were communicated to the legion of collaborators, many of whom never saw him, remains a mystery. "A scholar cannot idle" (Jean Paul, *Hesperus*), but his indefatigable activity was still amazing; he could not, even if he wanted to, turn away from the flow of questions and problems. In all the years I have known this remarkable man, there was no slackening in his work; he had an unfeigned respect for the importance of what he was doing, the guidance he was expected to furnish.

The contributors to *MGG* form the most distinguished panel of music scholars ever assembled, and one with a difference. An editor's natural inclination is to settle on an acknowledged expert in every particular field; but, while Blume knew this to be in many instances a mandatory process, he was resolved not to adhere to it to the extent of excluding able younger contributors not yet beatified. He correctly surmised that readers, in the main, are not overawed by the name of the contributor; they will pursue the article only if its author engages their interest and compels them to look hard at what he is saying. A wise editor will search for young scholars, invite and support them, knowing that it is the unexpected fresh reaction that is most rewarding to the reader. Such is exactly the course Blume followed, and not only in his own Germany, but on a global basis. This policy, though all articles by foreign scholars, celebrated or on their way up, were translated into German, made *MGG* into a truly international encyclopedia, a significant departure from the past. When "the Riemann" was translated into French, the only change the French editors made was to remove the hundreds of German provincial organists, forgotten singers, and obscure pedagogues who cluttered up the dictionary, replacing them with their own nonentities. This sort of thing was abolished in *MGG*. Instead, we have certain features of French, or English, or

Italian music as seen through French, or English, or Italian eyes. There was of course the great responsibility of making the often difficult choices. "Music is the universal language of mankind" is an idea loved and often quoted by the poets; unfortunately, this engaging notion is far short of being a universal truth. There are national idiosyncrasies that simply refuse to be laid to rest and which create what we may call the "unexportable" composer. To mention a few from our immediate experience, Reger could not penetrate beyond Germany's frontiers' Fauré is a national musical hero in France but meets with little enthusiasm elsewhere; Elgar is venerated as an English institution, but few are the performances of his works outside Britain; and such examples could be continued at some length. It is important and most enlightening to the reader, accustomed to seeing all composers through German spectacles, to observe these musicians and their music through spectacles with a different tint.

Just as the Blue Danube can have stretches of muddy river even around Strauss's Vienna, so a work of such magnitude cannot be free of dull spots and errors; Bärenreiter Verlag could not risk a counterpart to the long-standing offer of Oxford University Press to pay a guinea for every mistake found in its edition of the Bible. But MGG has a well-earned and well-deserved reputation for accuracy; we feel the general trustworthiness of the facts and opinions, even when they are not supported by our own experience. Many of the articles inevitably overlap; elements of a topic with wide ramifications may turn up in half a dozen articles. But that is all to the good, for it reduces the chance that the reader will miss the very item he most needs to know about. The bibliographies are copious, authoritatively selected, and well classified—though difficult to read. They cannot be exhaustive, but they give references to the books and articles likely to provide the reader with the information he wants. Those who quibble about the omission of an obscure item or two forget that bibliographies are the prime example of obsolescence. Theodore Besterman's *World Bibliography of Bibliographies* (1955–56) lists about 80,000 bibliographies on every conceivable subject; at that, he lists only those that were separately issued! With its inevitable shortcomings, errors, and omissions, MGG compared to its predecessors is like a floodlight to a candle. It is also a lasting monument to Friedrich Blume's lifework; he stands quietly but pervasively behind it.

The postwar musicologists assembled to create MGG went to work in the same shop that in the first half of our century was so well organized that the tools began to dictate to the workers. But these latter-day workers wanted new tools, a fresh tone, and they had different aims. No longer satisfied with the organization of known materials and the miscellany of curiosities of the old lexicography, they searched for additional new materials and changed the treatment of the old ones so that ideas as well as historical continuity became clearer. How different are the little essays that here follow the vital statistics in every entry devoted to a composer from the terse, reserved impersonality and apodictic judgments in the old dictionaries! As Goethe so well stated: "The poet sends his creation out into the world, it behooves the reader, the aesthete, the critic, to examine what he envisaged with his creation." This was the leitmotiv around which, like a wreath, *MGG*'s writers were deployed, their voices often rising to a chorus.

But the editor and his authors soon discovered that their newly furbished shop and their new tools were in turn in danger of being considered obsolescent, as vast new developments in social and scientific concepts, from which their predecessors were historically exempt, demanded acknowledgment. The force of the European tradition is constantly lessening, empires have fallen, dozens of new states have arisen, some of them not only politically but spiritually alien to the West and some with their own rigid interpretations of the arts. Then came the disconcerting inroads from the practitioners of the social sciences, to whom music is primarily a social product. The great composers and their achievements are slighted; it is the average composer who is important, the one who expresses docilely the average soul of the commonality. What really counts to the sociologist is this commonality; indeed, the public may be more important than the composer, musical life than music itself. Still other assaults came from the psychologists, who found the composer's character and personality more valuable than the examination of the work he created; in their hands art criticism became simply a branch of psychology. The attempt, becoming quite fashionable, to psychoanalyze long-dead musicians, the analyst addressing, as it were, an empty couch, virtually leads into the field of fiction. And finally, there came, in the wake of Heinrich Schenker, the new theorists, who with sharp and original minds placed music under a microscope, showing the ingenious alignment of its particles, but totally ignoring history and aesthetics. To deal with the history of the world's music seemed never more untimely—yet it has never been more needed.

Blume and his staff took notice of all these trends, but were not deflected from their original plan and ideas. In order to express the latter, we must once more turn to Goethe: "A man born into, and formed by, the so-called exact sciences, will find it difficult, even at his most perceptive, to understand that there can also be an exact sensuous imagination without which no art is possible." It was in this "imagination," the force of the creative individual, that

MGG's authors espied the essence of art, and while they provided the ample space that the new social and scientific thought demands and deserves, they affirmed that nothing social can avoid being also personal. We are made by history, and we make it; we are both actors and agents. Contrary to all appearances and to much social theory, it is the principle of individuality that binds humanity together; the collective spirit submerges them in impersonality. Man is an individual, and the world's music is the music of man as man. The historian realizes that to write about music in the spirit of the history of ideas appears to some as something old-fashioned and conservative, not in keeping with the progressive march of the sciences, both social and natural; but if so, from this conservatism emanates an unparalleled richness. Perhaps it is exactly what is needed in this confused world of ours; Robinson Crusoe must take inventory of his island. It is good and comforting to have in MGG such a superb summary and inventory of all the things that we are in danger of forgetting. Let us treasure it as a guide both for now and for the uncertain future.

New Thoughts on
Old Music

Palestrina across the Centuries:
A Review

Scholarship often proceeds as in a helix, recurring in the same place but at a higher level. So it is with the study of Palestrina and his music, though the unprejudiced attempt to discover the conscious aims of Palestrina the composer is a critical approach of fairly recent inception. Some of the nineteenth-century scholars and critics recognized the necessity of such an approach, without being quite able or willing to divorce it from the romantic Palestrina legend. The image of the Princeps musicae as a distant, almost supernatural, figure has long been familiar to every one, fully accepted even by Protestants; but if the picture is engaging, it nonetheless deserves closer contemplation; the romantic haze surrounding it almost completely obscures the artist. Palestrina was a master-composer, who achieved maturity under the iron discipline of a highly critical mind, a master whose knowledge of the métier was fabulous, and whose endeavor to perfect and polish this art of composition was as admirable as it was extraordinary, even in an age that produced great composers in abundance. That this impeccable art,

From *Festschrift Karl Gustav Fellerer zum sechzigsten Geburtstag*, ed. Heinrich Hüschen (Regensburg: Bosse, 1962)

tooled with infinite care, was placed in the service of the Church and was greatly influenced by a profound understanding of the spirit of the liturgy, causing the self-imposition of certain limits to which Palestrina adhered with earnest devotion, is unquestionable; but so is his abiding faith in the dignity and duties of the creative artist, his constant search for improvement and perfection. Unfortunately, the cool, reasoned, scholarly examination of this prodigious *Satzkunst* has been largely inhibited by the worship of the legendary hero "who saved church music."

The new edition of Karl Gustav Fellerer's *Palestrina* rekindles our gratitude to Professor Fellerer for having displayed an independence of mind unusual in the Palestrinian literature. The eager and arduous inquiry commands the reader's admiration: it is full of learning, wisdom, and sensibility. The work is free from the defects which disfigure so much contemporary musicography: it is well-proportioned; it is discriminating in its appraisal of its subject; it places Palestrina against an intelligible background; and it is written in an unpretentious and unsentimental style. Few scholars are so well versed in Palestrinian lore as the Cologne professor, yet the lore is barely touched upon; for this *Palestrina* is a strictly scholarly study of the composer and not of the symbol. This is the *Strenger Satz* of musicology, never straying from the sober path of scholarship, which is the more noteworthy because it is almost impossible to avoid metaphor and floral tribute when dealing with this Roman who occupies a unique position in the history of music. The absence of all rhetoric and preaching in the book so impressed me that I went on a little tour of my library to recapture the spirit *against* which Professor Fellerer had to armor his mind. What follows is nothing but a sketch, random excerpt from such documents as are available in my own library; yet they give some idea of the gradual growth of the Palestrina legend until, in the late Romantic era, it got completely out of hand, lost in the clouds.

In the immediate Palestrinian era, authors either referred to the composer with the genuine admiration of the fellow craftsman, respectfully stayed away from any criticism, or belittled him—but few remained neutral. Agazzari (*Dal suonare sopra il basso*) seems to have been the earliest to accept and record the legend of the salvation of church music by the composition of the *Marcellus* Mass.

> Music would have come very near to being banished from Holy Church by a sovereign pontiff had not Giovanni Palestrina found the remedy, showing that the fault and error lay, not with music, but with the composers, and composing in confirmation of this the Mass entitled *Missa Papae Marcelli*.

As we advance into the seventeenth and eighteenth centuries—and away from Italy—the references become fewer and a curious vagueness seems to dominate them. Mersenne nowhere mentions Palestrina; Athanasius Kircher simply remarks that "Praenestinus invented ornamental church music." Mattheson, being a practical musician of avant-garde learnings, calls upon the Bible to support his contention that the music of the church must be rich in resources and effect; in somewhat boisterous terms he calls for "loud and blaring, joyful music making", the emphasis being on the deliberate use of music as a tool of religious observance. Significantly, there seems to be no particular interest in Palestrina in his voluminous writings. Johann Gottfried Walther, too, makes little distinction between the sacred and the secular. His definition of *Musica Ecclesiastica* is almost primitively utilitarian: "Church music, or that which is suitable for performance in church." He does not offer to elaborate further on this definition, and there is no mention of religious music as such under a heading of its own, though individual technical terms are dealt with. In his article on Palestrina, a very brief entry in the *Lexikon* of about one-fourth the size used for comparatively minor musicians, Walther does mention the story that Palestrina was responsible for the saving of church music, but there is no indication that the offending "abuses of awkward and clumsy composers" might not just as well have been offenses against secular musical standards as against the requirements of "the Pope's music".

Having mentioned the two eminent German scholars of the late Baroque, both in the forefront of musical life, let us take a look at the professional historian, not involved directly in contemporary musical practice. To our surprise, we shall find that the romantic awe which characterizes the Palestrina literature after Thibaut and Baini is already present in the sober, cautious, and sharply critical Burney, the able co-founder of modern musical historiography, an English Protestant not given to dreamy generalizations.

> Palestrina having brought his style to such perfection that the best compositions which have been produced for the church since his time are proverbially said to be "alla Palestrina." In the compositions of Palestrina . . . little invention and few flights of fancy are required; yet there is a degree of happiness and genius in finding a few uncommon notes that are favourable to fugue and canon, as well as in creating new and graceful passages in melody.

Thus the "romantic" legend is already here, half a century before Thibaut; no particular gifts as a composer are granted to Palestrina, nor is a "flight of fancy" necessary, because while "ears not accustomed to ancient modulation would at first be surprised, and perhaps, offended, with some of the transitions," they should not remain "insensible to the solemnity and grandeur" of this music. There remains the question of the parody procedure, always embarrassing to biographers, then and now. Burney also considers the device a form of theft, but he has a very nice solution for its acceptance.

> However one chant may resemble another, and the subject and modulation of fugues may be stolen, yet they will still be in the style of choral music, and never awaken ideas of secular songs or profane transactions, as they will at least be decorous, if not learned and ingenious.

Burney's able colleague Sir John Hawkins, a less colorful author who is careful with his adjectives, nevertheless bows to the convention that made Palestrina immune to ordinary musical criticism and appreciation. Palestrina has "that noble and majestic style which has rendered him the admiration of all succeeding ages." The following is amusing, because Hawkins apparently attributes the deterioration of church music and the consequent need for the Palestrinian reform to—the Germans. (It is of course possible that in the still loose terminology of the time he is referring to the Netherlanders.)

> In the course of his studies Palestrina discovered the error of the German and other musicians, who had in a great measure corrupted the practice of music by the introduction of intricate proportions, and set about framing a style for the church, grave, decent, and plain.

We may jump a century and a quarter in English musicography but will find that with a very few exceptions the romantic effusion deepened while scholarship lessened, both of them considerably. Sir Hubert Parry was a triple doctor of music, a composer highly esteemed by his compatriots, holder of the chair of music at Oxford University, and author of a number of books, among them the volume on the seventeenth century in the first edition of the *Oxford History of Music*. Yet the reader wonders whether the distinguished baronet had ever read the volumes preceding his own in the *Oxford History*, for surely that eminent scholar, Wooldridge, could have saved him from the embarrassing nonsense one encounters in his *The Evolution of the Art of Music*.

> Up to the beginning of the seventeenth century was the period of the youth of modern music—a period most pure, serene and innocent—when mankind was yet too immature in things musical to express itself in terms of passion or of force, but used forms and moods of art which are like tranquil dreams and communings of man with his inner self. . . . The most comprehensive fact is that almost all the music of these two centuries is purely choral, that is, . . . without independent accompaniment. . . . All this music was unrhythmic, and consequently it was also divested of all that kind of regular orderliness of structure which seems so indispensable in the maturer art of modern times.

This was indeed a sorry state of affairs, this primitive music without rhythm and construction! But the Palestrina myth was so strong that even this convinced detractor of "old music" abandons all his condescension when he must deal with the Prince of Music, and his clichés faithfully follow the dogma.

> Palestrina without emotion embodies the most perfect representation of contemplative religious devotion. Bach, more touched by the secular spirit, and fully capable of strong emotion, formulates a more comprehensive and energetic type of religious sentiment, and foreshadows, by his new combination of rhythm and polyphony, the musical expression of every kind of human feeling. Beethoven expresses the complete emancipation of human emotion and mind.

One has the uncomfortable feeling that our triple doctor of music would have been willing to go beyond the emancipated Beethoven to find the ultimate of expression perhaps in Franck or Tchaikovsky.

Sir Hubert's senior colleague, William Rockstro, considered "an authority on ecclesiastic music," also believed that "the earlier contrapuntists gathered together the dry bones of counterpoint but made no attempt to arrange them in symmetrical order." But with the appearance of Palestrina, "music was no longer to be a dead letter, an exalted branch of arithmetic, but a living reality, an art speaking more directly to the heart of humanity than sculpture, or painting, or even poetry itself, its best loved sister."

Now let us leave the amiable scholars and see what some of the composers of the Romantic age thought about Palestrina. Schumann was strongly impressed by Thibaut's concept of church music; Palestrina remains a symbol, albeit a rather loosely used one. We are taken aback when reading such an application of it as the following: "Thibaut declared Palestrina the angel among composers, so among piano concertos is John Field's concerto in A flat." The reason for Schumann's somewhat distant espousal of the Palestrina cult was quite evidently the rising Bach cult, of which he was an enthusiastic partisan. The progressive composer in him was convinced that "the sources of music" were much closer to one another than they used to be in earlier centuries: "Beethoven, for instance, did not need to study all that Mozart studied—Mozart, not all that Handel—Handel, not all that Palestrina—because these had already absorbed the knowledge of their predecessors." But he goes on to remark: "Only one composer remains inexhaustible, J. S. Bach." The acknowledged coryphee of the Bach revival, Mendelssohn, did not find a conflict between his two allegiances. The *Lamentations* of Palestrina, heard in Rome, "sounded as if they came direct from heaven."

Other, somewhat later composers are much less honest in their pronouncements than was Schumann; with them the worship of the unknown Palestrina is in full bloom, and some are downright sanctimonious about it. A few examples will suffice to illuminate their attitude. Gounod had the unfortunate idea of expressing his admiration for Palestrina's unique loftiness by coupling him with Michelangelo! The poet in the composer of *Faust* gains full sway when he writes of the works of his two idols in his *Memoirs of an Artist*, which I possess in an English translation of 1875.

> The soul, unalterably fixed upon a higher world, strives only to express in an humble and subordinate form the sublimity of its contemplation. There is nothing, even to the general, uniform tone in which this painting and this music are enveloped, which does not seem to be created with a sort of voluntary renouncement of all colors. The art of these two men is, so to speak, a sacrament, where the visible sign is no more than a veil thrown over the divine and living reality. Thus, neither one nor the other of these two grand masters fascinates at first. In everything else it is the exterior that attracts, but here, not so; one must penetrate beyond the visible and the sensual.

Like most others who advance rhapsodic endorsements of the Palestrina legend, Gounod attributes the absolute inimitability of his works to the "absence of visible means, of worldly artifices, of vain coquetry, to the indifference to effect, and disdain of seductive attractions." The core of this concept is in fact the absence of such human qualities as we always associate with a great creative artist. Wagner no less than others stressed the absence of these qualities in the Roman, but he was in a dilemma. He who in *Parsifal* created a somewhat nebulous "Christian" drama, and whose religious skepticism in general and dislike of Catholicism in particular (until checked by Cosima) were well known from his many utterances, was nevertheless a full-blooded romanticist who could not ignore such an elevated legend. Accordingly, in his *Beethoven*, after appropriate scolding of Italian opera, the Jesuits, and other suitable subjects, he suddenly changes the tone to hushed awe as he discusses Palestrina's music. When listening to it, he says, "we get a picture almost as timeless as it is spaceless; a spiritual revelation throughout, that rouses unspeakable emotions as it brings us nearer than aught else to a notion of the essential nature of religion." Thus far the Lord of Bayreuth is on well-trod ground; every romantic of every denomination could subscribe to this. But the final sentence is thoroughly and amusingly Wagnerian; it violates an essential part of the myth as it categorically twists facts and ideas. "This music is free from all fictional dogmatic conception."

Richard Strauss, vaguely "scientific" in the long-since discredited evolutionary sense, sees Wagner as the peak toward which all species of music have striven. The origin of expression in music he places "in Gregorian chant, Palestrina, and the chorales of Bach," a rather curious grouping, even though linked by a consideration of "the necessity to give artistic form to religious prayer."

Frenchmen, of course, are seldom given to Gounod's ecstatic flights of fancy; some of them are very hostile not only to the legend, but to the composer *qua* composer. Berlioz (*Memoirs*), admits that

> the pure, calm harmony of the Palestrina style tends to a certain kind of reverie which is not without charm. But the charm is due to the harmonies themselves and is wholly independent of the so-called genius of the composers, if, indeed, you can dignify by that name musicians who spent their lives compiling chord successions like those which constitute a portion of the Improperia of Palestrina. . . It is quite possible that the musician who wrote them may have had some taste and a certain amount of scientific knowledge; but genius—the idea is too absurd!

Perhaps this outburst is understandable from the fiery composer of the *Witches' Sabbath*, but he is equally contemptuous of the great contrapuntal Masses.

> How, then, do such works as these, clever though they may be as regards their conquest of contrapuntal difficulties, contribute to the expression of religious feeling? How far are such specimens of the labor of a patient chord manufacturer indicative of single-minded absorption in the true object of his work? In no way that I can see.

At the opening of our century another Frenchman, Saint-Saëns, then very much à la mode, expressed disapproval of Palestrina, which is the more surprising because this eclectic near-salon-composer was at home in any style. "I am astonished," he writes to Camille Bellaigue in 1907, "at what you find in Palestrina's art. As for me, I can see only an insensible and inexpressive art . . . You will never make me find that the theme of the Pope Marcellus Mass expresses 'Lord, have mercy upon us.'" To do Saint-Saëns justice, should be added that he allows every man complete freedom to sing the praises of the Lord as he pleases, and while he recoils at the ideas propounded in the *Motu Proprio*, admits that "plain chant and Palestrina would be a hundred times preferable in church to the platitudes with which we are daily edified to the detriment of art and without profit to the individual."

Finally, a most interesting case is presented by Verdi. It is not always realized to what extent the Palsterinian ideal of suave, euphonious vocal sound had become a national ideal in Italy. Aside from the *stile antico*, or *stylus gravis*—that is, the archaizing a cappella style which never really died out and was practised either as a musical discipline or out of devotion to the Church (vide Matteo Palotta or Pasquale Pisani)—there was scarcely an Italian composer throughout the eighteenth century who did not acknowledge the Palestrinian vocal ideal as an Italian quality par excellence. Wherever we look, from Bassani to Lotti and the two Scarlattis, we find this, and Pasquini, in the preface to one of his volumes of motets, calls any musician unacquainted with Palestrina "a miserable wretch." This was not a mere patriotic or pious gesture; they believed in the Palestrinian ideal, if not quite in the sixteenth-century sense, for their concept did not exclude the participation of instruments. Evidently the old belief and veneration continued uninterrupted, judging from the following remark which Verdi made in a letter to Giuseppe Gagliani in 1891.

> I am particularly glad for the performance of Palestrina's music: he is the Eternal Father of Italian music. Palestrina cannot compete with the bold harmonic innovations of modern music, but if he were better known and studied, we would write in a more Italian spirit, and we would be better patriots (in music, I mean).

As can be seen, Verdi maintains a nice balance between the legend and the old Italian belief in the beauty of a pure vocal style which Italians consider their very own patrimony.

Our little excursion was perhaps like a cruise without definite ports of call; nevertheless, it showed that had he so wished, Professor Fellerer could have drawn from this quarry one of the rich psychological biographies fashionable today. But he judged that the scholar must bring down the heroic to be inspected on a level where familiarity will breed not contempt but enlightenment. This is the more noteworthy because, as recently as 1938, Henry Coates, in his *Palestrina*, one of the very few essay-biographies devoted to the master, still strikes a tone which—for an Englishman—is pretty close to being hysterical.

> To say that this was one of three or four greatest musical minds the world has ever known, and that this art has exercised a most profound influence upon the majority of the great composers who have followed him, might seem an exaggeration, were it not for the fact that the latter themselves, however diverse their musical creeds, have all acclaimed him as their equal, have even venerated him as master and teacher.

One is rather disappointed at not being told who the other "two or three" supreme musical minds may have been; but at least one of them is clearly suggested when Mr. Coates finds that he must come to the conclusion that Wagner's leading-motive system "may well have been suggested to him by the musical style of the older master." This conclusion, I venture to say, would have been difficult to endorse even by good old Torrefranca of pleasant memory, who firmly believed that if you scratch a German you will find an Italian under his musical skin.

As can be seen, until close to our very own times this failure of objective scholarship to adapt to changing requirements was inevitably accompanied by a tendency towards the deterioration and atrophy of the art which it sought to preserve. Professor Fellerer remained the scholar, scrupulously just, though not unmoved, and he demonstrated that the difference between the skilled hand at exploration and the romantic dreamer is that the former explores only the territory he traverses, while the latter explores, in addition, himself.

Purcell

Ⓘn the second half of the seventeenth century three great musical nations, England, Spain, and the Low Countries, left the mainstream of European music. After centuries of glorious production and leadership they no longer had anything individual to contribute and became a mere theater for the music coming from the new leaders. The world's musical headquarters was in Italy and it is significant that Purcell, the solitary great English composer of the age, stated in the preface to his sonatas that he "faithfully endeavour'd a just imitation of the most fam'd Italian Masters."

But he did not imitate; he simply accepted the dominant current as Mozart later did, within which his remained a sovereign personality. Nor did the young musician grow out from this style but from the choral music of the Chapel Royal and Westminster Abbey. This, alone and undiluted, would have stifled him, as it did every other English musician; for the Restoration Church was hidebound, stuffy, and uninspiring. But Purcell also learned to know the theater, Shakespeare's and Dryden's, and the composer of anthems

From *The New York Herald-Tribune*, 10 May 1959

and odes instantly realized that the breath of life was to be found not in the "welcome songs" but in the freedom of the theater.

"Dido and Aeneas," written for a girls' school in Chelsea, the music to "King Arthur," and "The Fairy Queen" are the artistic representation of this life.

The beauty of these works can be deceptive. The musician may see in them only remarkable lyricism; but in the great moments of his short life. Purcell was a true and profound dramatist who could create character and conflict and shape destinies.

It is remarkable how much the English Baroque inherited from the fantastically rich music of the English Renaissance; its out-of-doors spirit, its closeness to nature—and this in spite of the Cromwellian episode. In this wonderfully bold and original instrumental music, notably the sonatas and fantasias. Purcell fairly protests against the courtly Baroque, against the absolutism of Continental art, especially of the French, who made even nature conform to their ideals, as the gardeners in Louis XIV's Versailles made the trees grow in predetermined shapes.

Yet, from the point of view of English music, this hopeful portent is a mirage, for Purcell's is the last message of the island to Europe's music, a final flare-up to be followed by long smoldering silence. After his death English music had only strength to enrich Handel and prostrate itself before the giant. But in Handel's success Purcell had a large share.

While many of his anthems and odes are no more than well-wrought, "official" music—the Queen had many birthdays—others are of impressive beauty. Such works as his odes for St. Cecilia's Day, the "Yorkshire Feast Song," the burial anthems for Queen Mary should be universally known.

None of the anthems expresses Christian spirituality, for the Established Church was entirely secular-political; but their splendid festive vigor profoundly impressed Handel, who found in them the British tone par excellence, the tone of the proud and confident Englishman who knows on whose side God is.

It is most interesting to observe that whenever this British pomp and circumstance does not inspire him, and when his dramatic instinct is not aroused by the requirements of the theater, his music has an Italian or French cast. But when he is in his element, it is a final cry, the last voice of the English summer. And there never was another composer who could set the English language to music with such infinite grace, accuracy, and natural inflection.

Bach: Artist and Poet

How does the mid-twentieth century stand in relation to Bach? The music teachers, the music histories, and the performances of the Passions and the Mass worshipfully honor him as the teachers of literature, the literary manuals, and the theaters honor Shakespeare or Goethe: the embodiment of greatness in art, beyond reproach and beyond criticism. After two hundred years this greatness seems oppressive, and as we look back at the disappearing giant, we tend to be a little uneasy in the face of such Olympian grandeur. Our times do not enjoy a wondrous security not disturbed by external things and events, or rather, one that can merely use them to its own enrichment. We do not understand this infallible instinct and taste, this majestic self-sufficiency that can gather unto itself whatever is needed in the midst of a raging storm without being buffeted by it; dozens, scores, hundreds of works, composed with what seems to many an almost cold and mathematical certainty of craftsmanship. True, at times—*The Art of Fugue*—he reaches into forbidding and untrodden parts where the air is rare and the heights awesome. Yet this does not mean that his heart beat with less warmth than that of other musicians. On the contrary, Bach could live and

From *The Musical Quarterly*, vol. 36 (1950)

feel in regions where the ordinary musician could scarcely exist or could at best display the sheer knowledge of the métier that so many attribute to the "other" Bach, the Bach of the "abstract" instrumental works. The official opinion solves these perplexing problems by ascribing his unique greatness and position in the history of music to his sincerity, abiding religious faith, his upright, simple, and pious life, his incredible industry, and his phenomenal technique of composition. All this is true; yet how much life and how many living values escape this official exaltation!

Is sincerity an artistic value? It is certain that today we regard it as such, and perhaps we count it as the principal value in art. Yet it is certain too that true artistic value does not rest on deliberate sincerity; it arises, rather, from a lyric sincerity that breaks out of the soul because it must come to the surface, because it cannot be repressed. It is this sincerity that manifests itself even when the creative artist does not consciously reveal himself, for it finds expression in the shadings of thought, in the proportions of the composition, in rhythm, in style—style that was so aptly identified by a true son of the eighteenth century with the man himself. Such a type of sincerity is artistic value itself. Bach's sincerity is not that of Rousseau, whose *Confessions*, in spite of their incontestable literary excellence, savor a good deal of exhibitionism. Rousseau and many of his contemporaries were sincere before themselves and before man. They show the typical mixture of the spirit of the Enlightenment: cynicism and sentimentality. Bach, although he lived into the noon of the century, was not the typical genius of the times who brought new things from unknown regions. He was a stranger in this century, a man of the past, the embodiment of the heroic era of the Reformation, who made his confessions before God. Surrounded by the routine counterpoint making of innumerable cantors and municipal musicians, or by the puritanical doggerel manufacturers, the Pietists, he presents a phenomenon that is out of place in the declining Baroque: the meeting of religion and mind. To be sure, this is a difficult thesis to substantiate, for this unassuming man who left a vast collection of music to posterity expressed his ideas and beliefs so sparsely that the chronicle of his life, deeds, and utterances could all be collected in one modest volume. But the mind was always at work. Bach was an indefatigable "researcher," who examined everything pertaining to his art and tried his hand at every trick of his trade, only to cast away what did not agree with his sharp critical judgment and taste. The mind was there, and it is a grievous mistake to picture him, as is so often done, as a pious simpleton whose one and only accomplishment was the making of superb music for the weekly divine services he was engaged to conduct.

There can be no question of his strong faith, yet in his music there is neither preaching nor puritanism. Unlike that of other notable artists of Protestantism, his allegiance to the Reformed Faith brought with it neither fetters nor hard and fast doctrines, for to him faith was a liberating force. His task was the artistic embodiment of the tenets of the Reformed Church, and he stood for the Lutheran ideal at a time when this ideal was split into many fragments by divergent and warring factions. It is a great mistake to see in Bach a saintly Puritan, for to the Puritan everything revolves around the problems of evil—it is the large figure of Satan that lurks in the background—whereas to Bach the central problem of faith was redemption.

The profound and intimate, if somewhat mystic, stream that fired the Baroque spirit was already cooling by the time of Bach's birth. The devotion that filled both Counter-Reformers and Protestants came gradually and increasingly under the control of intellect. With it, lyricism departed from all branches of art. Angelus Silesius, the poet-mystic of the German Counter-Reformation, and Milton died at about the same time, a few years before Bach was born. After them there were no true lyricists (with the possible exception of Racine and Dryden) until the end of the eighteenth century. This was of course equally true of musical lyricism. What the era of Bach brought with it was rhetoric and the stage, philosophy and literature, but not poetry. True enough, that rhetoric was often noble and the stage powerful, philosophy was profound and literature spirited; but none of it was lyrical. And in the midst of this era that was no longer the poet's domain there appeared the chorale preludes of Bach, musical poetry and lyricism of the highest order. Those who see only the incredible contrapuntal mastery of the variations on *Vom Himmel hoch* should not forget the tenderness, the sweet melancholy, the tearful humility, and blissful abandon of such examples of the purest instrumental lyricism as *Das Alte Jahr vergangen ist, or O Mensch bewein' dein' Sünde*, or *An Wasserflüssen Babylon*. It is these most complicated simple poems of musical lyricism that afforded the key to the understanding of this seemingly forbidding giant.

Bach's lyric expressiveness in these preludes encompasses the whole gamut of the "affections" in forms of extraordinary virtuosity. This poetry has a unity that is not accessible to those who see in Bach's music the perfection of the métier or the expression of faith or the magnitude of architecture only; it is like the symbolic form-language of the Gothic: a secret language that is the bearer of more profound meanings. The body of the "poems"—like the verse of Dante—conceals a soul, and this soul dominates the body, for Bach is in the first place a spiritual poet. At the decisive point his eye always turns from the external world inward, into himself, and at this point reality is sublimated into an ideal; it becomes a vision broadened into universal significance, compelling us to divine the substance that is hidden under the colorful surface. Intuition and erudition, instinctive inspiration and conscious intellect, musical form and ideal content, are blended inextricably. It is for this reason that we are so liable to misjudge the uniformly high level of his output in all branches of music. It was not the supreme knowledge of the craft of music, the incessant exercising of his art, that led to this fantastically high average of artistic level. Other great musicians also were incredibly productive, yet much of what they composed is of little consequence, because none of them could approach the blend of receptivity, artistic curiosity, formative ability, critical judgment towards others and themselves, and ease of expression that this supposedly placid "pious musical workngman" exhibited from early youth.

How can we reconcile such a wide and colorful poetic range with the severe and sober structures of most of Bach's works? For we must not forget that such entirely "free" compositions as the fantasia that precedes the G minor organ fugue, some of the toccatas, and such of the chorale preludes as paraphrase the tune at the composer's pleasure, are outnumbered by the other, so-called strict forms—canon, fugue, *cantus firmus* settings, etc. The latter are of course strict only in our old-fashioned classroom sense, but they are architecturally bound and delineated. We might ask whether there is not some mysterious creative urge that makes the freest soul cling to the most circumscribed forms of expression. The creative man who is inwardly free willingly accepts— and even seeks—external artistic bonds, for he knows that by channeling his powers he can exploit them to better advantage. Only a free poet can be a perfect artist. And the reverse of this is equally true: the more disciplined the artist, the freer the poet. It is thus that in Bach form and *gebundener Stil* insure a comprehensive unity for everything to be expressed, whether pure lyricism, the epic-dramatic setting of *Ecce Homo*, abstract counterpoint, or innocuous birthday pasticcio. They all share in a defined form which is the artistically circumscribed consummation of a free poetic soul. This is probably the reason why Bach is more admired as an artist than as a poet. Yet even if form is the guardian of content, the essence is always there behind the symbol. The artist only plays what the poet composes.

On Handel Scholarship: An Introduction for a Symposium

When I entered upon the career of musicologist, back in the early 1920s, there were no such gatherings of Handelians as this, not because scholars, musicians, and the public did not know Handel, but because they were looking for him in the wrong places. His reputation was so firmly established that it was supposed that nothing could change it, but this confidence was based on the wrong premises. In England, this German-born Italianate Englishman was the "Composer in ordinary to the Protestant religion", in Germany, and on the Continent in general, he was one of *unsere Grossmeister*, and though he happened to spend all his mature years, nearly half a century, in England, he was hyphenated with Bach as the *other* great German Lutheran composer of the late Baroque. In America he was simply the composer of *Messiah* and a few contrafacta, like "Ombra mai fu," appropriately converted to inappropriate church music. Since he was indissolubly paired with Bach, few special studies were thought needed, because the *und* in "Bach und Händel" took care of him. That linking which connected Handel to the other Grossmeister, and therewith to Germany, became the point of departure for the appreciation of Handel and of his

From the *American Choral Review*, vol. 27 (1985)

standing in history, not only in Germany but, since the Germans were the originators of modern musicology, all over continental Europe and America. It can still be seen as late as in the writings of Leichtentritt, Gerber, Müller-Blattau, not to speak of the hapless Serauky. It is amazing how quickly the human image dissolves into the mythical image.

During the nineteenth century there was one outstanding figure who dedicated his lifework to Handel—Friedrich Chrysander—who almost single-handedly produced the old Händelgesellschaft edition. No one can dispute his dedication and his achievement, or even his scholarship, and until a few decades ago he dominated all writings on Handel. Unfortunately, it turned out, as Winton Dean has proved, that he often generously placed the facts on the side of his prejudices, and of the latter he had many. In England, as Novello published more and more of Handel's works, musicians and musicographers began to know larger portions of his oeuvre; but then came discoveries that gravely disturbed his admirers. They discovered that despite the hyphen, this paragon of sacred music did not share the great Thomas cantor's profound mysticism, and he did not peer into the beyond but lived very much in the present; that his music, for all its strong moral energy, also celebrates the attractions of the flesh and is devoted to sensuous beauty. The sages who looked at those sacred oratorios with Victorian eyes were taken aback to find that in uplifting biblical scenes he did not hesitate to include a great deal of very secular charm, and, horrible to contemplate, even carnal love (to use their favorite expression for this unseemly thing). The Victorians wanted to be edified, they were determined to preserve the halo effect hovering over Handel's head; so with Novello, and his straight-laced editor Prout concurring, a severe censorship was established.

Then there was another discovery: Handel's borrowings. Not being aware of Baroque musical mores, or of Bach's similar borrowings, the charge of larceny was directed against England's national composer by righteous, if ignorant, critics, and he had to be rescued by sentimental excuses of fatigue and ill health. They forgot that every artist is receptive, and sometimes the greatest, the consolidators, are the most indebted. Chaucer's opulence has fed many pensioners, but he was himself a huge borrower, as was Shakespeare. Every master is heir and dispenser, inheritor and progenitor. And all the great ones have something in common with Handel: even when what he borrowed was of little value, it was priceless when he left it. The romantics were also disappointed when they learned that Handel was a shrewd businessman, a speculator who played the stock market—successfully, I might say—surely not their idea of a serene artist.

But there was still another weighty fact to cause averted eyes: Handel composed operas—Italian operas at that. The composer in ordinary to the Protestant religion had no business playing the game of those "idolatrous popish showmen," as Swift called them. The old English aversion to opera, to a play "all sung," as they used to say, was tenacious, and it took Handel a long time and several dozen operas before he realized that the time had not yet come for opera in England. No one has diagnosed the roots of this aversion better than Edward Dent in his *Foundations of English Opera*. "Music for the Italians," he says, "is the exaggeration of personality, for the Englishman its annihilation."

But now a new myth was created. Handel's turn from Italian opera to English oratorio, which had many complicated causes, was interpreted as an abandonment of mundane frivolities for the service of God and religion. This conversion theory was widely accepted and is still encountered in popular books and program notes, but it was exploded by a great work that instantly changed everything: Winton Dean's book on Handel's dramatic oratorios, felicitously appearing on the bicentennial of Handel's death. Our entire view was altered and freed from the accumulated myths and the foliage that covered the fruit. We could see now that the thunder of Handel's great choruses, which ever since the artillery performances of the first commemoration services served as a catharsis for stout Christian lungs, and was felt to be the principal, if not the sole, quality of his music, is only part of his art. Handel was a musician of primal force, but he was not a preacher. We have to come to realize why Handel's anthems seem somewhat alien when heard in Protestant churches outside England, even in this English-speaking country, and are seldom used as service music. They are marvelous, but so thoroughly English, dynastic, celebrating the nation's triumphs—but also their own—that while the music is appreciated in concerts, its real message touches a Briton differently than it does any other listener. We have also learned that Handel was a fastidious composer, sumptuously delicate and exact, tender, sensitive, and luminous— indeed, elegant—as well as fiery and monumental. And we see the miraculous amalgam of the warmth of the Mediterranean with the cooler artistic climate of the tight little island, something unique with Handel.

Now I should like to address a few words to the fresh young scholars present here, who are working the Handelian vineyard. Despite the great advances made in Handelian studies, his picture is still like a partially cleaned old painting, and a great deal of restoring remains to be done. You must guard, however, against the two extremes of uncritical worship and narrow specialization. There are enthusiastic scholars who resemble the traveling ladies who fall in love with Neapolitan barbers and bell captains and take them for the very spirit of Italy. And there are others who doggedly sit at their desks, double-dotting every dottable note, and stuffing *notes inégales* in every nook and cranny from a dispenser, as painstakingly absorbed in the operation as an upper-class Englishman eating a soft-boiled egg. Remember, sources, references, concordances, and all the other paraphernalia of scholarly work are vital and indispensable, but there is a dimension above history, morphology, and even performance practice which now so agitates people, and before any aspect of music is capable of scholarly treatment, it must have passed inward, out of the mere region of the intellect and into the warm atmosphere of imaginative feeling, kindling the soul of the researcher into a glow.

Bach and Handel:
Ancillary Rivals

Every popular history of music reports with scorn the English bishops' reluctance to permit church choirs to assist in Handel's oratorio performances, which took place in secular halls. But the indignant authors forget that the oratorio was not considered church music but "musical entertainment," even though it had a strong moral, ethical, and religious tone. These bishops may have been unimaginative, but they were not ignorant. They recognized that the Handelian oratorio represented music that was deliberately moving out of the church and into a secular atmosphere; therefore they regarded it with apprehension.

A caustic writer of the times gives a lively picture of this new form of "entertainment."

> This oratorio being a new thing set the whole world a-madding. "Haven't you been at the Oratorio?" says one. "Oh, if you don't see the Oratorio you see nothing," says t'other; so away goes I to the Oratorio, where I saw indeed the finest assembly of People I ever beheld in my very Life, but to my great surprize, found this sacred Drama a mere Consort, no scenery, Dress or Action, so necessary to a drama; but Handel was placed in a Pulpit. I suppose they call that their oratory. By him sat

From the *American Choral Review*, vol. 17 (1975)

(singers) in their own Habits (and one of them) gave up a Hallelujah of Half an hour long.

This same movement from the church to the concert hall can be seen in Bach's Passions, though the genuinely churchly is still present to a fair degree.

Church music is by its very nature deeply influenced by the theological, philosophical, and social thought of the age. The great upheaval in Protestant religious thought caused by Pietism on the one hand and the Enlightenment on the other resulted in profound changes. The Enlightenment shook the edifice of theology when it proclaimed the adequacy of the mind unaided by faith. Now the old relationship of Church and State in the Protestant lands was changing. It must be understood, however, that this was not a total rejection of religion, though it did represent a shrinking of the sphere of the Church. At the same time, Pietism, within the Protestant churches, rejected elaborate art music and wanted the equivalent of what our own "old-time religion" revivalists favored: sentimental ditties.

Now religious thought does adjust itself to inevitable historical-cultural trends, but it is another matter with creative art. There were three ways open to the Protestant composer of the first half of the eighteenth century: stubborn adherence to hallowed tradition, which leads to antiquarianism; bowing to the dominant popular taste, which a powerful and creative mind will reject; or entering upon entirely new directions. The last was made feasible by the weakening of the hold of the organized Church which we have mentioned; religious music was able to strike out on its own without church sponsorship.

Handel, a "modern" composer, unhesitatingly selected the new ways. Brimming with creative power, he espoused the oratorio, and in thundering choruses, affecting arias, and gripping recitatives conjured up the majestic events of the Old Testament. The only work in which he touched upon the New Testament was *Messiah*, although in this, too, most of the texts are from the Old Testament.

Bach—the inheritor of a two-hundred-year-old tradition, and the issue of a family of musicians that had served the Lutheran Church through those centuries—was in a different position. His inner struggle was tremendous, for he was a convinced orthodox Lutheran, yet his musical imagination could not be restricted to the kind of music his contemporaries wanted. Therefore, if he were to give full range to his creative powers, there was nothing to do but join the artistic movement out of the church.

Bach's Passions are not liturgical, ritual music; they are essentially the same kind as Handel's oratorios, secular music with a religious subject. Although his texts show the Pietist influence, there is no compromise in his music. The difference between the two giants of the Baroque is not to be measured in musical values; both are incomparable. But one of them was a humble introspective German Lutheran; the other, a naturalized Briton who embraced the Established Church which, as we should remember, was an arm of the government in England and hence had a strong political coloring.

Although his whole heart, his warmest invention, and all his redoubtable skill were poured into his oratorio-Passions, in the end, Bach, tired of the meager support received from his superiors, gave up this particular form of music. The Leipzig cantor retires to his study to address himself to the solution of the final mysteries of music, while the London man of the world raises the oratorio to a national British genre.

Two musicians are before us, born in the same environment in 1685, two men of exceptional genius, who nevertheless were as far apart as the antipodes. As for Bach, at least four of his major choral works, a number of the smaller ones, and a wealth of his instrumental music are constantly before the public; but a Handelian oratorio other than *Messiah* is a rare event, and his operas are mere names. There are many misconceptions surrounding these two musicians, always mentioned together, with Handel always relegated to a lower eminence.

Bach was really not so little known by his contemporaries as sentimental biographers would lead us to believe; musicians knew and appreciated him. But the public did not know him until the Romantic rediscovery in the nineteenth century. In contradistinction, Handel was a celebrity in his life, and by the time he died he was revered as a national hero. Bach was a musician who composed for himself or for his immediate circle, without any contact with or regard for the larger public. A humble and sober Lutheran who saw his era with the moral eyes of the Bible-reading Protestant, he was not a man of his age and did not particularly care for that age.

Handel, on the contrary, was in everything a man of his times, a man of the present, interested neither in his historical forebears nor in his position in posterity. He had the pride of an active and highly successful man of the world, and he needed the world both as an inspiration and as a theater for his music; there was nothing of the hermit in him. There have been few composers so receptive to influences coming from outside, whether from nature, which he worshipped, or from the music of his contemporaries or immediate predecessors, from which he helped himself generously.

A robust and healthy soul, he does not look inward, examining himself with painfully searching conscience; he looks around, and with infinite receptivity takes in everything at a glance. His greatness rests on this fantastic responsiveness. His descriptive scenes, such as the two different pictures of the night in *Israel in Egypt*, which one of my able colleagues so perceptively noted the other day, are without parallel in the literature.

Handel, too, was a Bible-reader, but unlike Bach, who was preoccupied with the New Testament, notably with the ideas of death and redemption, Handel reveled in the powerful figures of the Old Testament, in the struggles of Israel, in the mighty clashes and curses, and gloried in the victory of the righteous which he set to music in triumphant sounds.

Bach has no sense whatever for nature, only for the soul. He feels everything and sees little; the absolute for him is beauty undisturbed by the outside world. There is at times a certain scholastic meticulousness in his music, which is characteristically medieval and Germanic, and which has its own peculiar charm. He is solicitous about every line, each of which must be a work of art by itself. His conscientiousness was unexcelled; there is no such thing as a trifle for him: the smallest choral prelude of a dozen measures or a little two-part invention receives the same all-absorbing care as the great choruses or fugues. These works are often geometric boulders, but behind them is a rich and eternally viable symbolic world.

Nevertheless, it is undeniable that this constant vigilance for the abstract musical line does at times obscure euphony; nor was Bach overconcerned with the beauty of vocal sound. Handel did not bother with trifles; he composed murals, and they are like a mirror that reflects every picture. This is wondrously clear and gives very sharp contours. It is this clarity and sharpness, the idiomatic writing, and the glorious sound that make Handel's music so engaging and irresistible. Through his straightforward and powerful mind we see the world in its natural colors, for he does not, like Bach, give a special light and color to everything.

It seems that it is Bach's unique immersion in what appears to be abstract beauty that has made him so popular in modern times. But there is precious little resemblance between Bach and the "back to Bach" moderns, for their ideas do not come from that region where the outside world vanishes and the soul alone remains; they only see and imitate the marvelous polyphonic texture in the music.

Better acquaintance with Handel would lead us to a fuller appreciation of both composers, for the two are not comparable—they are complementary.

Pergole∫i

Pergolesi's *Stabat Mater*, recently
performed in Carnegie Hall, is an utterly tender and delicate work, and although it was not meant to be heard in a large hall, from all accounts it appears
that Leonard Bernstein and the able soloists performed the cantata with a fine
feeling for style. Still, I wonder whether in our day its unique quality and
significance are properly appreciated.

The young Pergolesi, just out of the conservatory for the poor in Naples,
no longer represented the august Baroque; he was a thoroughly modern composer, far more so than his contemporaries, though not conforming to the type
as we imagine it. He came from unhealthy stock, his father and mother dying
in their forties, his brothers and sisters in infancy, while Giovanni Battista
himself, limping and frail, showed the effects of tuberculosis from his childhood. He died a mere youth, and the graduate of the conservatory for the poor
was buried in a pauper's grave. Yet this frail dreamer gave Western music a
new heart and a new pulse. His whole activity lasted but five years. At twenty-
three he wrote *La Serva Padrona*, the little opera that was to change operatic
history; at twenty-five, battered and distraught by failure upon failure, he

From the *American Choral Review*, vol. 17 (1975)

composed the *Stabat Mater*; at twenty-six he was dead. A tremendous talent, an original mind who in everything he did showed the way for a hundred years, the Fra Angelico of music passed away in the monastery of Pozzuoli, broken-hearted and perhaps not quite sane in mind.

Soon after his death he became famous. The marvelously fresh tone, the radiant color, lightness, and melodiousness, all undoubtedly influenced by the rich folk song of the Neapolitan countryside, struck Italians, Frenchmen, and Germans as a miracle. But color and radiance, gracefulness and lightness, meant far more in this music than mere virtuosity. Pergolesi caught the essence of the genius of his people, for in his music, life and the stage waited with open arms for the new impulses of form and expression.

Pergolesi's melodies are put together from the play of tiny, gamboling motifs; everything sings, even the instruments. But what most enchanted his contemporaries and followers was the virginally gentle, melancholy, dreamy lyricism we hear in *Stabat Mater*.

The means in the little opera were modest: three protagonists, one of whom is mute, a few strings, and a harpsichord (*Stabat Mater* calls for similar forces), but through this modest ensemble a whole new world speaks. The first to enter this new world, Pergolesi acts like the instinctive discoverer who, almost by accident, with childlike yet absolute certainty, makes a landing on a never-seen continent. In *La Serva Padrona* the sweet and flexible melody of Naples, with its fluent, smiling, and coquettish motifs in light, loose, and subjective forms, created a new genre. In the sacred cantata the brooding, longing lyricism created an atmosphere of tearful devotion. But even here the tears are gentle, and devotion genuflects without plaint, accusation, or mea culpa; Pergolesi only sighs and bows his head. This peculiar dualism is characteristic of Naples, and it was to conquer the world. It is to be found, at times more profoundly, more dramatically, in other composers' works, but never with such innocent abandon. And the double visage is present everywhere, whether oratorio or opera, Mass or fugue, sonata or concerto—the chiaroscuro reaching its culmination in Mozart, a direct descendant of the school.

To the northern, non-Italian listener this music is suspect, for indeed this warmth, this radiance, this sensuousness, recall the tone of amorous lyricism. But there was once a saint who called his verse *amor sanctus*—holy love—and there was a poet to whom poets "Are all but ministers of Love." Even the pious monk of the Middle Ages could not dismiss from his memory the secular folk song—the very melodies he helped to persecute. He could not forget them, and the warmth and beauty he learned from them he placed before the Crucifix, like the profane flowers he picked in the meadow.

Pergolesi's music is as subtle, pure, and naive as the monk's song, his *amor sanctus* as divine as Dante's love for Beatrice or Petrarch's for Laura. They were no longer earthly women; they became mystic desires, inexpressible divinations. And the bittersweet music of *Stabat Mater* was written to bittersweet words. A great medieval poet, Jacopone da Todi, composed the poem—a man who after he made religious vows suffered a terrible bereavement: his wife was buried under a collapsed row of theater seats. Theater? The dreaded word was always flung at the Italian composer of sacred music. What kind of a mystery or morality play could it have been in which the poet lost his wife and his mind? For ten years after the tragedy he was insane. But did not God select the insane to humiliate the wise?

These Latin-Italian religious poems and music cannot and must not be judged by the simple expedient of calling them "theatrical" or "secular"; they are heartfelt and sincere, come from the very bosom of the people, and contain a good deal of the eternity of beauty.

Mozart

I t may be said that there are composers who develop by constantly stepping out of their frame and following a new direction. Because they continually uproot themselves, they grow erratically and may perhaps fail to attain their full stature. Others circle their domain with their first steps; every circle brings them to known territory, yet every circling results in new discoveries and conquests.

Mozart was of the second type; he was always faithful to himself. Even in his early works most of the "themes" of his music are already present, and it is fascinating to watch how these "themes" reappear in successive works, always deepened and enriched. Such a composer does not constantly seek the new, trying to "advance"; he holds his ground ever more firmly, becomes stronger; every new work means more than the previous one, precisely because he is content to follow his natural growth. To change, and to proceed into new territories, is always an adventure; for the creative artist the only sure progress is into the depths of his own soul. And this is the most difficult and most exciting road.

From *The Creative World of Mozart* (New York: W. W. Norton, 1963)

Musical language is born before the ideas it will express. Mozart, too, began his career as a competent user of the musical language and very soon handled it with the skill of a virtuoso. We may recall that the early poems of Goethe also give the impression of exercises in style, and like him, Mozart early acquired discipline in a rigorous school. This discipline soon taught him the emptiness of external virtuosity, and he yearned for a different kind of virtuosity, greater and more difficult than the mere handling of the idiom. His youthful voice is tender and discreet, but it has a definite character; the well-known clichés of the idiom acquire an individual charm, and the thrice-familiar turns become in some incomprehensible way personal. In the hands of any one of his journeyman contemporaries these melodies and motifs are commonplace; when Mozart uses them, they become human wisdom. The most important utterances of poets and musicians, from Homer onward, have always been these commonplaces made their own. To rediscover the commonplaces and to dare to use them in one's own way requires more courage and judgment than to seek novelty at any price.

Still, this personal tone does not entail anything extraordinary or bizarre; on the contrary, there have been few great composers whose music was so intimately and organically tied to that of his predecessors as Mozart. Actually, one might call him a conservative, but a conservative who is fresh and unspoiled. This is an untouched youth, eyes alight with the first ideals. His idealism can remain conservative, for it is intimate and as yet unexposed to reality; there is nothing with which it can conflict. Revolutionary art is born where the ideal is in conflict with experience. But the young Mozart's music did not concern itself with external reality; there was no rebellion in him; at most he sighs, but this sigh fails to become concrete in his music for some time to come. Even when in Paris, in the fascinating bustle of the metropolis, he stands apart, like a wondering child whose dreams walk in purer and higher regions. This music originated before mankind had fallen into sin; it is angelic musical poetry, perhaps like the poetry of Shelley. But if Shelley is an angel with a sword, Mozart is an angel with a harp, though his wings are equally powerful.

The elements of Mozart's greatness are beyond analysis and discussion. Other great musicians can be discussed, but his music does not offer any opening—it is pure, unbroken, finished to the very end. There is no other such harmonious phenomenon in the entire history of music. Baudelaire's famous *mot*, "guileless poet," fits him, for indeed, he was guileless and straightforward, faithful to his vocation, which was to create beauty from such matter as happens to be, from the little and sad matter of our own life. How many things determine this life! But the composer transforms them into noble beauty which rises above the circumstances and remains, like the coral palaces, even after those who gathered and built them have gone. And he does it not so much consciously as with the instinct of the coral animals. This is the true and ancient instinct of the creative artist. It lived in him, creating the individual world of a peculiar beauty, both happy and tragic, formed from life, yet higher than life; for Mozart's poetry is always the highest lyricism, akin to the beauty of classical Greece even when he sang of frivolous barbers and swashbuckling adventurers.

This noble and guileless musical poetry, this pure creative greatness which remained untouched by the disorders of life, was looked upon as a miracle by posterity, which did not understand the composer's personality. It is sad to contemplate that this music was created by a composer who himself was not quite of this life, who always was a guest, one of us but not quite belonging among us. Not that this saint of song did not warmly feel the world—he was tied, like all of us, with a thousand threads of desire and love to this earthly life. But the desire abandoned the struggle, and the love became that of the wanderer who gladly sits down to our table but knows that he cannot stay for long.

Perhaps earthly things were more interesting and sad to him because he knew he was to leave them, or perhaps they seemed not so serious and sad to him as they seemed to others. It was easier for him to make beauty out of them. His was not a combative life but a contemplative one. How fantastic must life appear to him who looks at it, so to speak, from the outside, as at a strange exotic country, in which to live means squalor and sorrow, while to travel in it causes pleasure and nostalgia. It is this detachment that sheds a particular light on his music, on its perfection, sure and faultless composition, technical virtuosity, and infallible control. There is a certain single-minded determination for perfection in every elaboration of line and detail, which to the uninitiated appears as playfulness, and even the initiated may feel that at times this music is dictated less by necessary and logical progression from its beginning than by the playful joy of imagination. There is some truth in that, but if music ever had a Cellinian goldsmith, Mozart was he.

Thus he went, pouring out his song and his strength, through the indifferent world towards his sure death. But on his way he opened up for us an entirely new world. His progress was not struggle but sorrow, and perhaps it was sorrow because it was not struggle. Every force can be vanquished except one: resignation. At the bottom of this brilliant and playful music there burns the warmth of a great suffering, a doomed love and desire for life that are warmer than life itself. Many a person outlives his love of life; only the creative artist is outlived by it. Now the goldsmith's delicately traced melodies, his beautifully chiseled harmonies, receive a wonderful internal glow, and the glow fuses everything into great art. Thus the goldsmith becomes a great artist, beyond the accusation of playfulness. Here discussion ceases unless we are willing to question the very principle of beauty-creating poetry.

The soul has an ability to learn from another soul only what is its own, what is itself in another personality, somewhat as a magnet attracts its own kind of metal and leaves paper and wood untouched. Even the old contrapuntal forms, devices, and turns contained elements that suddenly became Mozartean; but somehow the severe lines end in personal phrases, the rhythm has a different mood, and in the midst of the most complicated part-writing there appear the simplest homophonic procedures, lightening the texture with a suddenness that may just as suddenly depart.

In Mozart's early works, some of which were virtual paraphrases of compositions of his elders, there is no plan or principle at work; art engrossed in itself flits from flower to flower. What was important to the youngster was to enjoy his own budding ability to handle the idiom. The new period began when he became convinced that every flower would not do, when he discovered that there are eternal flowers. The innocent pleasure in playing with models gave way to a desire to lay down serious principles, the principles of faithfulness to form and mood. Contemplating these later works, one is aware not only of what Mozart still retains from his heritage, but of what he no longer uses. He is disciplined, never accepts what obviously offers itself, and prefers the nuance to the easy solution. His greatest triumphs are reached not in works that rest on a pregnant idea or on a single impulse, but in those where every secret lies in the details and manners that escape the unwary. So he advances to the wellhead of true art, never thwarted by difficulty, never compromising with current taste, and never disturbed by indifference met with. He is akin to the magician of the fairy tale who, sensing his approaching death, prodigally shakes out his bag of tricks. A young magician, and yet old and wise like all those to whom death is close.

It is of course romantic criticism that sees the creative artist through his fate, but it would be difficult to understand Mozart without this romanticism. Young death permeated his life, his ideas, his accents, and colored his music. It was a young man who wrote to his father: "Since death, when we come to consider it closely, is the true goal of our existence, I have formed during the last few years such close relations with this best and truest friend of mankind, that his image is not only no longer terrifying to me, but is indeed very soothing and consoling!" He was lifted from our profane world, saved from further battles and mistakes, made wise, even transfigured, the poet of heroic resignation. Mozart did not beg for his life, he was acquainted with death.

Art arrests time. It continues life after death and illuminates the darkness. For Mozart art was the condition of life to which he could not be unfaithful, the strength, hope, and wealth of threatened life. He suffered from the lack of understanding for his art; the perfection he pursued interested few, perhaps only his devoted and wise old friend, Haydn. Success bypassed him; others less accomplished and less perfect attracted attention. This hurt him; but all this was a matter of time, the true content of his life was beyond time. To compromise his art would have meant the loss of his only hope, the secret health and security of a sick man.

We spoke of the guileless poet, and yet his greatness does not lie here. Creative greatness is not something so negative as guilelessness. It is not the absence of flaws that makes art great, not what is missing, but what is in it.

What a strange unfathomable thing, music! What is it that endows it with essence and value? Surely not content. We know well that great ideas are not sufficient for a great symphony; many a work that contains magnificent invention ends by being learned and naked. Could it be feeling? Hardly, for some of the warmest, most profoundly felt pieces are poor compositions. Perhaps form? Some of the most accomplished formal structures strike us as empty play with patterns. Or is it the sum total of all this? But experience has shown that any one of them may be missing and the composition may still be great. What, then? It is obvious that we are no more able to furnish an answer than the many thinkers from time immemorial who were equally baffled by this riddle. Only the hackneyed and much-abused word *magic* will be appropriate, and we use it as the mathematician uses x, the unknown, which cannot be named but at least can be indicated with a symbol.

The closer Mozart gets to his early grave, the more he is absorbed in this magic, even though the world is proportionately less interested in it. His music is no longer contemporary. With almost stubborn consistency he pares down everything "modern" and everywhere offers nothing but what, for want of a better term, we call pure classicism—the clarinet concerto, the divertimento for string trio, *Così fan tutte*. How incredibly happy this music of the magician ready to face death, offering the magic of a fulfilled life. Everything now is concentrated and telescoped. The intoxication of youth has not yet faltered when the first ideas of old age, far ahead of old age itself, add new subjects to the earlier themes. The composer begins to audit his life, to understand his fate and his destination. He looks at the cornucopia of his music, modestly, yet with pride. He thinks of death, too. He embraces music, the secret alchemy whereby he can create for himself joy out of misery. He holds on to music as to a lifeline, and in these last years pours out work after work without pause.

Perhaps every art should take its departure in this manner, like the sun throwing its most colorful rays in setting.

Beethoven

Musical historiography, especially in the nineteenth century, delighted in assigning exceptional positions to certain composers. Such men, like the Earth in the Ptolemaic system, were regarded as the energy center around which the rest of the musical world revolved. This tendency to idealize creative artists has grown, reaching its height in the case of Beethoven, who has long since become the heroic representative not only of his period but of all music, a symbol for all ages.

Beethoven was the first among the great masters to divorce the creative from the performing artist, the first to whom composing was a bitterly relentless affair, "perhaps the only language of his soul," as Marx says in his early biography. And the Beethoven of his last period attains to that degree of universality in which tendencies and forms lose their significance, melting into a vision that encompasses all that is human. Those who in the early nineteenth century heard his agitated and yearning themes, who were struck by the irresistible propulsive force of the allegros, the majesty of the adagios, the menacing humor of the scherzos, and the wild rhythms of the finales, recognized that this music, compared to that of his predecessors, is somewhat

From *The Creative World of Beethoven* (New York: W. W. Norton, 1971)

raw, gnarled, even unfinished. There were some who were repelled, among them such able composers as Spohr and Weber; but many more, despite or perhaps because of these qualities, found Beethoven's music to be warmer, more intense, and more fulfilling than any other they had known.

Beethoven proclaimed that art not only is personal confession but represents the divine itself, being a higher revelation than any wisdom. The boundaries of Haydn's beautifully closed real world gradually recede around him, clouding into metaphysics. At the same time, the revelation, the spirit which Beethoven so loved to emphasize, now gave a new nobility to the musician as artist—Beethoven called himself a *Tondichter* rather than a composer. Like Schiller, he fervently professed that the principal and highest repository of the dignity of humanity is the creative artist. It was this clear and courageous consciousness of his vocation and destiny, which he maintained under all conditions of life, that made him what the world sees in him: the epitome of the sovereign artist. Haydn, though always of a sunny disposition and a respecter of the prevailing order of the world, once admitted that he found it a galling thing to be forever a servant, but he quickly added that Providence decreed it that way. Beethoven proudly declared that a man should never humble himself before his fellows. At the celebrated encounter with Goethe in Teplitz, the whole assembled royalty could see that Beethoven would elbow them aside if they should get in his way. To Beethoven, unlike Goethe and most of his contemporaries, this independence was a cardinal necessity. With this new type of artist the old solidarity and commonality of the eighteenth century ended, and the solitary, individual, responsible, and challenging man steps forward. He in whom this overwhelming tempest took its course appeared to be no other than a Titan, the representative of humanity itself, and it is so indeed that not only romantic historiography but all the world sees Beethoven.

Those who expected to find in him Mozart's and Haydn's successor were taken aback when the young musician, only recently settled in Vienna, began to show the pride of a plebeian who jealously guards his independence and is filled with ambitions going far beyond those associated with his profession and social standing. There was something arrogant, wildly gauche, even offensive, in his attitude, and his supreme creed seems to have been pride and power; he believed that he was not only the equal of the men with whom he dealt, but their superior. His contemporaries felt that, in contrast to Mozart, a sun that illuminated and warmed without leaving its lawful orbit, Beethoven was a comet that followed uncharted paths without submitting to a systematic world order, giving rise by its very appearance to unsanctioned ideas. Then in our day the composer has been fair game for the psychoanalysts, with their explanations of guilt, remorse, and hostility; but Beethoven is a difficult subject, and the analyses are disconcertingly contradictory. Life's flame burned in Beethoven so vehemently, his mental travails were so intense and strenuous, that the passions of a decade in anyone else's life seem compressed more nearly into one year in his life. He was never calm or objective, for he reacted violently to everything, both embracing and hating life, and he could not remain indifferent toward anyone, nor forbear expressing his strong feelings. Those who knew and related to him as composer became, under the impact of his personality, his fervent partisans. His enemies defended themselves against his inescapable influence by excessive malignance, their every attack and every insult still a reaction to his prestige. He himself received homage as his due, and he was accustomed to mobilize nearly everyone in his retinue for his purposes. He was a republican who also like to work for royalty; he believed in the brotherhood of all men while priding himself on his German qualities and showing the old German prejudice toward Italian music and musicians; he preached the highest moral standards but could be less than fair in business matters and grossly abusive when inconvenienced. Much has been made of his yearning for the realization of the aims of the French Revolution, but these were only half-understood ideals with a romantic tinge. The younger Schlegel once held up *Wilhelm Meister* as the German counterpart of the French Revolution. Indeed, in Germany there could not be a real revolution at the turn of the century; no one would even think of it. The men born to action either were silenced or became mere utopians. It is in this sense that we must look at the *Eroica*, and even at the Ninth Symphony; for with the Germans in general and Beethoven in particular, every energetic impulse turned inward.

We have still not answered, however, the question of why Beethoven occupies such an exceptional position in the history of music, why he became the composer who more than any other speaks to all humanity beyond the German borders, the international composer in the best sense of the word. Different nations or cultural circles see and value works of art differently, and some works greatly esteemed in their homeland are rejected elsewhere. It may sound paradoxical, but an artist is none the less universal for being highly individual, and this particular universal individual who is everyone's hero had two qualities that no other musician possessed to such a degree: power and the desire for communication. "Was nennt ihr brave Kerls?" asks Goethe's Wieland. "Einer der mitteilt, was er hat," answers Hercules. Indeed, the desire for sharing, for communication, is as strong in Beethoven as the expression itself, but he makes excessive demands on the listener, creating a sense of urgency, always unwilling to make concessions, and refusing to soften his attitude. His listeners everywhere have felt that he strives to break into the processes of life itself, to reveal himself—not only himself but also the soul of humanity—with such courage, with such élan and passion, as has no one before or after him. The sketchbooks show the flaring up of passions, the struggle with ideas as they change their shapes like drifting clouds, the mixture of elation and pain that is creation, and the incompatibility of the finished work with the imagined one. And all this struggle is in his music; he communicates it with unparalleled directness, and the listener is overwhelmed by the nearly incredible willpower, the unexampled integrity of a creative artist who always strives for absolutes.

Bettina Brentano, reporting to Goethe, remarked that in no crowned ruler had she seen such consciousness of power. Goethe, for his part, could not fathom the composer and was intimidated by a man who could deduce: "Power is the morality of outstanding men, and it is my morality too." The boast may at first glance seem cynical, but we must remember that the relationship between genius and ideas is tortuous. The meaning of this statement becomes much clearer when we join to it the desperate resolution of the Heiligenstadt Testament, when his faith in power and human strength met a terrible trial. The realization that his growing deafness would deprive him of the voices of the outside world brought Beethoven to the brink of suicide; but then his characteristic courage gained the upper hand. "It seemed to me impossible," he said, "to quit before I had produced all that I felt myself called on to accomplish." Beethoven now realized this affliction to be the supreme test, and he lifted his head and accepted the challenge: "I will grab Fate by the throat." Popular tradition has it that Beethoven died during a storm with raised fist. Apocryphal or not, fist and storm could both be characteristic symbols of this man throughout most of his life, for he wanted to be a free man of power, a world conqueror. But this power, as well as his limitless will, he directed not to the purposes that animated the once admired Napoleon; his ambition was to conquer the more distant spheres of the spirit.

As the years went by, Beethoven broke with social conventions and accepted the unavoidable consequences: banishment and solitariness. He now knew that he must count on no one, need reckon with no one, and from this point onward he became increasingly ruthless, even in his composing, in the end trampling the instruments and violating the singing voice. It is idle speculation to attribute this solely to his physical affliction; deafness only liberated elemental and atavistic penchants, that ancient Germanic spirit which treasures the idea and has never bothered much with the means. In the last period of his creative activity, when the world saw in him an eccentric recluse, and Vienna greeted Rossini as the savior of music, his deafness seems almost to have been welcome; the material nature of music was less binding on him, he could advance into the realm of visions. There is in this music of Beethoven's last period something that was totally strange to nineteenth-century musicians: the delight in abstraction. The romantics were happy only when they could dress up the abstract, but works like Beethoven's *Grosse Fuge* are the great undressing act in art; the garments are thrown away, and only the naked ideas remain.

When in 1849 Millet arrived at the artists' colony in Barbizon, his colleagues, following their custom, tried to classify him according to "school." They could not agree, whereupon Millet exclaimed: "Well, if you are at a loss, place me in my own school." Beethoven could have said the same, for he too seems impossible to place in anyone else's category; yet to the romantics the man who was born in the same year as Hölderlin and Hegel and who died two years after Weber and one year before Schubert, was seen as the father and patron saint of Romanticism. The new movement could not defend itself against Beethoven's invincible art; all its instincts of self-preservation ceased when confronted with him, for there was everything in this music that the Romantics desired and valued. "Terrible!" exclaimed the enervated Pope Leo X at the sight of Michelangelo's murals; it is this *terribilità* that the romantics saw in the *Sonata appassionata* and the Fifth Symphony. But they saw only the means in this music, not its essence; they saw how Beethoven demolished the boundaries but did not see that he demolished only to force the unbounded into severe and logical unity. The secret longing of the romantics was for the no longer attainable classical ideal of form; the entire nineteenth century was a vast sigh of nostalgia for Bach and Beethoven. But Romanticism would have sawed the limb from under itself if it had admitted that its indulging in classicistic dreams was only a game, the equator dreaming of the poles. Berlioz saw himself as Beethoven's direct descendant, Brahms believed that he followed in Beethoven's footsteps, even Wagner incessantly declared that Beethoven—had he lived longer!—would have taken the path he himself took. The confusion has continued into our century, because many still mistakenly see in Beethoven emotion dominating the intellect; many see only the Titan, the hero, the fighter.

We tend to think that in Beethoven it is exclusively the heart that speaks to us, for we know about his deep interest in freedom and brotherly love, and our predecessors have already proclaimed him the liberator of music, or, as a book popular a generation ago was entitled, "The man who freed music." Even much earlier he was regarded as the first great composer who in his music withheld nothing of himself, and so was the first true romantic. And yet the voice of the intellect is never absent in Beethoven, even when he is rebellious, because he immediately proceeds to rebuild what he demolishes; he does not deny, he only contradicts. It was romantic anti-intellectualism in the arts that created the fashion of banishing from music logic of construction and procedure as inimical to poetry, thus creating the greatest impediment to true appreciation of Beethoven. This view created havoc as able composers denied their own healthy talents to follow the imagined Beethovenian code, and may have been the principal reason for the subsequent decline of symphony, quartet, and sonata. Yet we must also beware of considering Beethoven a belated product of the Enlightenment, for he represents the triumph of a new synthesis: the crowning of the "Classic era" in music as Dante crowned the Middle Ages.

The question arises, how far behind did Beethoven leave his heritage? How shall we measure his relationship to Haydn, Mozart, Cherubini, and others? He did not turn away from them; he abandoned nothing that was noble, nothing that he could not develop with historical logic. To be sure, this heritage was modified, it moved forward, and it rose in him to new heights.

We have already mentioned the surprising fact that this archclassic was still alive and creating when such full-blooded romantics as Weber and Byron were already dead. Together with such masters of the late Classic era as Clementi and Cherubini, Beethoven lived in an age when early Romanticism was in full bloom. This late Classicism endeavored to absorb and use the moods of the new movement, without, however, abandoning the principles of construction focused on a center. This almost paradoxical reconciliation of styles tempted many a composer of the era, but it led to half-solutions, Beethoven being the only one who knowingly and deliberately mastered this formidable problem. He took the large dimensions that Clementi and Cherubini introduced, eliminated what was inessential or watery, condensed and concentrated the texture, on the one hand, while giving a new meaning to the large forms, on the other, stretching them to their maximal tensile strength. The equilibrium often teeters on pinpoints and can be maintained only by overwhelming force, but it never sags. His solution is unique in the millennial history of Western music, and it is once more Beethoven's coercive power that so deeply affects the listener, who feels it even if he does not understand it. Surrounded by the stream of Romanticism, with all bonds and restrictions changing into relativism, Beethoven permits the new elements to pour in and be salvaged from dissolution. For we must remember—Goethe is our witness—that the late classics considered Romanticism an abuse of true art. It was the very fact that Beethoven's particular genius could admit so many romantic elements into an essentially classical concept that gave him his unique and revered position, the entire nineteenth century claiming him as its lawful progenitor. The romantics, however, since they could not really follow him, remade him in their own image, presenting his whole life as the manifestation of the Sturm and Drang, a movement with which he had little in common. *that's not true!*

When the theorists of the romantic age explain the harmonic practices of their movement, they cite Beethoven's great contributions to their art. They did notice in Beethoven's music the distant excursions from the tonal center; what they did not understand was that this is a modulatory maximum which still permits the work to be held within classical unity. Nor could they fathom the rate and complexity of the harmonic motion, the relationship of key centers to themes—in a word, they did not notice the brakes which Beethoven applied ceaselessly but which they had already abandoned. Beethoven does experiment a great deal, but his power of synthesis, of comprehensive summing up, was so strong that even in his early works we see a constant effort to strengthen cohesion. Though he received superbly developed forms from his predecessors, he had to conquer every bit of the territory upon which he built his music, and did so with unparalleled willpower. The classical perfection of the Viennese school, erroneously equated with formalism, does not signify merely faultless form; this is but the external expression of inner clarity. Man speaks in perfect sentences only if wholly conscious of self. What puzzled and misled the romantics was that within the barriers of this great self-control, Beethoven at times cannot carry his burden, and, as if from a burning house, runs wildly outside. But this does not change the fact that in him the spirit of the new age reconquers what in the first flush of excitement it had been ready to cast away: the disciplined métier and classical tradition.

Looking at the famous sketchbooks, one's first impression is that they are haphazard and sporadic; we also see that while Beethoven's imagination and inventiveness are inexhaustible, he often struggles with his material, notably with his themes, and there is a constant and ever-growing need to set things right, "order from disorder sprung." The approach is always analytical and synthetic; he raises questions and then answers them, often years later. He neither gives way to the impatience that characterizes the romantic, nor allows his expression to fail for want of craftsmanship. It seems as if the germ of every idea has been there in his soul from the beginning, growing slowly as Beethoven returns again and again, attempting to prune it down or extent it to the shape he desired. Indeed, the sketchbooks disclose the triumph of the *ars combinatoria* of old, or, as Lenz so engagingly says about the *Waldstein* Sonata: "In the development section Beethoven makes a nest from torn feathers."

These ideas and the problems of shaping they caused were purely musical and had little to do with the *Weltanschauung* music the romantics hung on Beethoven. Indeed, the romantics not only evinced a tendency to endow the notes with symbolic meanings, but turned this sincere and ardent lover of nature into a category: Beethoven, the father of romantic program music. Nature pictures have, of course, always attracted painters, poets, and musicians; but what did the word *nature* signify? The painter's and poet's representation of nature was background or lyricism, for nature provides man's surroundings, perhaps his dream world. That nature is a great truth independent of man, of which man is only part, but which makes possible and explains his life, was an altogether modern thought. Beethoven, who always found beauty in the simplest phenomena of nature, now discovers the greater truth, deriving from his discovery depth of feeling and a musical lesson whose motto, "More an expression of feeling than painting," he placed at the head of his Sixth Symphony. It was mainly this symphony that composers and writers from Berlioz onward used as the principal document to support their argument, but few stopped to ponder the significance of the motto.

Beethoven found in nature a liberating force—not in nature's individual manifestations, but in their effect on the beholder. Programmatic titles and superscriptions he did use in order to enhance a certain mood, but except for a few spots in the *Pastoral* Symphony, his so-called program music has little of the descriptive in it; as a rule he induces a mood not with experience described but with the musical association evoked. This is a purely poetic art, for programmatic interpretation can be justified only when the possibility of purely musical apprehension is not present, when music abandons its very own conditions of existence and depends on extramusical glosses. The mystery of poetic imagination defies scientific analysis, and it is easier to grasp Einstein's theory than to explain the essence of this supposed program music to one who is looking for pictorial verisimilitude in it. The deaf composer could not hear the sounds of nature; he could hear nothing but his own music. It is even immaterial in whose memory the funeral march in the *Eroica* was composed; it is not different from the one in the A-flat Sonata, which has no story attached to it. In the end, both are "absolute" music, conceived and executed on purely musical principles altogether free of extramusical, conceptual connotations. Even the overt, announced program can be very deceptive: the little concert of the birds in the *Pastoral* Symphony comes *after* the movement's musical construction is fully achieved. Beethoven, like most other great masters, created so many moods that any additional program is only a superfluous burden, as is well demonstrated in the sad aberrations with which Schering ended a distinguished career.

One would think that this universally admired and most performed composer, who gave a new heart and a new pulse to the world (to quote Tennyson's words about Shelley), was firmly ensconced on his throne; but there was no dearth of criticism even after Beethoven was beatified. The men of letters, with such notable exceptions as E. T. A. Hoffmann, seem to have been particularly at odds with him. Goethe never really understood Beethoven, remaining cool and reserved toward the composer whose power alarmed him. Grillparzer, who wrote a great deal about music with indifferent results, could not help recognizing Beethoven's greatness—we are in the 1830s and 1840s—but he too was frightened, denouncing the composer as the destroyer of form and too much devoted to power. We must jump over a large literature devoted to the master to consider the curious ambivalence of attitudes toward Beethoven in more recent times.

Spengler, who saw in the culture of a democratic society nothing but a spiritless material civilization, considered Beethoven the most typical agent of the transition from the perfection of eighteenth-century Classicism to the dullness and decadence of the middle-class world. To Spengler, and others as well, the last sonatas and quartets seemed to sunder classic construction. Is this not dissolution, the beginning of the abandonment of form? Is this not the beginning of decline, the autumn of Western music? These sonatas and quartets, and that vast choral symphony called a Mass, are they not harbingers of the fall that begins as the zenith is reached? We must deny all of it. The freeing of the individual from convention is always infinitely baffling and ambiguous, but the miracle of Beethoven's music is that in its liberty and individuality it is also finitely organic and compelling. In its caprice there lives the passionate logic of dissection and synthesis, in its dissolubility there is no looseness; for, despite all its arbitrariness and its many crises, this music reaches final harmony.

Today some young and impatient musicians find Beethoven objectionable; they are alienated by his security, by his imperious determination, they deride his majestic egotism, they resent his timelessness which still gives us lessons, but, above all, they are dismayed by the eternal presence of the hero who cannot be undone. As each new generation comes along, it sees its own place in the sun as requiring the downfall of its predecessors and of their idols and heroes, so that rebirth can follow. The world needs rebels in order to be able to move and preserve its rhythm. Beethoven does represent the highest heroism precisely because the revolutionary character of his music is kept powerfully within bounds; the mind of the classically schooled craftsman is always in command, ordering and organizing. Bartók and Stravinsky were still full of admiration for Beethoven, but many of today's musicians are completely estranged from him; they misjudge Beethoven's heroism, its humanity, its intensity of expression and communication. It is this passion that gives Beethoven's music its heroic clangor, its rhetorical force.

In the end, the grandeur and the heroism are Beethoven himself, the creative man who cannot be fulfilled, and it is this lack of complete creative fulfillment that paradoxically shows the richness of his soul. For he realized that he would never find the old Haydn's absolute peace, only relative calms in the struggle. This is what eternally drove him, from masterpiece to masterpiece, toward the unattainable fulfillment, and this is what creates in his music the great tensions that enthrall people all over the world.

Wagner: The Master of Tristan

Arecent performance of *Tristan and Isolde* recalled the astonishment, admiration, as well as the controversy aroused by this gigantic score in former years. Most of that is now forgotten, yet the work eternally fascinates because of its unique qualities. Wagner's grand plan for the creation of a national musico-dramatic epic had progressed satisfactorily, and he had reached the middle of the second act of *Siegfried*. So far everything was well ordered, if sprawling; the texture was diatonic and under good symphonic control. Then suddenly something happens; his brain is seized with convulsions, and his blood boils. The pictures turn into visions, the visions into yearning, and yearning into lust. The flesh is tormented, for this is the all-consuming passion of an aging man, more intense and dangerous than that of a young man.

Biographers have shown Wagner as a rather promiscuous person; as a matter of fact, he was completely amoral in sexual matters. From his fourteenth year, when he met the Pachta girls in Prague, there were innumerable women in his life, and since he traveled a great deal, he gives the impression of a musical sailor with a girl—or two—in every port.

From *The New York Herald-Tribune*, 30 June, 1963

He was not at all reticent about his views on a "liberal" concept of the relationship between men and women, but he put it in nebulous philosophical terms. There can be no question that Wagner exerted a tremendous attraction on women, young or old, aristocrat or commoner, single or married. Even those who managed to retain their distance, like the Princess Metternich or the great singer Schroeder-Devrient, went out of their way to help him, though sorely tried by his eternal borrowing of money.

But the situation that produced *Tristan* does not seem to accord with this characteristic pattern of rather casual love affairs. The cause of the upheaval must be sought elsewhere. There were two women in Wagner's life who do not fall into the usual category. One was Mathilde Wesendonck, the immediate source of *Tristan*, the other Cosima Liszt von Buelow, his second wife, who was finally his match and kept him in line for the rest of his life—or almost.

The stories about his passionate—if idealized—love for Mathilde Wesendonck are well known, but the key to the particular mental state that resulted in *Tristan* can be explained only if we refer to Wagner's writings, where there is a passage that sheds light on the situation: "To seek a pure, chaste virgin love, sprung from the soil of the fullest sensuousness, but which sensuousness as understood in modern society could not satisfy."

This is not really as cryptic a statement as it may seem. Wagner knew the obstacles, and they acted as a tonic on his imagination. Already under the spell of Schopenhauer's pessimistic philosophy, and gathering new ideas from Buddhism, he formed his own chaotic and mystic theory of catastrophe, of the oneness of highest rapture with death. What he needed was someone to personify all this, and he found her in Mathilde Wesendonck, an able, attractive, and cultured woman.

The vapors in his mind began to billow, and an entirely new composer is before us in *Tristan*. The diatonicism of the *Ring* cycle gave way to an agitated, gnawing, inflammatory, and seditious chromaticism that carried Western harmony to its limits.

But after a while this music, this frenetic, tumultuous tangle of motives and instruments, harmonies and counterpoints, becomes so complicated and overwrought that it reminds one of the battle picture on old tapestries where an inextricable maze of horses' hooves and warriors' legs trample the flowers of the meadow. Wagner would not omit anything he saw or felt; everything was retained in an intoxicating richness. Nevertheless, many of the individual scenes, and very long ones, are still overwhelmingly exciting.

And yet this paean of rapture and death, rich as it is, is really sad to contemplate, for it leads nowhere; it does not coalesce in a dramatic synthesis.

His overheated imagination, surging into the infinite, violently thirsted for the unheard-of and the unutterable, and these are not the ingredients of drama. Dramatic ideas and unity are not so much replaced by the music as they are drowned by the sheer power of it. Instead of great dramatic conflicts, the music gives lyric ecstasies, and those cannot be sustained through three tremendous acts.

When the madness departed—it was to return once more, greatly diminished, in *Parsifal*, and again with a "pure, chaste love," directed toward Judith Gautier—this incredible man had to turn back. And he returned to something so different, so far removed from the lethal voluptuousness of *Tristan*, that one is entirely at a loss to fathom his power of artistic regeneration.

The man who was capable of composing *Die Meistersinger* after *Tristan* remains the most forbiddingly powerful personality in the entire history of music, and perhaps of all the arts.

Music in Twentieth-Century Civilization

Dodecaphony

e should shrink with terror from the discussion of the recent history of music, where every character is a problem, and every reader a friend or an enemy; where a writer is supposed to hoist a flag or party and is devoted to damnation by the adverse faction.

The above sentence is not ours and, except for the insertion of the word *music*, should be in quotation marks, for it was written by Gibbon, the future author of the celebrated *Decline and Fall*, when he was casting about for a suitable subject. However, by substituting music for English history, we obtained an almost perfect description of the situation in general and our own state of mind in particular. Ever since the fourth century B.C., when Aristoxenus declared the music of his day "mendacious make-believe," through the fourteenth century A.D., when Jacobus of Liège bewailed the advent of the *ars nova*, to the twentieth century, when distinguished musicians and critics have used old Jacobus's words and arguments to condemn the composers active among us, the critic has run the risk of being completely disavowed by posterity. Yet most of us go at it with ever renewed vigor, convinced that errors widely disseminated with regard to current tendencies will continue to work mischief

From *The Musical Quarterly*, vol. 44 (1958)

unless brought into the open. What we have in mind is the place and role of dodecaphony in our present and future music, admittedly one of the most pressing questions of the day. Its proponents, with rather peremptory and heavy-handed authority, handle issues that are not always so abstruse and purely technical as they are made to appear.

If we look upon the music of the first half of our century as an island, then around the chaotic circle of Schoenberg everything seems calm and orderly, for Schoenberg and his school represent the first real breaking away from the legacy of the long nineteenth century. Stravinsky and Bartók are incomparably original and powerful composers, but only their thoughts, visions, and gestures are original, their manner of composing is not essentially different from that of the past. What they have to say rests on ancient tradition; their handwriting, though novel, is almost always decipherable to informed and progressive musicians. There are a good many persons who can recall the laughter and derision that rewarded the first performance of the *Sacre*, but in the meantime even the public has learned that Stravinsky's music is, so to speak, only a new application of musical perspective in which sounds have a different meaning and color. But dodecaphony has no traditions, and though the usual reproach leveled against it is that it is purely mathematical, logic does not get anywhere with it. The conventional symbols of music are gone, and at every moment we are in need of an imaginary glossary to follow the proceedings.

And yet without the post-Romantics we should not have Schoenberg and his school. It was the world of Mahler and others that awakened in Schoenberg his extraordinary curiosity and receptiveness towards novel techniques of composition. To the music he heard in Vienna at the opening of the century he listened not naively, but with the analytical skill of the philologist. This was his preliminary schooling, without which his art cannot be understood. Even in his earlier works he demanded far too much from his public. His style is a mixture of the most disparate elements and demands a great deal of knowledge and ingenuity on the part of the student.

Yet all these objections are stilled if we search for Schoenberg's place not on our little island but in the thousand-year-old recorded history of Western music. Then the chaotic Schoenberg will appear as a purposeful artist full of energies who created a new concept of musical space, and whose advent was foreordained. This new musical space, the result of "composing with twelve notes," created the most drastic illusion in recent music history. We say "in recent music history," because upheavals accompany every great stylistic change, for every fundamental change represents first of all a departure from the direction of Western music. The central problems of composing are shifted, though what we notice first is the more visible mass of peripheral problems. The calm and superior art of the Renaissance, the dramatically excited Baroque, were both oriented toward new dimensions, if each in its own way. The Rococo made this urge playful, the Classic era disciplined and tightened it, Romanticism set it boiling, but all of them wanted more room for their music. Then came critical times for music; in fact, ever since *Tristan* the situation has been critical, and some radical change was inevitable.

Able and distinguished composers attempted to channel the unavoidable change into something that did not demand a complete *tabula rasa*, and many of them have been entirely successful. Among them Hindemith, for example, deserves a conspicuous place, though he has lost the position that once placed him in the company of the coryphaei: Stravinsky, Bartók, and Schoenberg. Stravinsky, after shedding his original and invigorating Russian style, became the most brilliant and *raffiné* defender of the post-Impressionistic art of the West and a leader of the Neoclassicists. Though the frame and texture of his music remained admirably solid and artistic, the contents were diffident, objective, and cold to the point of being free of all passion and feeling. Then, after several other reorientations, the linear element came to the fore, and Debussy's astonishing prophecy became a reality. "Stravinsky inclines danger-ously towards the side of Schoenberg," said the clairvoyant French composer; and indeed, Stravinsky has capitulated to the dodecaphonists. Still, those who proclaim him the great liberator of music are as mistaken as those who see in his music nothing but a nihilistic conception of man, whose music he deval-ued into a fabulous machine. It is undeniable, though, that with every one of his conversions it becomes clearer that Stravinsky is not willing to face the higher moral issues confronting the artist, and is constantly looking for ready-made tracks upon which to launch his marvelous musicianship.

Only Bartók among these leaders stuck to his guns, living out his life undisturbed by any outside interference and influence that he could not in good conscience wholly absorb within his own art.

Like the collapse of the *prima prattica*, the deterioration of the post-Romantic world was due to several causes, of which the reaching of a stylistic impasse was decisive. In an era of extreme individualism, collective values cannot be established and preserved—music exhausts itself. When an extreme is reached, there is no longer any possibility of that slow assimilation which so often took place in the history of music. Schoenberg himself arrived at this point with his *Gurrelieder*. The only remedy is to swing boldly to the other extreme. When art is no longer produced within a social frame but consists of individual findings, when the great artist is a revolutionary not because of temperament but because there is no other avenue open to him, it means that art is no longer an essential necessity of man; or perhaps we should say that since art no longer fulfills its essential role, it becomes a mere agent and not a spiritual need. The post-Debussy Impressionists showed this clearly, for they surely were interested only in the peripheral, not in the central problems of composition. The color of sound, exotic sound, interested them more than musical ideas. In this they shared a preoccupation with their fellow artists, the painters. As the painters were beguiled with Japanese woodcuts and other oriental elements, which they proceeded to incorporate into their own style, the musicians flirted with gamelan, Hindu scales, and other exotic sounds and patterns, which they tried to reconcile with their Western heritage. How sad and unworkable this usually is can be seen in such an attempt as Messiaen's *Turangalila*. The chemical makeup of Western and Eastern musicians cannot be combined in this manner. The Western composer does not take over the Oriental's problems, he uses them only to solve his own—from without. The colors and rhythms may be wonderful and fascinating, and with their aid the composer frees himself of the dreaded ballast of "academic" music. He no longer depends on a demonstrable tonal plan; instead of harmonic and rhythmic motion his music exhibits only a tendency to move; his is a pure musical hedonism. At the same time, when the post-Impressionist is unable to wring more continuity out of the changing color scheme, he grasps with the impatience and pitilessness of the dilettante any and all means, no matter how foreign to his art. When this stage is reached, the rules of academic composition, or purely linear procedures, everything, is acceptable to him in order to reach his goal. Many a wayward fugato thus appears in the most unlikely context. This, however, never happens with the mature Schoenberg. His technique is solid, secure, and unwavering, even though the spirit of his architecture is and remains mysterious in spite of the logic of his tectonics.

There was one musician squarely athwart the careers of all composers during the first half of our century. Like the quartet composer, Haydn, whom no one, from Mozart to Brahms, could avoid without penalty, no one could avoid Debussy, and every one had to settle with him before being able to proceed on his own. There is something incomparably ethereal about the lightness and fluidity of Debussy's music which was buried with him, though all the results of his art survived. But no real school could be created, because with him the results were not commensurate with the means; they were far greater. If we compare him with, say, Florent Schmitt, this becomes instantly clear. Debussy's music is not hard or virile, his brush strokes are not imperious, and his colors are of the pastel variety; yet this music has an almost unnatural weight, and the contours, though softly, are nevertheless well drawn. The post-Impressionists could not continue this utterly refined, personal art; they became epilogue composers, elegant and sure-handed, but avoiding the essential problems. They were born into the bravura of orchestral wizardry, and for this reason the results appear with such seeming spontaneity, and it is for this reason also that their intentions could so easily be realized. But see where this leads: the depleted Ravel turns this wizardry to the exploitation of Mussorgsky, while the Busonis, Casellas, Respighis, and all the others (yes, even Schoenberg) belabor—Bach.

Schoenberg's relative position was not different from that of other musicians caught in this dilemma. He too inherited a lavish knowledge of the métier, but also a disordered situation. The decisive criterion was there: music no longer pressed with determination toward the development of a new style; it sought only to use the existing apparatus with more and more virtuosity. All of the three great masters—Stravinsky, Bartók, Schoenberg—together with many excellent composers of lesser stature, refused to acquiesce in this, though for different reasons and to varying degrees. While in Russia, Stravinsky was not aware of the bankruptcy of the West. Russian music was so new, the unspoiled energy of the Easterner so strong, that such a phenomenal talent could burst on the Western scene like a bombshell. Stravinsky could rival and far surpass the French among whom he settled, as once Hasse did the Italians; but like Hasse, he was unable to endow his prodigious musicianship with warmth and depth. Bartók, who started from Liszt, Wagner, and Strauss, may also appear to be an East European; but Hungary is contiguous with the West and not so close to Asia as Russia. He too brought the fresh and tightly coiled energies from the peripheries of Western music, but they did not suffer from contact with Impressionism. Bartók went his own way, unbowed and unintimidated, a supremely serene and strong artist.

Schoenberg had the opportunity to throw himself with ardor into the problem of what to do with this heritage, but he could not solve it: *Verklärte Nacht* and *Hängende Gärten* are the witnesses to this attempt at reconciliation with Impressionism. This earnest and honest artist was not satisfied, therefore he chose an altogether new road. That is why his mature art is so incredibly paradoxical and yet altogether logical and true. It was the result of the most personal and anarchistic work, and its far-reaching importance can be explained only by his exceptional place in his time.

Schoenberg's innovation is the greatest single event in the music of the first half of our century, and though it has the earmarks of a transitional phenomenon, the second half was to be dominated by it. As an individual artistic feat, it is very nearly unparalleled, and as it became generally known, few musicians could remain untouched by it. We can observe every day how among our own American composers some of the best, such as Copland, are turning to it at the height of their well-formed, pronouncedly individual, and successful careers. Thus Schoenberg is more than a unique eruptive phenomenon; he dislocated music from all its strata, and with his appearance a new geological formation took place. Since the advent of dodecaphony, the conditions of music have become different, and so are its possibilities. All this is no exaggeration—the facts speak. A number of years ago there was a flourishing musical culture from whose workshops emerged a host of fine works, among them great masterpieces by Bartók, Stravinsky, Ravel, Hindemith, Falla, Sibelius, Prokofiev, Vaughan Williams, and a little later Copland, Sessions, Piston, and many others. It seemed as if the good old days had returned, from Budapest to New York. But a sudden awakening chased away the dreams. The happy creative fervor has disappeared; the musicians are severely concentrated on doctrine. Yesterday they still had confidence in their own temperament and instinct; today they are unwilling to trust anything that cannot be justified by doctrine. There are still many able composers active who are willing to dispute the dogma successfully, but the young ones cannot seem to live without dogma. The moods are wilted; all we have are axioms and laws. It had to be thus, for there were too many musicians who played happily with some unessential beauties of their art. Schoenberg returned to the essence, and no one can play any more. This was the great accomplishment; the musicians were alerted, listening with awe, and the toys dropped from their hands. Schoenberg's art is inexorable, and it seems as if all the urge to self-preservation in the post-Impressionists is powerless against it. The Vienna composer was led to the hidden path with the inspiration of the chosen, and by following it he reached his domain. The path is no longer visible, it is overgrown with stubble and alders, and the great flaming instinct, the Messianic conviction, no longer flares. Gone also are the other distinguished captains, Webern and Berg, and we are faced with the legion of disciples, converts, and neophytes who are forced to manipulate the system of composing with twelve notes. They must resort to strategy and tactics, they believe in occult laws which they cannot really fathom, and they are, most of them, oblivious to the impulses and agitations of the outside world. It is impossible to evaluate Schoenberg at such a short perspective beyond establishing his exceptional importance, though we are somewhat better able to see the merits of the first two great disciples, Berg and Webern. His willpower and uncompromising artistic integrity compel admiration and respect, but whether his art will furnish the basis for the future aesthetics of music cannot be decided by dialectics; only time will tell.

The same cannot be said, with few exceptions, of the younger generation, and it is in their activity that the status of dodecaphony assumes a sinister aspect. Thus Schoenberg's legacy created a ghostly world, a frightened refuge for composers who have avoided clarity and single meaning. They have put on the whole armor of enigma, and within its burden have performed the motions of strenuous significance. They display the exploitation of a spearhead's victory by a competent but uninspired legion.

"Terrible," exclaimed the enervated Pope Leo X before Michelangelo's frescoes. This terribilità faces us in most present-day dodecaphony, but it is not now the heroic, frightening majesty of human moods and gestures, but rather the bald *logos* of music, a "stern and heartless petrification," to quote Constable. The great weakness of the many young composers who embraced the faith is that they do not penetrate below consciousness to the feelings and impulses that lie below the threshold of will; they merely sever all connections with the conventional language of music and all the conditions of musical life. They are not interested in personal tone and color; the real spiritual community, the joy and sorrow of creation are absent. This music no longer illustrates states of mind, and a separate and strange country is the musicians' domain. They give us acoustic impressions, acoustic relations, acoustic contrasts and balances, as if man were nothing but a pair of ears with which he takes in the world.

Dodecaphonism was the receiver for bankrupt post-Romanticism. It auctioned off tonality more completely than the Florentine monodists did counterpoint. But a substitute must be found for the swept-out conventions. Schoenberg and his school believed that with their new manner they were conjuring up the elemental, aboriginal strata of music. They were convinced that major and minor had been disposed of forever; and a new broom sweeps well. In order to be consistent, the doctrinaire twelve-note composer must relinquish, besides tonality, the principal agent of musical form, the alternation of tension and relaxation—that is, the opposition of consonance and dissonance. What he substitutes is something that resembles electric current—its tension is invariably 110 volts. That is the revenge taken by Schoenberg's musico-aesthetic misconception according to which consonance and dissonance do not represent contrast but only a difference in degree within the same phenomenon. This is palpably the result of a confusion of the physical with the aesthetic theory of consonance and dissonance.

The dodecaphonists correctly assessed the decadence of post-Romanticism, its cynical and hedonistic spirit, and the reaction led them to severe earnestness and ascetic immersion. The new style raised the inexorability of will and a masochistic self-denial to symbolic strength. It is a tragedy that a musical movement can remain so deaf to the requirements of aesthetics. It declared itself anti-Romantic, but in its contempt for the boundless freedom of Romanticism it landed in a vacuum. If composition meant the mere manipulation, no matter how skillful and logical, of the basic materials of music, of the twelve notes of the octave, we could not call it a revelation of humanity. The ranging and ordering of notes does not yet mean anything musically, for it does not yet bring it within the sphere of aesthetic formation.

Tonality as an institution is dying; and it can either die in foolish decrepitude or it can die mightily, merging itself with the principles brought to the fore by dodecaphonism for a final blow against philistinism. The fact is that the majority of musicians still firmly believe in a system of music that has benefited them, and will continue to believe in it as long as it can still produce fine and thoroughly modern works. When it ceases to do so, they will undoubtedly reconsider their position. But that time is not yet.

Marxist Theory and Music

Modern musicology often denies the "mystery" of historical reality, reducing it to morphology and style criticism, divorcing the human spirit from the historical. Musico-technical interpretation is far more scientifically applicable, especially in matters of detail, than historical-psychological interpretation; yet in order to approach any creation with understanding, we must know the period and conditions under which the artist labored. Full understanding can be achieved only by a combination of the technical-morphological with the aesthetic-historical; in this way we can assimilate the particular spirit that led the artist's inspiration to a style. And when we inquire into the meaning of the work of art, what it communicates, the incentive that crystallized its form, we must also inquire what the period itself considered important for communication—that is, from what source beyond his own inspiration the artist drew the particular spirit that characterizes him.

Every culture has its recognizable roots, from which grow the convoluted stalks of historical development. Since art is a social phenomenon, to perceive

From *The Musical Quarterly*, vol. 53 (1967)

them all requires the assistance of sociology; but here there are hazards for the historian and critic of the arts, because sociology tends to ignore the cultural significance of the examined elements. The dangers are twofold. At one extreme is the purely materialistic, even mechanical, application of the evolutionary principles of social science, at the other the magico-forensic. Granted, personalities must not be treated as isolated atoms, but the action of human beings depends not on external influence alone; it springs from motives deep within the personality. Men are not abstract, they are historical beings; individual men and historical forces interact upon each other, for it is in the historical context that the spiritual essence of the world is manifested, not in mere external phenomena. We must therefore penetrate into the historical-sociological strata and make ourselves at home in them. But history and sociology are not made of factual material pure and simple, nor do they exist in one definite form; they represent and call for an intellectual activity. This historical reality is above all something concrete. In history there is nothing abstract; it is sociology that operates with the abstract, because sociology often ignores individual concepts, whereas history always ends with them. Even the general becomes individual. The nation, too, is a general concept, but, at the same time, as a concrete historical nation it is an altogether individual concept. Therefore it is of considerable importance to us to see clearly the difference between the historical and the sociological.

No good social history can be written without a certain bias, but the bias should develop out of a study of the evidence. Such a bias is difficult to develop towards quite recent events precisely because the evidence is incomplete; yet the writer of these lines must face this task. I am about to attend a scholarly gathering behind the Iron Curtain and must formulate certain views and attitudes. One of the main topics to be discussed will be the influence of social conditions on the arts, a topic difficult enough under normal conditions, but forbidding in the setting where the deliberations will take place. I am not sure what I can and cannot say; some of the panelists will be hard-bitten Marxists who cannot be swayed, but others will be very eminent but very captive scholars. It would be most tactless to draw them into a discussion where they are not free to express their own ideas. A distinguished East German musicologist has just been removed from his professorship with forfeiture of his pension because he had the temerity to express his own ideas without reference to the official line. Still, I should like to communicate what I think and what, for reasons for collegial charity, I probably will not say at the congress of the International Musicological Society in September in Ljubljana. By the time these lines are printed, the congress will have taken place, and I shall be delighted if my apprehensions will prove to be unfounded.

The experiences of thousands of years of art teach us that the nature of the work of art is not determined by the laws of aesthetics but rather that those laws are an attempt to explain the mystery of creation. In a society where there are preconceived aesthetic tenets based, however tenuously, on social philosophy, artistic instinct is gravely impeded, and the projection of the artist's individuality restricted, if not made impossible. No form of "objective truth" or "ideology" can become the source of art, because art can be sublimated only from profound personal convictions and desire. With his creative instincts so hobbled, the composer must fall back on the practical everyday experiences of those upon whose musical taste the safety of his existence depends. The result is eclecticism, even though colored and strengthened in some measure by a dressing of more or less national or even near-contemporary idiom. But artistic power is born from creative experience. The eclectic composer utilizes the experience of another personality and invents only the details, and since inspiration cannot come secondhand, being utterly personal and penetrating every molecule of the work of art, the redigested substance loses its life-giving energies.

The Marxist theory that man's interests are both conditioned and controlled by the structure of his world is only partially true. The pervasive influence of "circumstances" may be acknowledged, but while the Marxists think exclusively of external circumstances, others also recognize internal ones. There is an extraordinary rigidity in the Marxist prescriptions, which they invest with theological certainty, and their theology is almost always puritan. Take, for instance, their hatred of Romanticism, which they consider the most pernicious form of bourgeois art. Their judgment is of course political rather than aesthetic, and yet what one disapproves of politically may be very good art. If the rulers of Russia examine carefully the writings of the founding fathers, they will see that even Marx and Lenin tacitly admit that aesthetic standards outweigh social significance in judging a work of art. Marx had the greatest admiration for Balzac, though from his point of view the French writer was a reactionary; and Lenin remained firm in his attachment to the Russian classics and had no use for the bright young writers who created in the name of the Revolution. What makes great art last across the centuries is that it is true to the continuum of human relations that subsist through all changes of differing social environment: love, friendship, loyalty, cruelty, selfishness, and so on. These things are of the nature of man and do not change with social circumstances. Also, there are many artists whose works survive by their style rather than their content. It is in judging a body of art or literature as a whole, as part of general history, that the social perspective becomes significant. Here Marxism as a method dealing with the history of culture may show some success. It can point out, for instance, such depressing examples of social irresponsibility as the case of the Public Libraries Act of 1850 in England. The bill evoked derisive comments from Members of Parliament, some fearing that "Parliament would next be thinking of supplying the working classes with quoits, pegtops and footballs." The bill passed into law by a very small margin of votes. But as aesthetic criticism Marxism is pitifully inadequate. One of the most unfortunate consequences of looking at art history from the standpoint of a social judge of past policies is the injustice done to artists who are condemned for failing to achieve what it did not come within their horizon to attempt. Also, many of the Marxist critics show a critical instinct that relies principally on suspicion. The witness is afraid that he is being bribed, or the judge that his code is being rejected and that his judgment will not be accepted.

The famous "Decree on Music" of the Central Committee of the Communist Party demands that, in order to be acceptable, music must have "high ideological content" and should not be "anti-people." This is mere gibberish to us. What it really means is that the masters of all the Russians allow that others do their artistic thinking for them, but they demand that those doing it think as they themselves would if they could. Interestingly enough, what the Central Committee advocates under the guise of socio-political thought is a falling back on the grandiloquent effects of that bourgeois Romanticism they despise so much. The situation is paradoxical and, if it were not so grim, one might say comical, when Communist doctrine lashes out at the "reactionary" aspects of Western art, then invites the Russian artist to base his music or painting on the least attractive features of this bourgeois style.

In the last quarter of the nineteenth century a certain painting was warmly admired by German official circles as well as by a large number of the public. It presents tall, rugged, and grim Prussian officers raising their beer steins while wiping their muddy boots on the Gobelin covers of the delicate Rococo furniture in a captured French chateau. This illustration of the war of 1870 became the painted national anthem of Germany, and its creator became His Excellency Anton von Werner. Today the embarrassed museum hides His Excellency's picture in the basement storeroom. What this proves is that "official" art bears little resemblance to what is innocently supposed to be patriotism expressed in art. Such works place before us the tawdry, tainted essence of dictated art, in the face of which the critic must surrender his role to the social historian. Anti-Romanticists though they are, the Marxists force the composer to use the means and even the symbols of that much-reviled era. It is fascinating to watch the characteristic reuse in disguise of the old arguments coming straight from fascism but now sounded in the name of the People's Democratic Republic. For it was Nietzsche, to whom all Fascist philosophy is deeply indebted, who first said that culture without slavery is not possible. He furthermore categorically denied that beauty is accessible to "sweaty plebeians" and insisted that in the multitude's art the beautiful is replaced by the gigantic, the suggestive, the spectacular, and the intoxicating. There is really little if any difference between von Werner's Prussian realism and Kabalevsky's Russian realism. Both of them aim at reducing individual inspiration, thought, and feeling to the lowest common denominator approved by those in power. Ironically, this socialist realism is the perfect expression of bourgeois comfort undisturbed by artistic problems.

The Marxist synthesis is ruthless and dogmatic, every vestige of initiative and originality is banished from its music, art, and letters. Look at one of Gorki's last works. He eliminated from his story every interesting personality, every psychological shade, all delicate transitions and situations, in order that his novel should represent nothing but the proletarian movement itself. Themes and motives, however, do not in themselves make art. A glance at Dmitri Kabalevsky's catalogue of works discloses such titles as *My Great Fatherland*, or *Before Moscow*, or *People's Avengers*, but this curious mixture of old-fashioned patriotism and socialist realism failed to produce a socialist art. All these noble-sounding compositions offer only a thoroughly conventional imitation of the music of the good old bourgeois days.

There were times when art did represent a collective spirit, when artists could raise a monument to the solidarity of man with his surroundings. The magnificent cathedral in Laon, built in the thirteenth century on a high ridge, bears as a diadem over the great portal the carved figures of the grave, tired, and gentle oxen that carried the heavy stones up the steep hill. But the People's Artists are unable to experience such warm human feelings; they are capable of producing nothing but very ordinary chromos. The more honest the artist is, the more compellingly he is borne along by his experience and convictions, even if the price is the interdiction of the very goal he is seeking. Being Russians who all grew up during the Soviet era, most composers in the USSR do not seem to realize this, though Dmitri Shostakovich, who rises above his colleagues, undoubtedly understands the problem and suffers from it. Several years ago we could see this with our own eyes. A group of Russian composers visited this country and met with the press. Shostakovich remained silent during the conference, and watching his sad face and averted eyes, we felt great sympathy for him. Whenever he was addressed, the glib music commissar, Khrennikov, took it upon himself to give the answers with smooth and well-trained efficiency by saying exactly nothing.

Today there seems to be a little stirring, at least among the literary people; some speak out, but most of them are just talking to pass eternity away. The absurd presumption of the Party being the sole repository of the one absolute artistic truth is not challenged. The explanation for the depression of artistic spirits must be sought in the enforced hypocrisy, which was there almost from the beginning of the Soviet state. Many years ago, returning from Russia, André Gide published a little book of "retouches," by which was meant a revision of his views on the USSR. What the erstwhile admirer could not forgive the Communists once he saw the scene at first hand was their falseness.

Great movements in society cast their shadow before and after upon arts and letters. The presentiment of change quickens the accents of music and poetry a generation before change is enacted in law or custom, and the signs of revolution have been visible in a people's literature and the arts before revolution has come to pass. The Russian novel is one of the shining ornaments of world literature in the nineteenth century; it expresses the Russian soul, the mystic devotion its author has for that soul and the people. The Russian writer of those days was openly subjective; he felt, commiserated, flailed, hated, loved, battled, but he also preached and taught. A number of them were as much revolutionaries as they were writers. They wrote for a lethargic people whom they wanted to arouse, and, however carefully—the censorship was rigid—they wanted to do away with an oppressive regime and evoke sympathy for untold miseries. Latent dangers appear in this profound striving of the Russian Hamlets: the dark distrust of Western ideas, the incompatibility of East and West, and a large gulf between the intellectual revolutionaries and the mass of the people itself. This is true even though a Turgenev was as popular in wide circles as any novelist in the West. And most of these Russians were xenophobes. Even Dostoevsky, whose sympathy for all forms of suffering was measureless, dreaded Western ideas. In Tolstoy, too, we can seldom divorce the artist from the philosopher-preacher and from the revolutionary— did he not want to banish and strangle all art? Here is the real Russian tragedy that is still haunting them: the great nobleman and the landowner, imbued with modern social ideas, who wants to make his moujiks happy, fails because stubborn and suspicious minds would not accept such foreign ideas. Then the great humanitarian himself succumbs to these doubts, becoming a sort of Cossack Rousseau. The octogenarian, dressed in rough peasant attire, advocates return to primitive Christianity, denounces Shakespeare and Beethoven and everything that is not addressed to the simple illiterate man of the people. As can be seen, there is a substantial prelude to the revolutionary play of 1917, except that some of these proto-revolutionaries also managed to create genuine masterpieces.

In all revolutionary periods literature and the arts have celebrated the new hopes and ideals that have fired men's imagination. Yet in this respect, as in many others, the Russian Revolution has a unique character, shared only by the short-lived Nazi era in Germany. It has not only infected the creative artist by its own mood but has contrived to invoke the authority of the state to impose upon the whole artistic imagination a specific task by which art is made to share the burden of a vast social experiment. How unwillingly the burden is borne can be seen from the many guarded and the few unguarded statements of the men of letters—though not of musicians. Whatever the precise truth in the matter, the conditions of musical activity in Soviet Russia are plain enough. Not only is there a censorship to suppress individual expression, but there is also an official philosophy of art to guide the artist in the true path. On the materialist reckoning, which assumes that culture is built on a system of class relations in society, art is seen not as self-expression, not disinterested imaginative creation, but a weapon of the proletariat in the revolutionary historic process. "Social Realism" is the latest and most authoritative of a remarkable assortment of slogans devised in the interest of Soviet art. But, as I have said, it has only a nebulous aesthetic significance and still begs the issue in disconcerting fashion. In artistic matters, as in all others, Communist policy has wavered between the claims of doctrine and of expediency, and has progressed by a series of sharp turns to the left and to the right and back again.

Neither literature nor music, needless to say, did begin anew in Russia after 1917. No tradition of art dies a sudden death, revolution or no revolution; society never makes a clean break with the past, it only destroys old bridges to build new ones in their place. But gradually there arose an illimitable emotional distance between the old and the new, the late Romantic era and the twentieth century. The party men—even the fellow travelers—backed by the facile optimism of political orthodoxy, would not fall in line with the advancing century. Inevitably the bolder of composers, notably Prokofiev, who returned home from the West, and Shostakovich, incurred the charge of disloyalty or, what was worse, artistic liberalism. Every once in a while moderation and common sense prevailed but would not last long. At any rate, once the good composers burned their fingers, they did not dare to assert themselves, and by the time they mustered enough courage to do so, the political winds had once more shifted. Ironically, there was nothing in their music that provides a shadow of excuse for the onslaught upon them by the philistines of the Left, but the Party wanted what Max Eastman called "artists in uniform."

It is clear, then, that the social ends that are being pursued by Russian artists at the order of a small band of assertive and obtuse theorists are not creative ends. Imaginative freedom cannot be reconciled with proletarian dictatorship. In Russia the individual citizen exists for the state, the supreme end of the state is power—physical, material, intellectual, moral, and spiritual—and since force is the instrument of power, the state can achieve its end only by force. This is done by concentrating in a collective unity all the powers and activities of the community's life and directing these powers, through unified control, to the achievement of the ends for which the state exists. The freedom of thought that we demand, and without which art cannot exist, can be neither secured nor exercised without securing and exercising other freedoms—political, moral, social, and economic. A creative artist cannot reach fulfillment under the conditions prevailing in the Communist world, for creative imagination cannot tolerate ideological restrictions.

It is commonly assumed that Russian art music achieved a national consciousness only in the nineteenth century—Russian musicographers all begin their tale with Glinka. If we realize that long after the Renaissance in the West, Russian arts and letters were still in their infancy, this assumption seems correct. We must remember that even Russian literature traces its beginnings to the reign of Catherine the Great, when the Russian language first acquired ordered written usages. Without the aid of foreign models, Russia could scarcely have made her great contribution to European letters. It is well known that English and French authors of the eighteenth and nineteenth centuries were immensely popular with the Russian reading public. What is commonly meant by "Byronism," for instance, is a much more integral part of Russian literature than of English. Similarly, Russian music discovered many sides of its own genius through appropriating French, German, and even some Italian characteristics and transforming them in the process. It is true, however, that each phase of Western imitation brought with it its own nemesis in the form of a resurgence of national consciousness. There were periodic awakenings, sudden reversions to the national idea and culture, during which Russia struggled against the constricting waves of foreign influence. But it remains a fact that throughout the struggle between Westerners and Slavophiles the process of assimilation of foreign music was an irresistible one. Soviet music has necessarily acquired a certain physiognomy of its own, but its characteristic forms and most of its means have all been taken from the past. Indeed, in all that pertains to questions of form and style Soviet music is merely a continuation of pre-revolutionary Russian music. The inescapable nineteenth-century influence is present not only in their plays but also in their compositions. Craftsmanship, so sadly missing in Russian Romantic music (except in that of the one genuine professional, Tchaikovsky), grew more important, however, and Russian music gained in polish, technique, and fluency. Even the minor composers are well trained in the métier and can turn out a well-made and fluent score. But polish is not nobility, as sanctimoniousness is not religion. The facility, the piquancy, the noisy orchestration are mere illusions of creative force. The fabrication can be distinguished from the real thing by the fact that it invariably exaggerates, that it is more so than the original. The empty boisterousness of a Khachaturian piece is merely low-grade Rimsky-Korsakov. Shostakovich has been overpraised in the West, largely because his imagination seems so much more distinguished than that of the commonplace poetasters like Khrennikov or Kabalevsky. Yet he does—or rather did—show genuine emotional and artistic sensibilities and poetical freshness. By now all this is nearly extinct; he is dehumanized, as was the bold, original, and elegant Prokofiev. Stravinsky escaped this fate by becoming a Western star; no stay-at-home could have composed the works he produced after the earlier "Russian" choreographic scores. All the other Russians remained within the atmosphere of an arrested post-Romanticism that had to feed on itself.

It is unfortunately a fact that this unhappy state of affairs is made more acute by the course of Russian music history, for in truth this supposedly popular art of the Communists has little if any rapport with the art of the people. Russian folk music is the catch basin of Eastern Slavic civilization. It is rich and original, but it is also isolated, unexplored, and little understood. The tragedy of Russian music is that this vast storehouse of melodies was called upon merely for the sake of local color in a musical style that was entirely conditioned by Western European currents. If the composer does not master the folk material as a natural heritage, when he merely quotes and imitates, such elements usually appear as rootless exoticism. This is as true of Rimsky as it is of Kabalevsky or Khachaturian—or, for that matter, Liszt. At best such a composer can bring the folk tunes into a simple relationship with more or less traditional harmony, and in the hands of a good musician this can be quite pleasant. But it could never advance beyond that level, for it represents a compromise between old and new music in which the Romantic tradition is still conspicuous.*

---

*It goes without saying that when a composer borrows foreign folk material, the risks are even greater. It was for this reason that when Beethoven used Russian themes in the Rasumovsky quartets, or

The Russians, with the exception of that most genuine of Russian composers, Mussorgsky, did not know how to absorb this heritage. Mussorgsky was close to the soil and the people, and even though his craftsmanship was wanting when compared to the finished Western technique and professional *savoir faire* of a Tchaikovsky, it was perhaps his independence from the West that brought out his authentic Russian genius. Even Stravinsky, in whose music the tremendous latent power of this folk music appeared with explosive force, failed to achieve a synthesis once he exchanged the Russian tunic for the Western dinner jacket. Prokofiev, also a fine and brilliant composer, was a man of the world with a Russian accent. As to the others, they are still largely prisoners of the very thing they are supposed to abhor: French and German post-Romanticism.

The trouble is that this wonderful Russian folk music never served as the starting point for an organic movement to be gradually absorbed, as in the West, by higher art. Russian "art" music arrived on the scene at such a late date that it was immediately engulfed by Western Romanticism. When this wealth of folk music began to be unearthed, it struck the Russians themselves as something strange and exotic, and since by that time manufactured popular music was present in Russia as in all other countries, they were easily misled into taking it for authentic folk art. Thus Western European culture and East European and Asian folk art without a genuine common denominator.

All these problems can be solved only by the artistic subjectivity of the individual, for where logic reaches a dead end, there enters the magic of genius. And again the fundamental rule of aesthetics reappears: first comes creation, then reasoning, and it is this very process that is not permitted in Russia. That in other countries, like Czechoslovakia or Poland, the situation is less strained is due to their geography, to the almost three decades of grace they enjoyed before joining the Communist orbit, and to their musical past. Unlike the Russians, both the Czechs and the Poles have an impressive music history that goes back to the Middle Ages. During these centuries they had a lively intercourse with Western Europe; as a matter of fact, until the curtain de-

---

Dvořák American tunes in his E minor Symphony, their sound musical instinct told them to disregard the nature of the borrowed tunes and manipulate them in their own altogether personal style. It is another matter with a composer like Bartók, who so completely assimilated the *spirit* and the *accents* of Hungarian folk music that it passed into his bloodstream. It is most interesting—and revealing—that the completely internationalized Stravinsky should so misunderstand this elemental, life-giving quality in Bartók. Speaking of the Hungarian composer, Stravinsky remarks: "I never could share his lifelong gusto for his native folklore. This devotion was certainly real and touching, but I couldn't help regretting it in the great musician" I. Stravinsky and Robert Craft, *Conversations with Igor Stravinsky*, (Garden City, NY: Doubleday, 1959), p. 82.

scended, Bohemia was considered an integral part of Central Europe, while Poland was the westernmost outpost of the Eastern Slavs. Finally, their fine folk music was absorbed at an early date and always nourished their higher art. Both countries weathered the important transition period from the nineteenth to the twentieth century and overcame a temporary Russian-imposed restriction. Today Hába's microtonal and athematic disciples are at work, and in Poland even electronic music is permitted and supported.

Comrade Lysenko made wheat grow according to the principles of Marx, Engels, and Lenin, and Comrade Zhdanov made symphonies emulate the procedure. I know nothing about agronomy, but I notice that something must have gone wrong with the indoctrinated wheat, because Comrade Lysenko has been relieved of his office, and the Russians are once more relying on apolitical wheat growing. I am sure, though, that this change was due to simple pragmatic rather than ideological reasons; such pragmatism they would not permit in the arts. When it comes to the arts, as in all other adventures of the mind, the highest collective aspirations will be frustrated in the absence of personal freedom, whether that frustration is brought about by the guardians of the totalitarian aesthetics or the "bourgeois" consumer of art who arrogates it to himself to say what shall and what shall not be played or written for his money. The philistine rhetoric with which the indignant conformists denounce the nonconformist is well known to us too, and there are in our affluent society shameful examples of neglect, ostracism—even starvation. But while we can ignore and neglect or pamper and reward our artists, we do not and cannot silence them.

Stravinsky

P roust used to say that he could judge an author's qualities after reading a single sentence of his work. There is a modicum of truth in this patent exaggeration, and in the recent history of arts and letters to no one could it be better applied than to Igor Stravinsky. His qualities could be recognized in one musical sentence, and these qualities made him an international musical institution, a leader acknowledged the world over. For half a century musicians' ears have been trained to the Stravinsky note as their ancestors' were to the Wagnerian strains. Two generations of musicians accepted him as norm, measure, and aesthetic; his highly individual freedom to turn in any direction he chose without losing the jeweled machinery of his style of composition awed everyone. Long ago it was realized that Stravinsky was one of those pivots on which the destiny of music turns. His vitality, rich inventiveness, extraordinary rhythmic and dynamic force, fantastic skill, elemental power, deep-rooted musicianship, and iron-willed consequence largely shaped the music of half of the twentieth century, and is still a potent force, at least with those who write music on lined paper.

From *The Musical Quarterly*, vol. 57 (1971)

His ability to set a course and then hold to the helm so steadily that the compass does not even quiver is almost incredible. Stravinsky lived a long life, and until very near the end his amazing vitality, which had triumphed over the many dissonances in his musical personality, continued to prevail, and there was still radiance in the faintly flowing stream at the end. Now the time has come for an *envoi*. Not a reckoning, for posterity will have its say, but for the verdict of this age. The critic at this moment must try to assist the jury to find that verdict, not as an advocate for or against—they have both been heard—but, so far as he can dare, as a friend of the court. Conscious of his own limitations and mindful of the disaster of many who have assumed the role, he may also attempt a harder task: prophecy. There is, we believe, no risk in the prophecy that Stravinsky will live and be admired as one of the most virile and skillful of master composers, and that he will remain, in years to come, as he now is: unique. But let us treat him as he treated his confreres, without timidity or hedging.

When Stravinsky came out of Russia, he knew little of the Western world and, like a good Russian, scorned what he did know. What he saw in Paris and elsewhere was stale, especially the parched if scented flowers of French music, for Debussy's influence was not yet pervasive. To the Russian the artificial colors, the broken and minced lines, the uncertain functional logic of the harmonies, and the labile equilibrium, all were strange; he could not be sure whether it was not a mirage he saw. This world Stravinsky entered violently, bringing Russia, the untamed East, suddenly to the door of hedonistic Paris. He swept into its music, driving out the languor and softness. *Le Sacre du printemps*, a natural bursting of his accumulated emotions, the cosmic apotheosis of the ancient barbaric Slavic world, is the kind of original work that can change the history of music overnight. Nothing like this had ever before been heard, and the first performance in 1913 erupted into a riot, scandalizing the artistic world. This was a totally new music, rigid in shaping, the presentation of primitive elements in the raw, themes repeated rather than developed, but with stunning dynamic shades and contrasts, and the whole exhibiting an orchestral apparatus of infinite sophistication. But *Le Sacre* was an end point—as *Elektra* was with Strauss—for such orgiastic vehemence could not be continued. Moreover, this music is like one of those drifting islets; its vegetation is lush, birds of many colors fly over it, but it is at the mercy of the currents, and one does not know its destination. While composers young and old eagerly tried to catch up with the creator of what has come to be called the "dynamic-barbaric" trend, Stravinsky took an altogether different turn. *Le Rossignol* ends the "Russian phase" of his career, for now the composer of eruptive rhythms and dynamics, the virtuoso of the magnificent orchestra of a thousand hues, turns his back on all this, on everything Russian. To be sure, there will be an occasional Russian subject or theme, but it will be handled by a pronouncedly international composer domiciled in France or Switzerland. *Pulcinella* opens the neoclassic phase in 1920. The worshipper of physical excitement and elementally direct expression became entranced with the new idea that the composer's own style is more important than what he communicates. It seemed to Stravinsky that the safest way out of both naturalism and enervated Impressionism was pure artistry; it is not content but style and form, where attention is centered on the writing itself, that offers a safe asylum.

It must have been the French influence that started Stravinsky on his new orientation. Mallarmé's *poésie pure*, which was a very special art of constructing sentences by giving the individual words an almost mathematical weight, led to the concept that the meaning of the words was secondary to their sound. Mallarmé's abstract art was greatly admired in the early twentieth century, and, following his lead, the poets no longer cared whether the public would understand their verse; it was addressed to an intellectual elite. This artistic elitism, so sharply opposed to the Russian psyche, is common in the modern West, whether in the poetry of Stefan George and Valéry or the music of Schoenberg and Webern. The man of intellect is not so much interested in reality as in ideas and possibilities. Stravinsky, observing that all around him were composers who had lost the third dimension in music, imaginative part-writing, gradually opened up this musical space, deliberately and almost scientifically refining his music until the last vestiges of any cliché or looseness were eliminated. The result was the counterpart of Mallarmé's "pure poetry," pure music, the abstract experience, form divorced from life—a new classicism. And once more Stravinsky managed all this with such marvelous dexterity and brilliance that we willingly surrendered to him our judgment.

When Dostoyevsky made his famous speech at the Pushkin festivities, he created a national event by announcing Russia's role as savior of the world. But was it true that everything was wrong with mankind, that we must give up the civilization and culture built through millennia and descend to a primitive peasant simplicity? Tolstoy was convinced that salvation lies in that direction, but Stravinsky, the one-time Russian composer, contradicts this spirit; he was no longer interested in any "message." To him art was finite, the combination of finite elements that can be mastered, for he had the impartial, analytical mind that can strip emotion from facts. For his new style Stravinsky adopted the eighteenth-century forms of divertimento, serenade, concerto, sonata— even *opera buffa*. The original spirit of these genres, as they are represented by

Bach, Pergolesi, Haydn, and Mozart, he disregarded to a large extent, but being a many-sided and impulsive artist who refused to mark time, he welcomed the new decorative frame, and loved the opportunities to engage in dazzling play and make-believe. Now the powerful—even demoniac—qualities of the Russian works and his marvelous sense for the grotesque gradually disappear from Stravinsky's music, and there is a marked turn toward the linear-contrapuntal. We are exhilarated by the fluent texture of the music as we are by the precise convolutions of a dancer, but hardly moved. The ingenuity that makes this music so smooth and seemingly simple and natural is almost incredible; the movement is flexible and unpredictable, wheeling, fluttering, hovering, diving like a great butterfly. And yet the impression is not that of mere ingenuity, but of perfect assurance and ease. We might wish that the voice would occasionally falter and the skill fail, so that we could see the mortal artist; but, no, it never does.

If Berlioz attempted to compose music that is nothing but expression, the faithful rendition through music of extramusical poetic subjects, Stravinsky's neoclassicism is the exact opposite, because in its increasing complexity simple humanity is absent, or stifled at birth. In neoclassicism the artist divorces himself from his creation, extracting from it the "I." This music has no relationships outside itself, either of feeling or of conscience; it simply lives of itself, in itself. Its ideal of beauty being to derive from human manifestations the pure essence, one would think that the musical universe is mechanistic, unaffected by life. A work of such consummate mastery of the craft of composition as *Oedipus Rex* is cold, its frigidity reinforced by the composer's remoteness from his characters; he reveals no hint of sympathy, no hope, and no kindness. *Apollon Musagète*, even more stunningly impressive in its warp and woof than *Oedipus*, is even more arid. The absolute compositional discipline and economy and the flexibility of the writing are admirable beyond words, but this art is so impassive that it becomes bleak and almost forbidding. Stravinsky appears omniscient and totally free of illusions, the ideal of the modern composer who is altogether unsentimental, who watches life but adds nothing to it. His art has become an apparatus for registering musical impulses without animating them; he no longer uses a brush, but rather lays out designs, and is solely concerned with his material and its manipulation.

Most of the young European and American composers enthusiastically accepted this new, puritanic, constructive trend in music. Let us have no ornament, they said; music should express the eternal beauty of its own substance, it should discard its garments and show its magnificent body. But how could this Russian assimilate the constructivism, the love of "engineering" so typical of the Germanic mind? Such an attitude was diametrically opposed to Eastern concepts of music, for the new Western movement was a great, sobering declaration of war against that pleasure in "decoration" that for centuries has warmly nourished all the arts. Now the composers evince a great desire for nakedness; they discard all masks, all costumes, they want the pure intellect in all its scintillating exclusivity. Stravinsky, assuming leadership in the neoclassic movement, insisted that there are immanent laws in music and that they are the sole criteria of art. But the art of music not only has laws, it also has secrets, and Stravinsky, restricted by the limitations of a marvelous intellect and endless knowledge of the composer's art not matched by feeling and passion, missed many of the secrets. He became the convinced ascetic of art, willing to sacrifice everything for perfection in creation.

Catchwords such as "antiromantic," "asentimental," "objective," and "neoclassic" (really neo-Baroque) were supposed to announce a return to truth. It is readily conceded that the highly egocentric music of late Romanticism had become trying to twentieth-century ears, and that music altogether subjected to literary fetters is only half art, can even be fake art; but this is not the whole truth. The reasoning behind the attitude of the composers of the 1920s was that Romanticism is opposed to all the natural requirements of modern life, and therefore its sentiments and excrescences must be eliminated. How? By composing music that does not even touch our own life. Let us just play with musical matter, our own and that of departed masters; let us return to Bach. But what has once passed away, no one can bring back, at least not in the arts. The freely running counterpoint with which the composers now played was flesh and blood in Bach's time, whereas neoclassic music lives only so long as it is in motion; it is carried solely by kinetic energy. The "Back to Bach" slogan which neoclassicism put on its banner is as logical as "Back to the Greeks"; it can be no more than a hypothetical reconstruction achieved by artifice, and Stravinsky carried this artificial classicism to icy lengths.

It seemed that neoclassicism, the longest-held of Stravinsky's stylistic periods, would be the last of his conversions; but the septuagenarian turned to serialism. His espousal of dodecaphony and serialism in general is interesting, because, as was generally known, Stravinsky was contemptuous of Schoenberg as well as of his school, which by that time was decidedly followed by composers everywhere; not since the Netherlanders had there been such an international style. This hostility is understandable, because in many ways Schoenberg was Stravinsky's antipode, and surely in the lifetime of his Hollywood neighbor, whom he ignored, the Russian would never have made his way into the Austrian camp. Perhaps he acted out of a kind of daring, both as a stimulant and as a test for his ebbing creative strength, and certainly at the urging of the sycophants around him who needed a standard-bearer now that all three coryphaei of the new Viennese school were dead. Though little except deprecating remarks about Schoenberg was heard from Stravinsky before Robert Craft took it upon himself to edit the master's statements, there can be no question that during the vacillating years between 1914 and 1919 Stravinsky could no more escape the impact of *Pierrot Lunaire* than could other composers of the age, and serialism was actually suited to his particular gifts of compression, logic, and clarity. Since for some time now as a composer he had elaborately insulated himself from life, this was understandably the ultimate step, the final stylistic conversion. Needless to say, we do not dispute the legitimacy of serialism as a style of composition; it has produced authentic masterpieces, though it can also be the deadliest exercise in planned boredom. Stravinsky's dodecaphonic pieces are written with his usual and unparalleled skill, for he had an ear that can apprehend anything and everything and an ability to elaborate it all with the unerring hand of a virtuoso unequaled today in the craft of composition. Nevertheless, here he is on alien territory, and his embracing of the Viennese faith is the final and total rejection of his Russian past. The ultimate stage, the Webernian, borders on a renunciation of the imaginative, a farewell to life and to the art in which he was born. These little cryptograms, some lasting less than a minute, must be decoded phrase by phrase, a difficult task without the visual help of the score. And after all, these microscopic pieces are really *vieux jeu*; Webern did them long ago, and in his works there is an otherworldly sensitivity, an infinitely expressive subtlety, whereas in Stravinsky's the artistic labor seems more important than the result. A creative genius has here become competent rather than compelling, giving the impression of a most accomplished composer working mechanically. The musical lines have become too explicit, stating facts rather than expressing moments of vision.

Stravinsky's aesthetic creed is conveyed to us in his *Poetics of Music*, an exasperating book, a sort of inverted ostentation, enigmatic and insolent. As evidence of his beliefs, he offers not logic but new dogma—a new hedonism of the composer "in quest of his pleasure," "pleasure" here meaning the freedom and ability to play with sounds. While the degree to which Stravinsky shared in the authorship of this book is uncertain, it does reflect his views, and he certainly carries them out in his post-Russian period. Widespread belief notwithstanding, he was not a revolutionary avant-gardist; on the contrary, like most great masters, he was basically conservative. His slogan could have been

"Let us save what can be saved." Art is revolutionary just by being itself. It is only when it sets out to be revolutionary that art ceases to be so. Indeed, Stravinsky was far more willing to learn than to rebel; he consistently tried to make use of his heritage, and in a way he remained consequent in his numerous stylistic about-faces, for he did not lose sight of musical values that he felt could be further developed. But what happens to this conservatism when a new generation asserts itself? The collective spirit of each generation, its tastes and its aspirations, its fashionable views and judgments, demand favorites as well as whipping boys. Stravinsky, who outlived several artistic generations, always fell in line with the changing tastes, from Rimsky-Korsakov to Webern, but only, it must be emphasized, after he had studied the new trends to see whether he could go along on his own terms. This is what makes the enormous difference between him and the other fellow artistic travelers—he always remained his sovereign self. Furthermore, he had the uncanny power of making others see things as he saw them. In the end, however, this incredible versatility and virtuosity betray a lack of fundamental stylistic concept, such as Webern, for instance, did have. Stravinsky's Russian works shook the West not because of their revolutionary idiom, but because of their uninhibited and original power. *Firebird* is super Rimsky, full of rich color, good tunes, nerve-tingling rhythms, and wild Russian abandon; this is dynamic music, always lively, and infectiously attractive. When Stravinsky exchanged the Russian tunic, boots, and fur cap for the dinner jacket, patent leather pumps, and top hat of the West, everything but his phenomenal compositional skill changed. Then in *Oedipus* he wears a toga, and the classical garment is as distant from us as the language its wearers spoke. The works of his neoclassic period are far removed from the fires of youth, yet there is in them a concealed youthfulness which increased their appeal to young composers. Once more, far from being a revolutionary, Stravinsky presents here a carefully calculated, conscious artistry that has many roots in the past.

Le Sacre was still a naturalistic vision, but *Threni* and what followed it reach the final consequences of naturalism: asceticism. These late works offer objectivized counterpoint and harmony; they are like messages addressed "to whom it may concern." And in the last of his "new directions," the Webernesque, Stravinsky's passionless style tends of itself to create an impression of unreality, as if a theorem were being discussed rather than music composed. Within this wide gamut of stylistic variations, one is conscious of perplexing extremes. The neoclassic music is presented with a certain disdain, with a nonchalant coquetry, and with an art of cool and subtle artifice in which nothing is routine, nothing accidental, every small detail receiving the same meticulous attention. But when we hear the *Symphony of Psalms*, we feel that this sorcerer had a heart, a warm Russian heart, and that he could kneel before an icon and pray. Listening to the Alleluia, one is enthralled by its magic, hoping that the gently undulating song punctuated by the soft beats of the timpani will never end. How marvelously fresh and moving this great work remains; yet it was composed amidst the neoclassic clatter, and immediately following the costume jewelry glitter of *Capriccio*. Then again we were treated to a most curious composition which caused the opposite sensation: we could not wait for it to end. *Noah and the Flood* is a modern mystery play for television, attempting to apply the most modern means of mass communication devised by twentieth-century technology to the oldest form of the music drama. Regrettably, the whole thing amounted to nothing but a twenty-minute vignette within an hour-long show generously padded with credits, commercials, bits of art history, and biographical sketches. One really hated to see the aging master involved in such an affair, for the suspicion cannot be dismissed that he was somehow enticed to become part of a scenario partly juvenile, partly commercial.

Throughout his career Stravinsky showed a strong penchant for parodying the styles of other composers. In this case "parody" must be understood both in the everyday meaning of the word and also in the musicological sense, for Stravinsky borrowed, in the best Renaissance and Baroque tradition, from Gesualdo to Tchaikovsky. This method of composition served many great masters well; these borrowed goods are elaborated somewhat as historical novels take small details, anecdotes, stories, as well as facts, to use in constructing a larger whole. Stravinsky delved into all manner of music, including jazz; he seized the documents and color patches and fashioned from them highly successful musical scores. The workmanship in these compositions is of such high quality that praise is impertinent; it is when we come to seek underlying motives that we are once more puzzled. Whatever a Bach or a Handel borrowed became Bach or Handel; in Stravinsky's case the procedure results only in a brilliant game. The composers from whom he borrowed ideas and materials were musicians of a warm, emotionally communicative disposition, not in accord, certainly, with neoclassic frigidity. A particularly surprising choice, that of Gesualdo, was made late in Stravinsky's life, at a time when he had completely banished the soul in favor of a creed of total emotional abstinence. What on earth could have attracted the composer and his counselor, Craft, these lovers of the arctic, to so tropical a climate? Gesualdo's music is the most passionate expression of self-denunciation; it is all emotion and little logic and discipline, all impulse and little calculation. What did these puritans seek in

Gesualdo? Was it the warmth of life and emotional fervor they themselves were unable to experience?

Stravinsky's theatrical talent was inborn, and his stage instinct marvelous; the terpsichorean Stravinsky at his best is delectably irresistible. The wonderfully characteristic themes and the infectious lift of *Petrushka* have no equal in this genre. It was a most happy stroke of fate that brought together Diaghilev and the composer; we should not underestimate the role this splendid impresario played in Stravinsky's life. He recognized and encouraged genius before anyone else had become aware of it. Yet, as an opera composer, Stravinsky was not nearly as successful, because in his theatrical imagination the mimic moment always received priority over the dramatic. *Mavra*, a comic opera on the "classic Russo-Italian model" (by which Stravinsky undoubtedly meant Glinka), is merely pretty; *Oedipus* is not a real opera but a scenic oratorio, while *Les Noces* is a *ballet chanté*. *The Rake's Progress*, though full of elegant detail, is too studiously a parody of eighteenth-century procedures to be convincing. Moreover, Stravinsky's aesthetic theories are most damaging when applied to opera. The abstract vocal texture is made even more expressionless by the deliberate favoring of "syllabic values," which Stravinsky considered more important than the customary setting of words in their entirety. We are dealing here with two poles of art: with beauty and with what Stravinsky calls "truth." In reality the two have always lived together, but have usually balanced each other as expressive communication and constructive force, creating a potential stress between exterior and interior. As in the modern biological-psychological concept which does not recognize absolute masculinity and absolute femininity, only proportions in their mixture, so in art there could not be a total separation of construction and expression—unless deliberately sought and carried out. The creative artist used to be indivisible; his was the world of beauty which soared over the material world, he was the *maître de plaisir* of life. In Stravinsky's stations following his Russian phase we fail to see a convincing view of life, only a hedonism of the métier. Still, those who see nothing here but a nihilistic concept of man, his reduction to a machine, are as wrong as those who see a great liberation of human powers. What Stravinsky desired was occasion and frame for the deployment of his ever fresh and activity-seeking musical imagination. He was always fired with a craving for action, for new material that he could maneuver; he made music with immense gusto, and with the total immersion of the chess player. It was highly characteristic—and moving—of the old master, devastated by illness, and with only a thin thread holding him to life, to have triumphantly confided to Robert Craft that on that day he managed to write two measures. This absorbing preoccupation often permits a musical thought to become a mere center of diffusion, but he could always summon the ability to do justice to these problems. Neither liberation nor mechanization interested him, only problems of craft and style. It would never have occurred to him to claim for his music what Beethoven, writing to Prince Galitzin, claimed for his, that it "may help suffering mankind."

Stravinsky's insatiable intellect always demanded to be occupied, and when he was not composing, he wrote essays, autobiographical sketches, and submitted to interviews that subsequently took the form of books in dialogue form. This variety discloses the cultivated modern man of the world who turns with vivid interest toward every intriguing subject. Since Stravinsky was blessed with a generous gift of wit, was widely read, and was a connoisseur of the musical literature, one would expect in his verbal activity the same ease and brilliance he exhibits in his scores. These qualities are present, indeed; but here we face a grave problem that will bedevil the work of his future biographers. Stravinsky himself readily admitted that his *Poetics of Music* was largely the work of Alexis Roland-Manuel, while his autobiography, *Chronique de ma vie*, depended in equal measure on Walter Nouvel's helping hand. More recent than these works are the volumes of conversations with his long-time amanuensis Robert Craft. A look at Craft's writings, as for instance his series of articles in the *New York Review of Books*, discloses an easily recognizable personal style, suggesting more than simple editorial assistance in these volumes. Craft's idiosyncratic mannerisms, the eclectic chichi, the boulevard pleasantries, the foreign or big oblong words in every other sentence, are typical of a good many American would-be cosmopolites. The unfortunate consequence of Craft's running of the show is that the astonishing intellectual curiosity, which is perhaps the greatest virtue of Stravinsky's writings, is smothered by a no less astonishing deficiency of discrimination and sensibility. Though it is well known that Stravinsky was the most egocentric autocrat among musicians since Wagner, some of his statements about other composers disclose a contempt so bottomless that one is hard put to believe that this can come from a man who knew and understood music as few have in any time. He seems to have turned the old saying "tout comprendre c'est tout pardonner" into "tout comprendre c'est tout mépriser." Though acknowledging that Stravinsky does not claim impartiality, that he was a good hater, that his statements are more pugnacious than provocative, we are still unwilling altogether to accept the picture that emerges from the dialogues. The great composer answers questions, some straight, some leading, some loaded, as Craft consistently tries to entice the bull into his china shop. Baffled and deterred by the jungle of digressions, quotations, and allusions, as well as by the rank confusion and variety of the material, we are often either pulled up with a jar by a remark that is inappropriate, totally lacking in taste and dignity—even unpardonable—or, if we escape that, remarks that on subsequent reflection seem to indicate a flaw in taste or charity. Nevertheless, there are in these volumes many interesting observations that only an exceptional musician could make, and when Stravinsky reminisces on the episodes of his colorful career and explains the genesis of his works, he makes for absorbing reading.

When a composer writes as a critic, he may be sure of his readers' attention, since his views on aesthetic problems carry a particular authority, and anything he may say about the mysterious process of making music is bound to be of interest. It is true, however (and composers themselves are the first to acknowledge this), that there is a difference between the creative and the analytical-critical mind. The composer-critic can destroy confidence in his judgment by special pleading and a propensity to erect straw men for the pleasure of knocking them down. The reader may justly hesitate to accept a composer's views of other composers' music, for much of such criticism is invalidated by being wholly negative or wholly adulatory; it is the danger of the comparative method that denigration or apotheosis of one composer does nothing to reveal the qualities of another with whom he is compared. Categorical value judgments in the arts are difficult to make, yet Stravinsky's answers to Craft's promptings are full of them. Perhaps they come easily only to those who have unlimited self-assurance, like Bernard Shaw, who in one of his prefaces asked himself whether he was greater than Shakespeare.

Stravinsky subscribes to Schumann's amusing romantic theory that "only genius can fully understand genius." His own cold dismissal of other composers—at times amounting to abuse—and his studied silences inspire little confidence, however, on this score. The critic must speak the truth about things, whereas the creative artist's themes and materials are not bound by any particular truth—art is illusion. It is in the nature of criticism that it does not create independently but deals with the prior creation of the artist, placing it in a new perspective. Stravinsky's attitude toward critics recalls what Macauley wrote to Sir James Mackintosh: "I am in the right, and you are in the wrong. When you are the stronger you ought to tolerate me, for it is your duty to tolerate truth. But when I am stronger, I shall persecute you; for it is my duty to persecute error."

The millennial stream of Western music still flows, and it is too early to pronounce its doom; but its giants have disappeared—Stravinsky was the last of them. His lifework if a curious complex, an encyclopedic mirror of music containing its own aesthetics and critique. The excitement generated by his "Russian" works, the tremendous sonic boom he threw into the tired music of the West, he could never again recapture, but his failures were the failures of the too well made; they do not diminish his stature, only help explain his qualities—for in the end Stravinsky emerges as a true giant. The musical world watched him with awe, with the elation one experiences when seeing a juggler work with three platters, then four, then five, and so on. After a while this does not satisfy him, and he throws them behind him, between his legs, and finally whistles a tune as if to show that all this is a trifle for him. Is not the bulk of Stravinsky's oeuvre, the great amount of fastidious music, the minute solution of stylistic problems, out of proportion with the content? Would it not have been better to avoid the hairline finesse and jewel-studded clockwork? No, because here this prodigious craftsmanship is art itself; born perhaps from acquired rather than from inner truth, but nevertheless real. The musicians who were his contemporaries and who followed him could not approach his sovereign virtuosity, his subtle *art pour l'art*, which he wore like a carnation in his buttonhole, while looking with disdain beyond the rest of his confreres, past and present. And if his admirers did put a similar carnation in their buttonholes, it soon drooped because they could not keep it fresh, they could not keep up with the changing world. At no stage in music history have styles, trends, and attitudes risen and fallen with such rapidity as in this century, but Stravinsky stayed the course. His character and historical position made him a symbol of the cultural aspirations and disappointments of Russia, the symbol of her great powers and of her failures. The struggle between East and West is exemplified in this great Russian-born master, whose elemental force was sacrificed to the blandishments of the ultra-cultivated West, and the Eastern musician ended by becoming the hero, the apostle, and the uncontested leader of Western music. He battled for the West, yet it was his adopted world that hobbled him, that sapped his original strength. Thus it is that Stravinsky's music, always fascinating in its thousand-and-one-nights splendor, remains without real issue.

Bartók at Columbia University

It sometimes appears that man's worst scourges are not accidental catastrophes that engulf us indiscriminately, but tragedies measured to each of us individually, tragedies that complete our own little destinies. Something of the kind can be seen in the fate of Béla Bartók. His was a strong soul in a body frail but intense, with penetrating bright eyes, lively gestures, precise and ready words, always alert and courageous, as if the whole man were the blade of intelligence drawn from its sheath. Both war and injustice—and his firm response—rudely disrupted his life's course.

Bartók started his career at a time and place auspicious for a young and gifted musician. At the turn of the century there still existed in Central Europe, notably in Hungary, a great liberal tradition that nourished the arts. Wealth and fame seldom companion the service of serious and forward-looking art, but in those days an artist and scholar could indeed live and work in peace, his activity sanctioned even by officialdom. Though as a "radically modern" composer Bartók did meet opposition—often violent—he steadily rose in status; some of his compositions were published, his concert tours were

From *High Fidelity/Musical America*, March 1981

successful, and he became professor of piano at the Royal Academy of Music in Budapest. Universal Edition of Vienna welcomed him into a company that would come to include the elite of twentieth-century music: Mahler, Schoenberg, and other leading lights of the age.

Acclaim greeted not only the creative artist and the piano virtuoso, but also the path-breaking scholar, the folklorist, who attacked a vast fortress of misconceptions. He demolished bit by bit the picture the world had of Hungarian music as reflected in the Hungarian dances, rhapsodies, *csárda* scenes; and other fabricated urban export articles. By collecting, transcribing, and publishing in impeccably researched and annotated collections the unspoiled music of the peasantry, he revealed the true national heritage. This was iconoclasm, albeit in the best sense of the word, and it did not sit well with many people, especially when he explored the music of Czechoslovakia, Rumania, and other neighboring nations then regarded as enemies of a Hungary dismembered by the Treaty of Trianon. At the outbreak of the Second World War, his position in Hungarian and European music was so assured that nothing could hurt him. So why was it that he left the security of Budapest and set sail for the New World, arriving in New York in October 1940 as a little-appreciated and impecunious refugee?

A man can be characterized by the relationship of his intellectual and moral qualities; when equally elevated, they are in balance, yielding a rare integrity and nobility. Such a noble mind was Bartók's: he could see the truth and had the courage to hew to it and to speak it. And when the evils of Nazism plunged Europe, and subsequently the entire world, into misery and anguish, he voluntarily relinquished his prominent position, because he refused to have commerce with the legions of hatred and destruction. Had he but taken a passive attitude, like Richard Strauss, he could have remained the commanding musical figure in Hungary, for he could not have been denounced as a *Kulturbolschevik* or non-Aryan. But he refused to condone evil, raised his voice in the defense of friends and colleagues now hunted and humiliated, forbade that his works be performed in Germany, and chose exile in defense of principle.

The man who arrived in New York was a little-known pilgrim. It is sadly ironical and not a little uncomfortable to recall that the New York newspapers, announcing the arrival of several musicians seeking refuge in this country, casually mentioned his name as a "Hungarian pianist and composer," singling out from the group Vladimir Golschmann, a perfectly decent but minor musician, as the most important new arrival. It was painfully clear that Bartók had to start life anew, from the bottom.

Yet—and this is not generally known—the difficulties he encountered were to a considerable extent of his own making; his integrity was so fierce that he could not make even reasonable compromises. There were enlightened musicians in this country who fully realized his standing in twentieth-century music, and there were offers of good positions—always to teach composition. His reasons for refusing are not altogether clear. He was, however, a "national" composer, his idiom outside the international current of contemporary music, and he may have felt that his own style would conflict with teaching composition in a foreign setting. I believe he was unwilling also to expose young students to so decided an influence, remembering his own apprenticeship at the academy under the thoroughly Germanic Hans Koessler—a period he later considered a false start. He wanted to teach piano or ethnomusicology, but the country was then overstaffed with piano teachers, while ethnomusicology was almost totally unknown in 1940. There was not a single chair in our universities for this discipline. We did have a few able scholars hidden in anthropology departments, yet anthropology itself was then a new discipline; an opening for a *musical* folklorist was indeed a rarity.

There was, however, a first-class ethnomusicologist at Columbia University. George Herzog, a professor in the anthropology department, was working in the field of American Indian music and linguistics. Based on this contact, a genial conspiracy was initiated. Such fellow Hungarians as Fritz Reiner, Joseph Szigeti, and Eugene Ormandy got the money. Herzog and I, who had known Bartók since our student days at the conservatory, did the rest, aided by Douglas Moore. Bartók was appointed research fellow in Columbia's department of anthropology without teaching duties. The university had access to a large collection of Serbo-Croatian folk music, and he went to work with gusto, transcribing and analyzing it with a view to publication. (Columbia University Press, after agonizing delays, published the fine volume after his death.) All this had to be done informally and *sub rosa*, as this proud man would not accept anything resembling charity.

During his stay at Columbia, we "colleagues" had a very pleasant relationship with Bartók. Although he was an almost fanatically private person, he often visited the music department. We had small dinner parties at the faculty club or in our homes, and we hung on his words, because most of us realized that we were in the presence of genius. And when, at the piano, he would show us some fabulous rhythmic combinations he had found in his research (he very seldom spoke of his own music), we were enthralled. He, in turn, always prodded Herzog to show him the results of his research in American Indian music, which interested him very much.

Then things took a bad turn. By 1942 the funds gave out, and what with wartime conditions, the university felt unable to budget a nonteaching position. Performances of his work were few, as were concert engagements—and both, it was only later known, were pitifully underpaid. Our renewed efforts to persuade him to accept a position as teacher of composition were unavailing.

This episode in Bartók's life in America has been misinterpreted. Understandably, we did not want to reveal the background of his appointment, and Columbia was accused of ignorance and heartlessness, even though it graciously played along with the conspirators, bending the rules to do so, and made an appointment that was—to say the least—unconventional. It also bestowed on Bartók the honorary degree of doctor of music, which pleased him very much. The chief source of the misunderstandings of his stay in the United States was a "biography" by Agatha Fassett, full of inaccuracies, lengthy quoted conversations that never took place, and all sorts of hearsay anecdotes. The 1954 edition of *Grove's Dictionary of Music and Musicians*, displaying editor Eric Blom's well-known dislike for everything American, called Bartók's treatment in this country "shameful," though the article admits that "of how [he] lived during his last years we still have no clear picture."

Beyond question, all of us, caught up in our own problems and trying to cope with wartime restrictions, failed to improve his lot, and we deeply regret this failure. ASCAP, in sharp contrast to the behavior of his publishers and managers, came generously to his assistance when apprised of the situation, but by then it was too late; leukemia soon claimed its victim. Those who see nothing but deplorable indifference toward a great artist overlook the difficult and confused situation—and Bartók's own inflexible resistance to accepting any contribution not earned. The privacy he so ardently desired became a loneliness no one could breach. Only after his death did Victor Bator, his Hungarian-born friend, mentor, and executor, discover the extent of his deprivation.

Bartók's persevering idealism counted on no reward; through exile and illness, living from hand to mouth, it kept him above the waves, sustaining his creative activity until his dying day. In the end, he succumbed, the soul vanquished by the frail organism that had never really contained it. The world that showers its gratitude on the fashionable idols of the day does not understand artistic and moral integrity of so stern a nature; his funeral was attended by a mere handful. Succeeding generations may consider him another of those geniuses an unresponsive society has permitted to perish; yet perhaps it was inevitable that a man of his character would, like many others, appear to be fate's victim. Whatever his hardships, however deep his disappointments, his art was triumphant. Even in the *Concerto for Orchestra*, composed in the shadow of death, that vernal energy that always characterized his activity still shows through, unbroken, without resignation—indeed, transfigured.

A Tribute to Music Scholarship at Mid-Century

W hen Alfred Einstein published the rediscovered autograph of Mozart's Kyrie K. 90 in *The Musical Quarterly*, he did so with a dedicatory message to Paul Hirsch—patron of music scholarship rivaled in largesse, understanding, loving care, and public spirit only by the grand seigneurs of the past—who had then reached the proverbial three score and ten years. But was not the dedicator himself about to reach this age which Cicero so beautifully characterized as man's second creative period? "The soul is no longer the servant of passions but has become its own master." Nor was he the only distinguished septuagenarian musicologist among us, for he was flanked by a senior and a junior: Otto Kinkeldey and Curt Sachs. These three eminent men have left a profound impress on international scholarship, but we greeted them affectionately especially for their contribution to our scholarly well-being in this country.

The period in which a good part of their work was done was not urbane and well disciplined, and they were not representative of its spirit. Nor did it accord them their due. The ivory tower of the scholar was not so isolated and

From *The Musical Quarterly*, vol. 37 (1951)

innocuous as it may have appeared to the uninitiated; in fact, the slender towers bore cannonaded embrasures. The public watched the battle with indifference, unaware of the reasons that called it forth. It preferred to ignore the warring factions and lent its support to the dilettante and the charlatan who dominated the musico-literary field—and market. The three to whom we pay tribute were men of marked personalities yet were alike in an unflinching moral compulsion and a high sense of responsibility. They had known adversity—even humiliation—yet they went their own way serenely to earn the gratitude of new generations who dip their colors to them in genuine admiration.

Otto Kinkeldey's career as a scholar, like those of his two colleagues, began with the century and at the place where the new issues of modern musicology were being raised: Germany. But the similarity ends here, for Kinkeldey was an American who went to Berlin because at that time this country could not offer him the training he desired. Thus the handicap for the young scholar was a considerable one, for not only was he to take part on equal terms with veterans of music scholarship in a foreign land and language, but in place of the long traditions and training of his German colleagues he could bring only native musicianship and a fresh and inquisitive mind. But when his generation—one that was to produce many illustrious names—began to publish the interesting and often provocative essays that characterized the times around 1910, we see him among them. In the rather animated if not noisy atmosphere he appears serious, confident, and assured. He immediately shows such mature scholarship as is seldom encountered in a first essay. *Orgel und Klavier in der Musik des 16. Jahrhunderts* turned out to be a major contribution to our knowledge of music history, and a work that remains valid and concrete in a field of scholarship where books age rapidly. There are no flamboyant statements, and the controversial tone is missing; instead, we feel the unselfconscious security of a man whose second nature is to weigh and to judge, whose taste is impeccable, and who can see beyond the horizon.

When he came home in 1915, he found that the situation had not appreciably changed from the days when he found it necessary to seek competent instruction elsewhere: the universities wanted no part of scholarship in music. This may sound rather ridiculous to us, even though the enemies of musicology are by no means an extinct race, but it was grimly serious to the distinguished professor from Breslau University who came home to become a prophet in his own land.

He began to gather the bricks with which to build the structure of American musicology. That it was built, and that today we have a flourishing and ever growing confraternity of American musicologists, is largely due to his perseverance and devotion. This is not to belittle the contributions of the Pratts, Sonnecks, and Engels, but the fight had to be made in the colleges and in the musical and other societies and committees where the real adversaries lurked. Of this struggle we personally did not witness the first and most difficult fifteen years, but we did see the last twenty, when at every convention, convocation, committee meeting, and sundry gathering Kinkeldey was a force to reckon with. When the discussion began to get diffuse or out of hand, he arose and in his own quiet manner immediately organized matters in a logical order. Never belligerent, always forbearing, but uncompromising, and with a devastating ability to marshal facts, he usually carried the day. This dedication to a task he carried out without the slightest sign of ostentation or recrimination, yet the arduous work must have entailed many disappointments. Chief among them must have been the lack of time and opportunity to engage in additional capital studies to follow *Orgel und Klavier.* The shorter essays are all important and show him at his best: masterful in exposition and felicitous in expression, but they also make us feel keenly our loss of further large works. On the other hand, directly or indirectly, our first professor of musicology (Cornell, 1930) helped to shape almost every American contribution to musical letters, and every one of us of a younger generation is indebted to him for friendly and unselfish guidance.

The discoverer of the little Kyrie of Mozart who is responsible for reminding us of the distinguished septuagenarians has been acclaimed for his monumental *The Italian Madrigal.* How dry and professional the title, and how great the reader's delight after the very first pages as he is carried along. A picture here, a brilliantly contrived characterization there, or an idea that uncovers the essence of things, and he is led into a world no longer nebulous, but now acquiring a living force. The man who speaks here is not only an eminent scholar but an artist in expression and communication. At times a seemingly chance remark, a clause, makes us realize the presence of far-reaching musicological-philological erudition; yet the narrative remains elegantly polished, for there is no scholarly pretension in the old-fashioned manner, only a warm enthusiasm for the subject. This warmth and love shape and elevate the work, which becomes light and clear precisely where it probes into the richest depths. Yet everything is very serious here; a great cause is hidden in the easily flowing prose: introduction to great music experienced through the receptive soul of a great seeker.

The range of Einstein's interest is something to behold. There are people who spend a lifetime in amassing learning. They know the entire literature of their own field and a good deal of neighboring territory, yet what they do resembles more the work of the horticulturist: they come up with something that is not new, merely the more or less successful cross among several species. Einstein knew that the essence of scholarly performance is not dependent on technique alone, nor even on command of the spiritual and material realities, although these are of the utmost important, but on the love—the *eros* as the ancients used to say—with which he grasps the matter and which urges him to a dedicated service. If this eros is living and is communicated to the audience, creative scholarship becomes a reality and an art. And whether it is Mozart, de Rore, or Lasso, Einstein is talking about, we feel this creative process from the very first, and therefore his essays are never hybrids but original and very personal creations. Upon reading them no one can escape the feeling that he is beholding a new Mozart, a new de Rore, a new Lasso.

When compared to the other arts, the history of music shows an appalling tendency toward the ephemeral; works and whole schools once acclaimed to the skies are forgotten in a generation or two. On the other hand this very same history gives the scholar a thousand opportunities, amidst the changing realities of subjects, approaches, schools, amidst philosophical and moral, social and political aims, to point out the ideal, the lasting, the beautiful. Curt Sachs, the "junior" of the trio of musicologists then looking back on a past rich in achievements, had brought a deeply searching mind wealthy in scholarly inventiveness to a lifetime spent in trying to apprehend the ideal. This ideal cannot be measured with any exactitude, even though our eminent investigator gives the impression when at work that, like the experienced jeweler, he can tell the gold content of an object by its weight. But perhaps it is not very difficult to find beauty when one is so well equipped with a magic wand as is Curt Sachs; what is difficult is to guide others in the search. A legion of devoted followers and disciples testifies to the success of the guide.

It is unnecessary for us to enumerate the many works of Sachs, works that set the model for research in many an unknown region of music. He does not admit special bias or even sympathies, yet we cannot help feeling an especially warm stream flowing from his writing when he deals with the question of the commonwealth of the arts, when he probes into the regions we consider a no-man's-land contiguous to all arts yet not specifically claimed by any. We feel when reading his writings that the destiny of music is formed by many influences coming from a multitude of sources which we, who are closely identified with the music of the Occident, are inclined to overlook or belittle. He knows that the history of music is a great epic without frontiers and cannot be fitted into small compartments. His is a noble conception presented with the skill and insight of a true humanist.

What appears to be the play of blind and unconscious forces of nature reveals design when it is subjected to the scrutiny of a searching and critical mind. This is the nature and chief benefit of the work of the scholars we are saluting, for it is the scholar-critic who sheds light into this darkness. The cultural work carried out by them—and by all men of the same artistic-scholarly persuasion—does not emanate from some chance exercise of a profession, from the following of some rules or precepts, but from the essence of things. What they have to say is what a civilized being has to say; what they feel or think is the experience of civilized beings who have traversed every flowering field of arts and letters, who have thought with the great thinkers the great thoughts of humanity, who have learned the life of all manner of people and peoples. May new generations, enriched by the expressive force of these masters, share in their creative insight.

Devotional Music at Mid-Century

hristmas is approaching, and all the hidden Christian virtues that during the rest of the year lay somnolent in people's bosoms begin to stir. The stores remind us that the greatest of these virtues is "giving"; the magazines, swollen to double their normal size by the same zealous appeal for brotherly giving, are resplendent with pictures of happy families opening packages; while Santa Claus, preferring the warm and congenial atmosphere of the department store to the cold climate of the bleak North Pole, gravely takes suggestions from the wide-eyed young citizenry, not yet able to practice the Christian virtues unaided.

There is music in the air too, reactivated for the specific purpose of providing Christmas cheer and edification. The church choirs are dusting off the dog-eared copies of *Messiah* and prettying up good old "King Wenceslaus," as well as *Adeste Fideles*. The organists will ready suitable transcriptions of unsuitable music and make sure that their accompaniments are properly sweet and dragging, so as to create what is believed to be a religious atmosphere. The newspapers will publish the list of music to be given at the Christmas services,

From the *American Choral Review*, vol. 17 (1975)

and a more impoverished, sad, and inartistic collection of third-rate "sacred art" could not be imagined. What happened to this sacred art, for many centuries the core, main support, nay the very substance of the art of music? The great Christian denominations are infinitely rich in masterworks that sum up their creeds, aspirations, and convictions, yet only an isolated church here and there is aware of that.

In Bach's time, Christmas services consisted of cantatas and oratorios with chorus, soloists, and orchestra; and of the singing of those magnificent hymns, the chorales, that were born with the Reformation and express its spirit as nothing else does. Today we hear these cantatas in the concert hall, in white tie and tails. In church the chorales are replaced by Victorian ditties, most of which are pretty nearly insufferable as music, and the cantatas by anthems of equally watery consistency.

This adopted son of the Republic has vivid recollections of his bewilderment when, in the early days of his Americanization, he was thrown off his religious and musical balance when listening to the hymns. There was "Glorious things of Thee are spoken," which turned out to be Haydn's grand old Hapsburg anthem in praise of the Emperor. I had to stand at attention when I heard it in my youth (and still later, once again, to the words of "*Stand Columbia!*"). Then again the edifying words "God the omnipotent King who ordainest" were accompanied by music that used to glorify another autocratic monarchy, for this is the old Czarist anthem. My remembrances, going back to the fateful years 1914–18, recalled the sound of artillery when the strains of this tune were heard—but now I had a hymnal in my hands.

Well, this is a curious world. Not that the use of secular tunes for sacred texts was unheard of; it was practiced in the older centuries, but today there is no excuse for it in the face of the immense store of great original church song.

The Catholic Church, older and wealthier in sacred music, is just as backward as her Protestant cousins. The backbone and foundation of her music, Gregorian chant, is performed in a perfunctory manner and often disfigured by incongruous organ accompaniments. Few are the churches that have a true appreciation of it. And where are the great choral works of the legion of hallowed composers of Masses and motets? Perhaps the *Marcellus Mass* of Palestrina is sung on occasion, but he composed ninety-odd other great Masses. And where are Josquin, Lasso, Victoria, Byrd, and all the others? The Church, justly proud, conferred the title "Prince of Music" on a number of them, but now they are replaced by commoners such as Refice, Yon or Carlo Rossini—all well-meaning and devout persons, no doubt, but pathetically short on talent. And what of the solemn Masses of the great

Baroque and Classic composers, from Monteverdi to Mozart, Haydn, and Schubert? They were composed by believers who gave their best to the Church.

This brings us to the question of the orchestra in church. In Europe even small village churches had an orchestra of sorts, and the great churches and cathedrals had very substantial ones. In our Catholic churches they are banished because of a mistaken conception of "worldliness." If this is valid, several centuries of Catholic church life must be condemned as having been in error—something that is rather unlikely. Just what logic silences the scruples when Gounod's *St. Cecilia* Mass, perennial favorite with American Catholics, is performed? This music is as worldly with organ accompaniment as a Schubert Mass with trumpets and kettle drums is deeply religious.

When Handel's *Messiah* is performed without the orchestra, it is preciously close to a caricature. The wondrous orchestrally accompanied Protestant church music of the great biblical composers, Schütz, Buxtehude, Purcell, Bach, to mention a few, is heard only in some college chapels in its true magnificence. The other churches prefer the "safe" works of F. Flaxington Harker, H. Alexander Matthews, or Harry Roe Shelley—all true and tried Christians—and wretched composers.

One of the principal reasons for our low musical literacy is the lowly quality of church music. In the days when Sunday services were carried out to the sound of glorious music by the masters, the congregations imbibed an understanding for good music that formed their tastes and made them receptive to other great music outside the church. The church composers, up to the Beethovenian era, were the great composers of the day, incredible as it may seem: the avant-gardists. Today, new church music by a master is a rarity, and then it is usually performed in the concert hall.

It does not follow that true religious feeling can be achieved only by truly great religious music, but the churches of old were the great patrons of music and believed that only true art is worthy to fill the nave with its sounds. The department store Santa Claus is the symbol of our sacred art, and we too put on his false whiskers for Christmastide, and offer manufactured gifts instead of the dedicated works of those "in whom dwelleth the gift of God"—genius.

The present celebration of Christmas may seem to be based on very ancient practices, but in reality it assumed its familiar tone and mood in very recent times. An immense store of fable invests Christmas in all northern countries. They are biblical and liturgical, but also thoroughly mixed with a great deal of pre-Christian practice, to which our advanced age has added the glamour of commerce and advertising. Christmas presents, as well as the tree and other accretions, were totally unknown before the nineteenth century and are of distinctly Germanic origin. The poetry of Christmas, Christian and pagan, gave way to creature comforts of the season.

The feast of the birth of Our Lord was placed at the winter solstice, which is the date of the rebirth of the pagan sun god. Many of the fine East European folk songs, such as those that Bartók collected, actually go back to old Roman solstice celebrations danced in animal skins. At the opening of this century Bartók still saw this done, and while the melodies are equipped with suitable Christian texts, there is no mistaking their origin. Such age-old pagan elements are numerous in the Christmas music of most countries, and they are well absorbed, even though for a long time they were censured—without success—by the ecclesiastic authorities. When the first broadcast of a Christmas service was made in England on the newfangled radio, there were still grave misgivings among the more conservative that it might be listened to by someone with his hat on.

The great literature of motets, cantatas, and other highly artistic Christmas pieces is seldom heard today in our churches, though half a dozen standbys do reappear every year. After the middle of the last century a specific category of Christmas music, the carols and noels, became very popular; unfortunately, what we hear is only a pale reflection of what they used to be.

The beginnings of the carol go back to the Middle Ages, for it descended from the hymns of the church services, as well as from dance songs, rounds, marches, and folk songs, and there are unmistakable connections with the liturgical play. The dramatic instinct of the Middle Ages was responsible for the introduction of the practice of displaying the crib of Bethlehem to furnish the humble, unlettered peasants with a pictorial representation of the Nativity. Then there were the Italian shepherds who on Christmas morning came to Rome, like their biblical ancestors, to play their bagpipes before the pictures of the Madonna. As is usually the case, this delightful custom inspired the great composers, and many fine Christmas concertos and pastorals were the result. Every one knows the gently undulating "Pastoral Symphony" from *Messiah*; Handel borrowed it from one of the old Italian pastorals.

We must beware of the romantic-popular concept that the carols stand for spontaneous folk song; the best of the genuine ones were written by gifted, if anonymous, masters, some of the tunes later becoming known as "traditional," or "folk song." There are some five hundred old English carols extant, both in English and in Latin. With their freshness, lilt, and rhythmic vigor they represent some of the finest music of the late Middle Ages, the counterpart of the Christmas-inspired paintings of the period. But who knows them?

The carols were composed for ecclesiastical use, especially for processions, and often had moral, didactic—even political—undertones. If this seems strange to us, we must remember that the Middle Ages did not know the distinction between "sacred" and "secular" we make with rather startling incongruity. Those good people, whose entire life was infused with religion, would certainly be amazed by the saccharine trivialities we declare "sacred" music.

There can be no doubt that the carol was danced to, marched to; that it was used in church for the greatest solemnities and also as banquet music. "Wassail," which is a cry of elation, like "Nowell," proves this, for it was most certainly sung on convivial occasions and accompanied by the appropriate spirits drunk from the wassail bowl.

Many of the later carols in general use today are far less significant musically, though some, such as the well-known "God rest you merry, gentlemen," have very fine tunes. And, of course, some of the great ones have survived, while still others of exceptional artistic value were adapted from Continental sources. An example of the former is the famous "Good King Wenceslaus" which descended from a beautiful old carol to serve the trite words of its present form, while among the latter we may mention *Puer natus est in Bethlehem.* Unfortunately, many of these grand tunes were mangled when set to careless English translations. The French with their sparkling noels created a delightful body of Christmas songs, and the Germans are noted for their beautiful cradle songs and lullabies, of which Gruber's ubiquitous "Silent Night" is a late Romantic descendant.

The Reformation diverted interest from the virgin and child motif, putting emphasis elsewhere, and Protestant music followed suit. Even so, the Puritans frowned upon it (as upon Christmas in general), and after 1700 the carol fell into neglect in the English-speaking countries. It was the Victorians who revived its use, but the musical originality and verve of the original carol were largely lost in the sentimental products of the last hundred years.

Though still very pleasant, joyful, convivial, and often artistic, the carol no longer reflects its characteristic naive religious spirit. If we want to capture that, we must turn to the many fine paintings of the old masters devoted to the manger, to Mary, the child Jesus, and the adoration of the Magi, which depict the unutterable mystery of Christmas. The musician no longer knows how to sing about this mystery, and the old one, who did, is forgotten.

A year or two ago this column commented on the display of shallow and unchurchly music. In response to the article, I received several communications, a few coming from highly respected church musicians, disputing my contentions and asking for "proof." Now I am happy to acknowledge that there is an increasing number of organists and choirmasters not only well trained but literate, with a knowledge of the great masterpieces, and a progressive attitude, and that a palpable improvement is observable in the country; yet I must renew my charges, and this time with documentation.

The April 20 (1957) newspapers printed the complete musical program of the Easter services in ninety-seven Protestant and ten Catholic churches in the metropolitan area. This does not account, of course, for all churches, but represents a fair enough cross-section for statistical purposes. Of these hundred-odd churches, only seven offered music that in its entirety honors both worship and art. We may be sure that these seven are not the only ones to be faithful to the great traditions of Christian devotional music; nevertheless, the statistics still hold.

The two New York cathedrals win the prize for inartistic hodgepodge, reflecting no credit on their trusteeship of sacred art. A number of other churches had a sprinkling of genuine church music combined with "religious" war-horses, while a large group had nothing but blasphemous trash. On the other hand, among the seven uncompromisingly serious and artistic programs, I might mention St. Thomas Chapel, Episcopal (Pachelbel, Walther, Bach, Charpentier, Viadana, Handel, and Gibbons), and St. Ignatius Loyola Church, Catholic (Palestrina, Lotti, Byrd, and a wealth of Gregorian chant), as offering an object lesson to the others.

If we look at the remaining hundred programs listed, the situation is even sadder than the figures would indicate. Let us mention the few respectable staples many churches produce for Easter: the "Hallelujah" chorus (and a few other numbers) from Handel's *Messiah*, though it is not church music, Bach's chorale prelude "Christ lay in death's dark prison," and Vulpius's Easter Hallelujah are the most frequent. Now subtract these from the programs, and dozens of churches are left with nothing but pitiful fabrications. What glorious names in music! Speaks, Wacks, Banks, Holler, Pfohl, Spinney, Bogatto, etc. Then, of course, comes Gounod's notorious Ave Maria, and there are many other arrangements, considered the *pièces de résistance*. Among them may be mentioned Kreisler's Chanson, Mendelssohn's "On wings of song," Wild's "Blow golden trumpet," Mariott's "Lilies of the dawn," the Easter chorus from *Cavalleria rusticana*, and, most frequently of all, something entitled "In Joseph's lovely gardens." One church recalled the Resurrection by offering

Pierné's Impromptu caprice—for harp solo. As I said, a number of churches had a few decent numbers, but demonstrated no understanding for a balanced musical offering. They may start out with impeccable religious masterpieces—Hassler, Palestrina, Eccard, Bach—but end up with the inevitable Willan, Gaul, Refice, Yon, and all the other journeymen musicians.

The basic reason for this regrettable state of affairs is the fact that society as an organization is no longer interested in sacred art, an attitude that took its inception with the French Revolution. By the second half of the nineteenth century, church music was considered "an affair of the clergy," but the clergy, in the wake of Jansenism, Josephinism, Puritanism, and Fundamentalism, turned into a conscientious and hard-working body of ecclesiastical bureaucrats serving the church and the parishioners with zeal, but showing no sense for the great and traditionally elevating role of art in religion.

What has happened since the times when the clergy itself took the leading role in fostering and developing the arts for the greater glory of God, when the inventive genius of the Abbot of Beauvais created the Gothic arch, the Renaissance, the Florentine Baptistery, when the canons at the cathedrals of Paris or Dijon or Canterbury, the cantors of Lübeck or Leipzig, created the most profoundly devotional—and modern—musical movements of the day? The ambitions of the younger clergy, if they transcend the boundaries of the pastorate, are almost exclusively in the field of the social sciences and politics. Therefore, paradoxical as it may seem, the church musician is the lesser offender, as is the sculptor who provides the atrocious plaster statues of Christ and the saints, manufactured, as are the hymns, anthems, and Masses, by the commercial artists of religion. It is up to the churches and their administrators to realize that God's house is not an artistic attic from which on certain occasions odds and ends are temporarily retrieved for practical use.

This column's discussion of the musical programs at the Easter services in New York churches elicited a volume of correspondence rivaling the Callas controversy. It is cheering to this writer to realize—as he suspected—that many church musicians are aware of the bad state of affairs, though they are powerless before their superiors and their congregations. On the other hand, some of the correspondents do not seem to understand what "artistic hodgepodge" means and, citing all manner of great names from their general repertory, cry "Unfair" and want "equal space" on the editorial pages.

If someone is slighted or injured, every possible courtesy is extended to him on our pages, but in this particular case I commented on 107 printed musical programs and reported on unquestioned facts. I deliberately dealt only with those churches whose programs were published on Palm Sunday, and certain excellent unlisted programs have since been brought to my attention. But the overall picture remains.

Let us take for an example the program offered by the Cathedral of St. John the Divine, where a very able and knowledgeable organist and choirmaster officiates. But on Easter Day, when traditionally something notable is expected, he did put together a program embracing Jackson, Shaw, Titcomb, Stanford, Gibbons, and Beethoven. Only one item on this very mixed program is great and bona fide church music: the anthem by Gibbons. As to the pièce de résistance—the final chorus from Beethoven's oratorio *Christ on the Mount of Olives*—I submit that this composition, presented in a truncated manner, that is, without orchestra, is neither church music nor a particularly outstanding work. Where is the great sacred art especially composed for Easter services?

No, gentlemen of the choir loft, I used the printed programs not "to criticize the chef merely by reading the menu," but because without such documentation your indignation would have been the greater. The fact remains that on Easter Day, Anno Domini 1957, most churches in New York presented in whole or in part "sacred music" that is anemic, sentimental, sweet, and empty, unworthy to accompany the great event celebrated on that day. One might debate whether the pyre upon which Savonarola threw every artistic product he regarded as being conducive to sin was an instrument of purification or of destruction; we might debate whether religion, morals, art, and culture gained or lost by this radical act; but it is beyond doubt that both religion and art would gain if a modern Savonarola were to collect and burn to ashes the trash that under the heading of sacred art has been introduced into our religious life within the last hundred years.

At the bottom of this situation is the fact that sacred art—not only music, but all the arts—has been stagnating for a century or so. A certain frozen concept of the churchly in art gained acceptance during the Romantic era, and the great masters ceased to compose, paint, and build for the church. Until recently, to most modern Christians, whether Protestant or Catholic, only the Gothic has been the acceptable churchly style of architecture; it does not matter how eclectic or even atrocious, as long as it has pointed arches, it is par excellence religious and Christian. Similarly, in church music the ideal is a nondescript "anthem" style that is supposed to represent whatever Palestrina is imagined to have stood for. It too has pointed arches in a musical sense, and it too is eclectic but even more atrocious than the architecture.

But let us assume that it were possible to re-create music in the image of

Palestrina or Bach; what would we gain? Antiquarians can never restore the milieu that produced a certain style; the man of the twentieth century will never think with the mind of his ancestor, nor can he feel his mood. No one expects a contemporary poet to write in Dante's style, but the architect and the composer are supposed to create in a deliberately archaic way. If every age has had the right to express its own ideas and feelings—I reiterate that the hallowed church musicians of the era of "classic polyphony" were absolutely modern masters, in the vanguard of their day—why is this right denied to our musicians? In the world of ideas stagnation means death.

It is not true that modern composers are unwilling or unable to compose for the Church; it is the church, the clergy, and the unenlightened congregation that keep them out. The crux of the matter is that either the church accepts art, true art, both old and new, as it did in its youth, or it abdicates its cultural mission, permitting insignificant journeyman musicians, painters, and architects to carry sacred art to the sad fate of Byzantium.

There is, of course, such a thing as a liturgical attitude; but it must be remembered that a true composer will do in his own way exactly as did Veronese when he placed the *Wedding at Cana* in the house of an Italian patrician, or when Rembrandt presented the soldiers who guard Christ in Dutch army uniforms. This is natural. Artists are not historians; they see the past through their own creative eyes. Many, many people have prayed reverently before such "modern" and "inaccurate" pictures.

The same is true in music. Even the severe papal encyclicals on church music recognize the validity of modern art in the church; all they demand is the observance of liturgical propriety, which emphatically does not exclude the musical equivalent of the patrician's house and the Dutch army uniforms. The church musicians, many of whom are aware of the need, should undertake to educate their superiors and their congregations; it can be done gradually. But as long as they merely entertain them with sweet music, they are not true to their calling.

The Film Amadeus

In the Romantic era, novels and plays based on long-past, often mythical events, mostly drawn from medieval tales and handled with untrammeled poetic license, became very popular. But presently men of letters began to wonder whether real historical characters might not be more convincing than fictional ones, and whether, rather than being used as props upon which to hang a story, they might not serve as means of conjuring up a period's soul in a way that would transcend archeological minutiae. This concept is artistically challenging and potentially fruitful, but it places the author in a quandary. To what extent may actual events be modified for the sake of dramatic effect? At what point do historical persons become so changed as to be falsified, so that the very reason for calling on them—to provide new insight, sharper illumination, a clearer vision of history—is negated, and they become little more than easy devices to catch the attention of the audience? To pass that point may create a theatrical triumph at the cost of essential truth.

This is what happens in Peter Schaffer's sparkling *Amadeus*, which won a

From *Opus*, October 1985

bushel of honors in both its stage and its lavishly mounted film versions. It is well wrought, and the audience is both moved and entertained. We do not go to the theater to learn history, and historical accuracy, as the author acknowledges, was not his concern. The outlines of Mozart's and Salieri's careers during the years they shared in Vienna are actually pretty well respected, the notable exception being the circumstances of the composition of the great Requiem Mass by the dying Mozart. Here, as we shall see, the interchange of roles between Salieri and Count Walsegg-Stuppach (and also, in the film, Süssmayr) serves the play's thesis, and in fact the scene is the plot's linchpin. As the portrait painter Kokoschka said to a client: "Those who know you will not recognize you, but those who do not know you will recognize you very well."

Artistic biography, whether in the form of the theater or the novel, that lingers on the contrast between creative grandeur and personal squalor is in its way as banal as the Romantic leaning toward the jejune. To avert one's eyes from Mozart's shortcomings, which are in any case trivial and can be attributed to his hothouse childhood, is unnecessary; but to make of him a giggling buffoon is unpardonable to "those who know" him. The play is further removed than the film from both the literal facts and the psychological truth. For example, it carries the scatological repartee to much greater lengths—whether to amuse the audience or to blacken Mozart's reputation is unclear. The Viennese did tend to be rather free in their use of such vulgarity, as has been the case in other times and places, but not to the extent implied here. The playwright obviously extended the ribald language the very young Mozart used in his well-known letters to his equally young cousin, the "Bäsle," to his everyday conversation, false both to the period and to Mozart. As a matter of fact, while Constanze is maligned in both versions, in the play she seems to have acquired the personality of that rather inelegant young lady, the "Bäsle," and is the vehicle for the copious flow of gutter language. Constanze came from a musical family and was herself a singer. Leopold Mozart strongly opposed the marriage as an impediment to his son's career and a financial burden Wolfgang was ill equipped to carry. In this he was correct; but Constanze was a faithful wife. Mozart himself relates that both wept for joy at the wedding, and we know that he wrote the C Minor Mass (in which Constanze sang) as thanksgiving for his marriage. Schaffer's scene of the two lewdly romping under the table in the archbishop's anteroom is libelous beyond the needs of the author's thesis.

The dramatic idea that a man whose entire life is devoutly dedicated to his art can attain only mediocrity, while he sees a young man—empty-headed, sluttish, unworthy, yet mysteriously "beloved by God"—effortlessly pouring forth incomparable music, and that this divine injustice should drive him beyond endurance: this is a powerful theme. To have based the play on fictional characters would have deprived it of the illustrative value of Mozart's music; to hear this (superbly performed on the film soundtrack by Neville Mariner) gives conviction. In fact, the play would have been rather thin without it. (The entire tremendous final scene from *Don Giovanni* is performed in the film, and there is no such dramatic finale in the whole operatic literature.) Nevertheless, it is regrettable that, to serve the needs of the theater, an able and important historical figure, Antonio Salieri (1750–1825), is demolished as man and artist, and Mozart is made into a silly genius who simply shakes masterpieces from his sleeves.

That Salieri, although his official position was secure, could have become so insanely jealous as to plot the murder of his young rival is no recent invention. Mozart himself unwittingly gave the story some plausibility when, sick and miserable with a devastating illness (now thought to have been typhoid fever and nephritis), he expressed the suspicion that he was being poisoned. The rumor that Salieri actually succeeded in doing so seems to have started in Austrian and Czech nationalistic circles that were trying to breach the entrenched musical reign of the Italians, typified by the court composer, Salieri. First mentioned in 1798 by Franz Xaver Niemetschek, a man of letters and friend of the Mozarts, the idea was later embellished by the belief that Salieri had confessed his crime on his deathbed. This was emphatically repudiated by all Mozart's friends familiar with both his illness and Salieri. The two nurses who attended the dying composer day and night in his final days also refuted the story of the poisoning. Still, the tale, long since disproved, was too titillating to be discarded. Salieri came to be depicted as a vain, fast-thinking, and unscrupulous cynic, a mediocre musician at the head of an Italian cabal that aimed to get rid of Mozart as the chief threat to Italian musical supremacy. In 1830, Pushkin wrote a dramatic poem entitled *Mozart and Salieri*, and in 1897, Rimsky-Korsakov followed with an opera of the same title.

Amadeus had its predecessors, therefore, but this play does not press the poisoning theory. rather, it makes Salieri a psychological murderer, obsessed in his old age by the memory of his consuming desire to kill "Amadeus," and his recollection of the deathbed scene when he willed to drive the exhausted composer to his final collapse. It is here that the alternation of events is most serious. Salieri is represented as the mysterious commissioner of the Requiem (actually, Count Walsegg-Stuppach, who, like Salieri in this account, planned to pass the finished work off as his own, if only its true composer would die), and he is also substituted in the film for Mozart's pupil Süssmayr. It was

Süssmayr to whom the dying composer gave directions how to complete his great Mass. Schaffer's play (more than the film) imagines Salieri as going to considerable lengths to convince Mozart of the approach of his death and thus hasten it, and in fact Mozart was convinced that he was writing his own Requiem.

Let us now sketch Salieri's real life story. Born to a well-to-do family, he was discovered in Venice by Florian Gassmann, a prominent Viennese composer, who took the unusually gifted sixteen-year-old (whose father had died) back with him to Vienna, treating him as his own son and providing him with an excellent humanistic and musical education. Salieri was well-read, fluent in German, French, and Latin, and even in his youth became admired as a very versatile musician. Contemporaries described the mature artist as full of *joie de vivre*, warm-hearted, always helpful to others, especially solicitous about getting jobs for young musicians (among them, Mozart's son, Franz Xaver!), witty, open, and decisive. He was widely respected, even by the crotchety Beethoven, who dedicated his Op. 12 Violin Sonatas to the Italian and sought his advice even after he himself had become a famous composer. Among his many other pupils were Schubert, Weigl, Hummel, Liszt, and several of Mozart's favorite singers, as well as Pauline Anna Milder-Hauptmann, for whom Beethoven wrote the part of Fidelio.

Salieri was recognized as a master musician in all genres, a great conductor and teacher, and one of the best vocal coaches. An authority on all matters musical of the day, he was consulted by everybody from the emperor on down. As imperial conductor, the highest musical position in the land, he was in charge of opera and all other music at the court, and an intimate of the emperor. He maintained friendly terms with Metastasio, da Ponte, Spontini, and Gluck; indeed, the last-named considered him his potential successor as an opera composer. Perhaps the last late Neapolitan master, he was more versatile than his colleagues. Whether in *opera buffa*, or *tragédie lyrique*, or *Singspiel*, he always found the proper style, and in his fine church music he ranged from the Palestrina manner to the grand concerted idiom. Like Rossini, Salieri ceased to compose operas when he saw that a new aesthetic was gaining over the Classical French style as represented by Gluck, but he continued to compose elaborate sacred music. Many of his operas were successful all over Europe.

Salieri was very civic-minded, one of the founders of the Society of Musical Artists, whose concerts he conducted until 1818, and of the Friends of Music. Indeed, he was responsible for the high level of Viennese bourgeois musical culture. He received many honors: member of the Institut de France and of the Conservatoire, knight of the Legion of Honor, and a fellow of many European musical societies.

Obviously, Salieri was a formidable personality who could not be dethroned and was in the way not only of Mozart but of everyone climbing the professional ladder at the court. Despite his unassailable position, Salieri fully realized Mozart's genius; as a sign of his admiration, he walked in the small procession with Süssmayr and a few other musicians at Mozart's funeral. (Incidentally, the shabby funeral, the interment in a mass grave, and the pelting storm that scattered the mourners are all now disproved. Among the reforms of the "enlightened monarch" Joseph II was a strict regulation of obsequies, mainly to help impecunious families. Since, as usual, there was little money in the Mozart family coffers, a third-class funeral was selected. The wealthy Baron van Swieten, who arranged things, should have helped; but perhaps, as a member of the nobility, he considered a modest funeral proper for a poor musician. The third-class affair still provided for a single grave, which was later mixed up with others when the lax attendants rearranged the graves as was customarily done every eight years. The weather was fine, and the mourners turned back after following the bier part way to the cemetery; this, too, was according to the edict.)

Well, now, how did Salieri's exalted reputation plunge to that of a murderer in posterity's eyes? To understand so startling a change, we must also examine Mozart's place in this gloomy legend. Both Leopold Mozart and his son resented the dominance of Italian musicians in Austria, but unlike his diplomatic and cautious father, Wolfgang made no secret of it. His feelings are defensible because the Italian musicians occupied most important positions at the Catholic courts, preventing native Austrians and Germans from advancing their cause; Weber and the young Wagner still had to contend with them.

Mozart did have one or two opportunities that he could have cultivated more assiduously. The first, a good if provincial post at the court of Archbishop Colloredo in Salzburg, was ruined by Wolfgang's frequent and long concert tours. The archbishop was a thoroughly unpleasant autocrat who treated Mozart insultingly, but one can hardly blame him for being annoyed at the inopportune absences of his concertmaster. In Vienna, the way might have been open to Mozart, because the emperor, a good and well-trained amateur musician like many of the Habsburgs (and not the bumbling two-finger pianist shown in *Amadeus*), espied the genius in him.

Unfortunately, Wolfgang, a fascinating and profuse letter-writer who missed nothing and had an opinion on everything, was an incorrigible and often unkind gossip, though repeatedly warned by Leopold to watch his tongue. Peter von Winter, a well-known composer and friend of the Mozart family, told Mozart *père* that his son was "heartily disliked at the court" because of his reckless remarks, which naturally got back to those at whose expense they were made.

And of course, like everyone else, Mozart had competitors, both Italian and domestic, some of whom he treated with belittling sarcasm, even though they expressed admiration for his music. At the famous confrontation with the world-renowned pianist Muzio Clementi, which the emperor arranged at court, each heard the other for the first time. Clementi, who was one of the creators of the new, delicately nuanced legato playing on the fortepiano, and whose sonatas profoundly influenced Beethoven, said after the encounter: "Until now I have never heard such spirited and expressive playing." And Mozart's verdict? "He has not a penny's worth of feeling and taste." But he did not hesitate a few years later to make use of the opening theme of the sonata Clementi played at the tournament for the overture to *The Magic Flute*. That he made something out of it, as he did of Salieri's little march, that neither Clementi nor anyone else could touch is another matter.

Among the temporary rivals was Pasquale Anfossi (1727–97), a well-regarded composer, about whose opera *Il Curioso indiscreto* Mozart said that "not a single piece of the opera was liked except the aria of mine that was used as an insert." (The aria was written for Aloysia Lang, Mozart's sister-in-law, who sang at the performance.) The outstanding domestic rival was Carl Ditters von Dittersdorf (1739–99), a self-created noble like Weber and Gluck, and like them, a distinguished composer and virtuoso performer, a favorite of the emperor, who had long conversations with him about music. On one of these occasions the emperor asked him what he thought of the "talented" Mozart: "He has more than talent, Sire, he has genius." Dittersdorf and Mozart were on friendly terms, but the young master could not help being disheartened when Dittersdorf's opera *Doctor und Apotheker*, a tremendous success, displaced *Figaro* in the repertory. There were also important transient competitors acclaimed at court, among them Cimarosa and Martin y Soler.

In addition, there was plenty of intrigue—opera is unimaginable without it, and so is Vienna—as well as all sorts of bad luck that made difficulties for Mozart. He had to wait months on end for the *Figaro* libretto because da Ponte was busy with another libretto—for Salieri, of course. Yet all the decent musicians, not only Salieri, knew that this mercurial young man was not of this world. There is the moving story told by several witnesses who attended the dress rehearsal of *Le Nozze di Figaro*, when both stage and pit spontaneously erupted with bravos. *Don Giovanni*, though a triumph in Prague, did not elicit bravos in Vienna; except for Haydn, a generous admirer of Mozart, and the emperor, no one liked it, and Mozart was counseled to rework the score. He and da Ponte made some changes (K. 540a–c), but success did not come in the composer's lifetime, and in 1788 the great opera disappeared from the repertory.

We may guess from the foregoing what happened to Mozart's efforts to obtain a good court appointment. The emperor, though he really admired Mozart's music, was aware of the constant jockeying for position among the members of his large musical establishment, often necessitating his intervention, and he may well have been reluctant to add to the turmoil such a potentially divisive person, who by his sheer overwhelming musical presence would exacerbate the situation. All Mozart got for his petition, submitted with such hope, was a minor title at a very low salary. Incidentally, in his application for the post of second court conductor, he referred to the principal conductor as "the able Salieri."

If Salieri was guilty of anything, it is here that we could find fault. Neither his secure appointment nor his numerous successes would have made him immune from feelings of jealousy toward the incredibly gifted young master who produced one masterpiece after another that put every other's work in the shade. Perhaps he did wish to safeguard his own position at Mozart's expense. It does seem that, as the emperor's principal musical advisor, he might have overcome any resistance the monarch might have had, but we do not know whether he attempted to do so, whether he sat by passively, or whether he actually opposed the appointment. All we know is that neither Dittersdorf nor even the mighty chancellor of the realm, Prince Kaunitz, who did try to sway the emperor on Mozart's behalf, got anywhere.

With the death of the great and knowledgeable patron of music Joseph II, all hope for obtaining the position that Mozart and his father had so eagerly sought also died. Leopold II, although he retained the court music establishment—noblesse oblige—did not care for music; among the changes he ordered were plans for a new opera house with considerably enlarged loges to permit card-playing and chess, the favored way to sit out the recitatives. Salieri, dissatisfied with the situation, resigned his directorship of the opera but retained his title and the administration of church music and of musical events at court; he was too famous and too much of an ornament to the court to be dismissed.

Essentially, Mozart's tragedy was that because he could not attain a suitable position, which was partly bad luck, partly the fault of his temperament, he was reduced to the existence of a freelance artist, a career in those days not yet possible for a composer in Central Europe; only a few traveling virtuosos could make a living that way. Handel did achieve such independence on a grand scale in England, where the free-enterprise system, not yet known in the arts in Austria, was in full swing, and where he could create his own position as a solid English businessman-impresario. But even if that had been possible, Mozart's congenital inability to manage his finances would have doomed him. Constanze, too, was a poor manager of what little money they had, and was borne down by pregnancies and ill health.

After a brief life that started with success and ended amid many privations and unfulfilled hopes, leaving behind a host of incomparable works, Mozart died at only thirty-six, but his memory will live forever. Salieri's instinct was correct—a divine light shines from his music.

Salieri, although he lived a full span, covered with honors, admired by colleagues and distinguished pupils unpersuaded by the ugly rumors, is almost completely forgotten. It is regrettable that his large output has not yet been thoroughly investigated; the scurrilous legend of his unsavory doings is to some extent responsible for the neglect of his music.

Amadeus, whatever its virtues as entertainment, is offensive in its injustice to both Mozart and Salieri, and will unfortunately give many in its extensive audience an enduringly twisted view of these composers. Its author, adept at the mystifying clarification, offers feuilleton psychology instead of genuine appraisal of the soul. In Mozart he gives us a coarse naif; but Mozart had a maturity of artistic vision that could not exist in so shallow a personality. He had the power to will himself into a serenity, a wholeness of spirit that cannot be doubted. Even faithful and insightful biographies cannot make plausible such a miracle.

In the end, *Amadeus* is an amorphous muddle of ideas crippled by their contradiction of recorded facts, yet slick and overlaid with a varnish of cinematic éclat. The contention, advanced by Schaffer in the play's preface, that one may freely indulge in this kind of "edited" truth without paying a price for distortion is contradicted by an earlier playwright, Ben Jonson: "Man may securely sinne, but safely never."

A Music Master for
the White House

Some of the London papers took Queen Elizabeth gently to task for the type of music performed at her receptions. It riled the British, who look back upon a proud past of "official" ceremonial music, that their well-educated Queen should have such mediocre taste, and that she should be unaware of some of the magnificent traditions that surround court functions. The papers tactfully refrained from comparing her musical taste with that of her predecessor of the same name, though they could have pointed out that Good Queen Bess was indeed a connoisseur.

Under the first two Hanoverians, the man called to furnish music for ceremonial occasions was none other than Handel. Whenever there was a state function they put on a fine show, mostly with music especially composed for the occasion, but also performing great music of the past.

I don't have to mention the magnificence of the court music at Versailles, but Vienna, Dresden, Madrid, St. Petersburg, and other seats of government always saw to it that at important state functions, representative music should be heard instead of mere facile entertainment. The office of Master of the

From the *New York Herald-Tribune*, 27 September 1959

Queen's Music is still in existence, but unfortunately, the royal family no longer pays any heed to it. What they do these days in Madrid or Berlin I do not know, but in Moscow they usually put on a first-class musical demonstration whenever they want to entertain visiting dignitaries. As to our own White House, last week the newspapers again reported in detail the artistic fare on a state occasion in Washington, and it does not make for heart-warming reading.

Lest anyone counter with the usual argument that we don't go in for royal trappings, I should like to state at the outset that the founders of the Republic did envision the creation of such a tradition and that their musical tastes were by no means negligible.

Jefferson, a man of great culture, was a pretty good violinist who played duets with Patrick Henry. Benjamin Franklin played on half a dozen instruments, was the inventor of a seventh, and also wrote some penetrating observations that can be put down as the first American musical criticism. There were many other American gentleman musicians who were respected amateurs, but I am singling out Jefferson and Franklin because they were convinced that this country should emulate the state functions they had witnessed in Europe. They saw no reason why only a monarchy should have the privilege of putting its best artistic foot forward when the nation's prestige was involved. Jefferson, an ardent democrat who hated class institutions and arbitrary rule so much that he refused to read Walter Scott because of the latter's feudal sentiments, cannot be accused of wanting America to ape royal manners. And, indeed, if we look at such bourgeois-commercial political states as, for instance, the Hanseatic free cities, we can see that he was right. Hamburg had no royal pomp and circumstance on state occasions, but plenty of good and elaborate music.

These thoughts were prompted by the musicale given at the White House for Mr. Khrushchev and a large assembly of prominent guests. The occasion was an important one, for time and again it has been claimed that the Russian premier was invited principally to see for himself the United States, its people, its institutions, and its culture.

The comrades must have been properly impressed by our standard of living; gold plates to sop up the gravy from, sterling silver knives to lick, crystal glasses to slurp from, the highest in the culinary arts, beautiful flowers everywhere, and the most expert service by waiters whose wages would be the envy of our college professors. All this was doubtless overwhelming, but the music that accompanied this splendid affair must have been puzzling to them—and to a good many of the Americans present.

During the dinner the famous Marine Band played what the papers called "classical Russian airs—Prokofiev, Shostakovitch and Rimsky-Korsakov—as well as songs from Broadway musicals." This was a little ambiguous, for one cannot tell whether the "classical airs" were meant for the Russians, the Broadway ditties for the Americans, or vice versa. But the formal part of the evening clarified the artistic policies. After dinner the distinguished company was treated to a concert by Fred Waring and his Pennsylvanians in a program that included "Oh, What a Beautiful Morning," "Zippity Doo Dah," "Happy Wanderer," "Ah Sweet Mystery of Life," and "Over the Rainbow."

Now I have, of course, no quarrel with anyone's private musical taste. If he prefers "Zippity Doo Dah" to a Schubert song, that is his unquestioned privilege—but not on an occasion such as a state dinner. There were quite a few persons in the assembly who must have been acutely embarrassed, and there were also undoubtedly some Russians who know the difference between popular jingles and art. Ever since Stalin set the precedent, Russian commissars have doubled in music criticism, as Mr. Shostakovitch can tell you.

The White House has a consulting architect, an arbiter for etiquette; it uses the best interior decorators; it does not hang chromos on the walls; and of course it does not call in the short order cook from the nearest diner to plan the menu for the meal. Would it not be proper to have a "Master of the President's Music" to be consulted for ceremonial occasions so that such a primitive cultural demonstration might be avoided? It would not cost a red cent to the taxpayer, because any distinguished American musician would gladly assume the office as a matter of patriotic duty.

Menace of the Machine

In a recent issue *Time* magazine, under the heading "Science," reports a meeting held at Britain's National Physical Laboratory during an international conference on the "Mechanization of Thought Processes." The assembled scientists bewailed "the irrational human reverence for human intelligence," and in particular, Dr. Marvin L. Minsky of M. I. T. seemed to be convinced that there is nothing special about creativity, while Dr. S. Gill of Ferranti Ltd. was confident that machines will be made in the near future that will compose music.

Now I am going by what I have read in *Time*, and their reporting may be inaccurate and slanted toward the paradoxical, flippant, and the deliberately controversial, which they love so much, but there is no getting away from the motto of the conference: "Whatever a human being can do, an appropriate machine can do too."

Such a "scientific" view gives one the horrible feeling of the disenchantment of the world, that there are no more dreams or aspirations left, only "mechanized thought processes." The men who advance this atrocious idea

From the *New York Herald-Tribune*, 4 January 1959

are not charlatans, they are acknowledged scientists, but with all their technical training and experience, they are utterly naive and myopic dilettantes in
human affairs.

The great knowledge gained from the tremendous progress achieved in
physics, chemistry, biology, and other natural sciences should contribute
immensely to the enrichment of our world, not rob it of its beauties. What
these scientists offer is a radical changing of the world, its order and sense, a
new relationship of things spiritual and material; in a word, a new order of life
itself. But this demands a new type of mankind whose *raison d'être* no longer
rests in the human spirit. We shall have many technicians and artisans but no
artists, many scientists but no scholars, many believers but no mystics. And
there will be the great mass of blind worshippers of the gracious living afforded
by the machine.

There are no real cultural attainments without high human values. Every
true civilization can be recognized by the degree of humanity it embodies, for
all culture, and more specifically all art, is a process of ennoblement. What
will happen to that inspiration which envelopes musical creation with poetic
warmth and color: will the composing machine construct it by mechanical
means? Can the machine experience a mood, an atmosphere, can it be supra-
rational, can it face truth? And above all, will it have moral and ethical
convictions?

A great masterpiece is unique, it is never duplicated, and it never returns,
for it is the creation of an individual soul. But even the type is not made a type
because of its averageness, but because in it are entwined all human and social
moments of an entire historical period. Real art gives the whole man and his
whole society and does not offer samples, and the aesthetic point of view itself
is saturated with humanistic, moral, and social points of view, for the world
grows from man's soul and mind, it is not an abstraction.

All this may seem faded truism, but it must be reaffirmed as the final
wisdom of our existence, now threatened by the miserable and sad caricature
of culture created by an inanimate machine. Music, like the other arts,
brightens and darkens according to the brightening and darkening of the
spiritual human substance, for the spiritual first rules from within and then
impresses itself on the outside. There was no time—and never will be—when
this was otherwise; yet these men of science want to grow the bloom from the
fruit.

We are living in the chaos of a disintegrating civilization. What is old has
been lost and abandoned; the new, only dimly divined, is yet far from crystalli-
zation. But we cannot abandon our fervent belief that if there is to arise a new

edifice of life and faith, it will be built on the eternally old foundations of the human spirit.

What these scientists offer is the philosophy of despair, the apotheosis of the destruction of human culture. It is tragic that in their naiveté they are advocating something essentially similar to the brutal conformity of thought the Communists and the Fascists extract from their artists and writers. If our champions of the mechanization of thought processes have their way—and our education, now hysterical because of the sputniks, is dangerously inclined to follow them—they will not kill the artist if he does not fall in line with their machine, but they will just as surely starve him to death.

They might profitably read a little confession Mozart made, for in their calculations they have forgotten something that no machine can experience and convey: "Real genius without a heart is a monstrosity. For it is neither intelligence nor imagination alone, not even both together that make a genius; love, love is the soul of genius."

On Performance Practice

From the Preface for a Book
on Performance Practice

> Where you come from is gone, where you think
> you are going to never was, and where you are is
> no good unless you get away from it.
> —FLANNERY O'CONNOR

The present book began some time ago in a rather chance encounter with an ensemble playing early Haydn quartets. The occasion had an aura of reverential solemnity, the program notes containing excellent information (this was a resident quartet in a major university) as well as the entire history and pedigree of each of the four instruments upon which the quartet was playing. But the sound was thin and matte, the playing very cautious, and the tuning slipped perceptibly, requiring considerable corrective activity between movements (all gut strings and old bows were used). Well, it was a rather dull evening, and I put it down as one of those well-meant but naive historical demonstrations that greatly inhibit performers used to different instruments as well as to different playing conventions and standard pitch. One thing intrigued me, however: the cello player held his fine large eighteenth-century instrument between his knees, as one holds a viola da gamba; yet I could plainly see the tip of the withdrawn peg protruding from the instrument. I learned that the cellist did not use the pin that anchors the instrument safely to the floor because he was instructed to refrain from using that helpful gadget: "it was not invented until the second half of the nineteenth century and therefore could not be used in eighteenth-century music without creating a historical anachronism." This waiting for the exact historical moment to make its appearance conjures up the vision of a traveler about to cross the equator watching for the bump when the wheels of his carriage hit the line. The poor cellist was visibly inconvenienced, sitting and playing in an awkward position, as busy adjusting his hold as he was attending to his artistic duties. From this encounter and many later such experiences comes this venture. (The question why such unconditionally rigid historicism is so exquisitely absorbing to some scholars and musicians takes us from the realm of art to that of psychology which, I am afraid, is far removed from my competence.)

This book is, then, not a systematic historical study of performance practice; it is concerned not so much with the exact restoration of old music as with the interplay of scholarship with that dynamic process of assimilation by which a contemporary artist re-creates in his own terms the masterpieces of the past. I do not impose solutions; I propose a critical, reflective questioning of the Orphic mysteries of performance practice. The principles advanced on the following pages are modest: they attempt to mediate between the opposing factions, seeking not a merely convenient compromise, but a *modus vivendi* faithful to the requirements of scholarship while responsive to the needs of artistic performance.

Music that is removed from our cultural environment is not readily accessible, because it cannot be directly connected with our experience and to the symbols with which we are accustomed; we have lost the consensus that supported it. Some old music is as distant and puzzling to us as the dinosaurs, with only some bones and footprints left behind, and there is no easy way of telling how this music was played and how it sounded. As Burney said, "It is with Musick as with delicate Wines which are injured by Time however well kept." Our knowledge is incomplete, the issues themselves are formidably complex, and there are an extraordinary number of variables. Musicology, which opened many doors that had been closed for centuries, must approach the task of resuscitating the great treasure of old music with respect and forbearance, weighing the possible against the probable, with a willingness to accommodate our own music sensibilities.

The arts of each epoch are unique and can never be duplicated or even fully recalled, for art is vision. Furthermore, every age finds in the past those elements in which it can discern something of itself. We know the spirit of other eras only to a certain degree; we see in them what our own age enables us to see. Medieval man read Christ into Virgil, the French Revolution found the expression of its own civic freedom in the Roman Republic, and Gounod heard Bach with Werther's ears. Similarly, when we identify ourselves with Josquin or Schütz, we do it with our feet still in the present. Yet it is precisely this dualism that makes the enjoyment of this long-departed music possible. Because our own musical institutions are largely the creations of the nineteenth century, ideas and concepts concerning the performance of "early" or "old" music have until recently been too frequently the residue of that period, reflecting practices then acceptable.

As the exploration and restoration of the authentic performance practice of earlier music became an important branch of musicology, all of us felt like discoverers glimpsing through the fog the shores of an unknown land, marveling at the new vistas opened by scholarship. To the extent that the study of performance practice by scholars has opened entirely new insights into what is vaguely called old or early music, it has been a most welcome spur to fruitful activity both in education and in practice; but to the extent that the new discipline attempts to structure and regiment the whole experience of musicians concerned with pre-Romantic music, it may actually become an impediment to the revival of old music. Unfortunately, there is an ever-growing party that claims privileged intimacy with the private qualities of the old masters, worshipping a purism unsullied by the realities of life. Such elitism threatens the all-important relationship of music to social needs and social purposes; the perils are as great as the promises. We must search for comparative cultural values, expose the contemporary relevance of artistic traditions—historical and cultural. Otherwise we are likely to create "cultural clutter rather than a culture" (T. S. Eliot).

We must not forget that in any branch of learning, if it is not a mere collection of dogmas, certain propositions are always appearing in connection with new circumstances, new conditions, and new relationships; we ourselves are in the midst of a historical process of change. To present as universal verities matters admitting quite variable interpretations is to ignore the fact that there is no absolute consistency in the spirit of even a well-delineated age, and that many a great work reaches out well beyond the limits of its birth. A great artist's horizon is broad; he sees further than the conventions of his time; he offers visions that allow him to speak directly to, and be understood by, people who live in entirely different periods. Then again, an equally great artist may defy the march of time and lag behind without in the least diminishing his stature. Bach, in whom the German Baroque reached its peak, hit his stride at a time when the stylistic metamorphosis that was to lead to another culmination at the end of the same century was already under way, and Palestrina was still active when the Venetians were inaugurating an entirely new style. It goes without saying that aesthetic standards cannot claim permanence either. Thus the champions of absolute historical authenticity in performance are in error when in their efforts to seek universal precepts of performance practice they use the same procedures at diverse levels and in diverse proportions. The same process established for one era may work for only a section of that era, or even contradict a slightly earlier or later practice. The rich diversity of music certainly negates the rigidly stereotyped image of a style, and hence performance; for it creates many exceptions to the rule. It is not possible to establish a system from which to extract predictive, manipulative information for the performance of "old music," for there are no absolute or constant interpretive values that can be ranged into concrete categories.

No matter how we phrase the question, we cannot obtain unequivocal answers, because we have no photocopy of the past. We are trying to penetrate the intriguing forest of this past to recapture moods and feelings long since vanished. The excessive weight of historical, archival, and ideological considerations; the vast, inchoate, and by no means integrated areas of musical experience, with their absence of fixed reference points and their reverberations too faint to be trusted; the avalanche of research material that can suffocate the genuinely interesting aspects of the music—all this can lead only to what Whitehead called the "fallacy of misplaced correctness."

No doubt exception will be taken to many of my suggestions; on the other hand, my personal experience with musicians as performers—I was once in their ranks—persuades me that many, even among those raised in the new faith, may welcome them. I regret to say that it would be quite impossible these days to do what the famous lutenist, Denis Gaultier, offered so amiably in the preface to his *Pièces de luth* (1669): "If anyone has trouble making sense of what is in my book, I shall enlighten him with the greatest pleasure if he does me the honor of coming to see me."

Authenticity

The great of literature and the visual arts who have cast off earthly dust have triumphantly taken their place in the pantheon of memory. Literary works are published in collected editions, while museums and private patrons vie for the canvases and sculptures of "old masters." Millennia have not made us forget the *Iliad* or *Oedipus*, the *Winged Victory*, or the *Discus Thrower*; they are alive, because they are seen afresh with the eyes of each new generation. But among the great of music there are many whose works are never heard, whose very names are unfamiliar to highly cultivated persons cognizant even of the minor poets and painters of the past. Medieval music—indeed, much later music too—remained forgotten until musical historiographers began to discover it. Yet, though musicologists exposed to view much magnificent art of past composers, we have been unable to recapture for them the celebrity and popularity they once enjoyed as the equals of their great contemporaries in literature, painting, and architecture. To publish the collected works of one of these musicians, the necessary funds, amounting to a small fraction of the millions that museums gladly pay for a single painting, must be begged, cajoled, or borrowed from governments, foundations, or individual patrons.

The question has been raised whether the modern age represents a qualitative break with the past, whether we who live in this century can really cross a historical divide. As nineteenth-century progressivism devalued the past, traditions were seen as the means by which institutions imposed outgrown patterns on the present. Our argument is not, however, that one generation is bound to the limits of perception established as standard by another, but that new interpretive patterns may contradict the circumstances of history, that "authenticity" may be self-defeating. Enlightened as we are by modern musicology, our historical sense does not permit anachronistic performances such as were popular only a few decades ago. We no longer hear performances of Handel oratorios, like Sir Thomas Beecham's recordings of *Messiah* and *Solomon*, that attribute to an eighteenth-century composer the premises of a nineteenth-century churchman and a twentieth-century orchestrator. It is not that such artistic practices were not known in the past. Mattheson relates as a matter of fact that he prepared Giuseppe Orlandini's opera *Nerone* for performances by "rearranging the order of arias, setting the recitatives anew, and adding a number of my own pieces"; Bach doctored Palestrina; Schütz fixed up Gabrieli; Christian Bach lent a little help to Gluck even though that composer was still alive and active; and Mozart reorchestrated Handel. Later we have Mendelssohn retouching Bach, Berlioz bowdlerizing Gluck, Mahler recomposing Weber, and Grieg adding harmonic spice to Mozart's sonatas. We have seen the spoken dialogues in the German Singspiel and Bach's recitatives orchestrated, and so forth. But as authenticity becomes a battle cry, we are no less in danger of counterfeiting history.

The cardinal criterion of performance practice is often the use of instruments coeval with the composition, without any of the devices that came into use after the time in question. Although to many of us the sound of old instruments as they are played today, especially the vibrato-less strings, as well as the low pitch, is strange, at times even unpleasant, the principle seems at first so self-evident that one hesitates to dismiss it. Yet it cannot be granted, as many insist, that authenticity and stylistic integrity demand the retention of "original instruments," no matter how unwieldy and obsolete they may be. Such practices have contributed to the exaggerated polarization of "old" and "new" music, a posthumous piety bestowing a sepulchral respectability on an imagined world. It is this antiquarianism that prevents the true revival of old music, because what it is essentially doing is recapturing the external raiment but not the heart of the music. A few original instruments, as a matter of fact, are preserved in fairly good repair, and excellent replicas are made with the aid of modern research and craftsmanship; but we still do not know exactly how those instruments were played and what the ensembles sounded like. What Burney said about the music of antiquity is still valid for the centuries before the nineteenth: "Who will be bold enough to say how these immortal bards did play and sing?" Not only have the instruments' timbres changed, but so have the techniques of voice production; for each age creates its own ideal of sound. We are simply unable to hear music with the ears of Frescobaldi's or Haydn's audiences, and old instruments and other period-bound agents may actually fail to translate the composer's meaning for us.

The composer of an earlier time did not necessarily regard his work as definitive in its first version; to him every finished work was also fair material for another one. Throughout the sixteenth century, certain composers were fond of adding, perhaps years later, one or more parts to a finished composition of their own or of someone else; many a fine polyphonic chanson exists in four, in five, or in six-voice versions. Then there are the architectural second thoughts, like the momentous addition of a single measure to the beginning of the second movement of the *Hammerklavier* Sonata, after the movement had once been finished. Nor did the composer, especially in the Baroque era, write down every detail in the score, because when he did not play or conduct his own work he could count on the performer, a musician thoroughly familiar with the reigning convention; indeed, the latter was a veritable coauthor, and he customarily played with a good deal of latitude. In addition, the audience brought to the occasion a consensus, a rapport with the conventions of the day, which the composer also counted upon.

We are now attempting to fill in for ourselves the omitted details; to restore, with the aid of contemporaneous treatises, the grace notes and other ornamentation, to spike the da capo arias with our embellishments, and so forth. This can and should be done, but with tact and moderation. Performance practice is not like taxidermy; yet in many instances the purportedly authentic embellishments made by twentieth-century minds are like glass eyes and plastic tongues. The laudable aim is to enable us to hear a piece of music as it was heard by its contemporaries; but the assumption that this is possible is clearly questionable, because it equates a group in one society with another of a considerably different nature. We cannot determine with precision to what extent our concept, our projection of an earlier style, is genuine or even approximate, because interaction of the three entities—composer, performer, and audience—as we experience it can be quite different from the experience of another age. We cannot hear even later composers, such as Beethoven, quite as their contemporaries did, because in the intervening years our musical techniques, listening habits, concepts of sound and pitch have all changed. Although Schindler, Beethoven's amanuensis, described the master's piano playing from actual firsthand experience, his *words* still leave us with our own conjectures and imagination, because described sound is as far short of reality as are described meals.

Performance based mainly on archival evidence risks the danger of becoming independent of reality and ending by living for its own sake, seemingly to freeze and encapsulate the archival findings rather than to transcend them. The industrious search for authenticity threatens to become an abstract business divorced from the enjoyment of art; it bureaucratizes the performance of music. If we say that a work must be understood historically, there is the possibility that it will not be appreciated for its own sake, but will merely appear as a specimen of a stylistic development. It is a mistake to assume that, by ascertaining through historical studies the conditions and practical application of principles contemporaneous with a composition, the essence of the work had been accounted for. So long as we insist on operating on a categorical plane of historical authenticity to the exclusion of artistic intuition, dictating the one "right" concept, we simply make performance practice an end in itself. When it becomes a "body of knowledge," as it is respectfully called in the university, it is in a sense a dead body, usually overloaded with terminology and interpretive hermeneutics.

An argument can be compelling in print, but far less so carried into actual performance; and it may turn out that its historical basis has no relevance whatever to the artistic situation. A good example is the exclusion of women from the choir, which was not a musical but a *theological* fiat long since abandoned; yet the great dramatic choral works are still often performed with treble and alto sung by boys in the name of faithfulness to historical facts. This is simply a surrender of musical instinct and judgment to superseded conditions.

The premises of the authenticity movement are briefly that facts and figures pertaining to the performance of old music can be researched, collated, coordinated, and brought into a comprehensive, unified, and logical system on the basis of which historically authentic performances can be achieved. Such data must be interpreted, however; and there are usually alternative interpretations, cross-cutting, tangled, case-based academic reconstructions. Since there is no such thing as one unquestionable set of rules, precedent must be given to musical niceties, and every case must be judged on its musical merits.

Nikolaus Harnoncourt, one of the *chefs d'école* of the movement, has flatly stated that he believes only in the original manuscripts and does not accept any modern critical edition. This is a sentimental delusion, and it can be seriously misleading. It must be stated that he, and many like-minded specialists, though often excellent musicians, are not breveted and hardly know how to deal with old manuscripts, notational systems, tablatures (Bach and Handel still used them!), and so forth; these disciplines call for arduous studies—a nodding acquaintance with them is not enough. Since archival evidence concerning the musical practices of past centuries is graphic, not auditory, our deductions and conclusions depend on assumptions; and it is better to end with definitions than to begin with them. The relationship between data and conclusions is far more complex and admits far more intervening variables than is often imagined. Also, many of the data are anecdotal, and their origin nebulous. A cursory look at thematic catalogues will show the frequent unhappy note: "Original manuscript lost," so we do depend on copies and both early and modern editions, and are compelled to use our own critical faculties in searching for authenticity. Obviously, there is a long way from manuscript to actual performance.

Though the past reverberates in the present, we cannot replay history because it permits only one run-through. The fact is that historical authenticity alone will never lead us to a true revival without an admixture of a degree of our own artistic beliefs and instincts. The advocates of unconditional conformity to authenticity in the interpretation of old music, in depending on archival fidelity, may fail in fidelity to the composer's artistic intentions. To approach old music, scholarship is manifestly needed; but when scholarship alone proves to be inadequate, we must break through the carapace of theoretical and historical facts and seek an artistic solution. This is what the brave Solesmes Benedictines did with their revival of Gregorian chant; they tried hard to arrive at the truth with superb scholarship, but ended up with beautiful artistic creativity. While much genuine progress has been made and some convincing conclusions reached, many others are hypotheses noteworthy chiefly for their ingenuity. But no art is understandable from history alone. There are the imponderables. And the first thing about imponderables is to recognize their existence. The discontinuity between the old and the new should not be exaggerated, since aspects of a later musical culture bear the impress of the earlier practices in spite of the differences in external features.

There are also independent variables which are involved in intricate ways with the subsequent history of music. The purely historical approach may enumerate many facts that are undeniable in themselves but whose connections with one another are often tenuous or nonexistent. Their rigid observance can lead to painful collisions with sociology, economics, and, above all, aesthetics.

Performance practices so established contain implicit biases which hinder the instincts of sensitive musicians; and we end not with a gracious resurrection, but with living art reduced to abstractions. But we do want, most of us, a sense of wonder and mystery in art, not merely abstract cause and effect relationships. Evidently, worship is often offered to an ideal, and the supreme achievement sometimes seems to be to present old music in a way that is quite at variance with our experiences, customs, and sensibilities. At times it is difficult to tell whether the antiquarians are perpetuating artistic values or embalming them. There is also a tendency to look for greatness in everything that is old, and not infrequently rust is taken for patina.

Abstract antiquarianism cannot give a valid picture of art; its formal mechanism can lead only to a technicized music making in which the performer's natural musical sensibilities are anesthetized. It negates the very concept of interpretation by placing abstraction ahead of immediate experience, causing the performance to lose its qualities of spontaneous creativity and to become not so much a performance of a work of art as an example selected and prepared. A distinction must be made between exemplification and expression, and care must be taken not to imitate too closely the restoration techniques practised in art museums. We also have our musical restorers who are adept at dealing with worm holes, cracks, and darkened varnish, and their work is very valuable; but it is not final, for old music cannot be handled like old paintings. Sound is a living thing. It is always part of the present. It is produced by living persons for living ears.

A new branch of learning such as performance practice, whose scholarly existence is still somewhat uncertain because of the considerable number of amateurs flocking to its flag, tends to assume sectarian traits and attitudes. Its partisans, with admirable devotion, want to present the past to us with unsoiled hands. But such pursuits of Utopia are accompanied by an implicit opposition between the enlightened and the benighted, the refined and the philistines, the "right" and the "wrong," together with a certain xenophobia toward anything outside the devotees' world. The severely circumscribed restorations that avoid any concessions to our own musical sensibilities create a dismaying gulf around old music. The so-called authentic performances with original instruments cannot be transferred from the recording studio and its cleverly manipulated microphones, or from the congenial small auditorium to a concert hall large enough to accommodate more than a token audience, so that the resuscitated old music could become part of our musical life. The economic and sociocultural problems are topped by an aesthetic paradox: the more secure and polished the performances have become, the more it becomes obvious that they do not represent historical reality and authenticity so much as an ideal rendition that never existed. Their procedures may apply in some cases. They may have confirmation from archival sources, or from general local conditions; but in their total commitment, they are unable to compromise. Reality is more fragile, unstable, and, above all, more diverse than theory.

The theory and practice of authentic performances is well advanced, but its advocates seldom consider how these performances are heard. The sight of instruments no longer in use and the unfamiliar sound of those whose shape is familiar give the music an unavoidable tinge of exoticism. The intention of being strictly faithful to history therefore results in an aesthetic impression false to history, because the exoticism is an accretion. All this indicates that our real aim should be to approximate the musical experience of the original listeners, not to strive for an unattainable absolute authenticity. Thorough historical studies are emphatically required, but what is also required is an acknowledgment of the validity of our own aesthetic norms and ideals of live sound. Our aesthetic concepts of the sound of a balanced instrumental ensemble and a good mixed chorus is opposed to the pallid strings, the weak-toned winds, the unnatural voice of falsettists and countertenors, and even the immature and neutral voice of boys when used in the great dramatic works which they sing without understanding the meaning of the words. Germicidally clean performances, the rigorous application of the sacred cosmetics of ornamentation and embellishments, the asceticism that is opposed to creativity; all these, if they prevail unconditionally, may separate the intransigent reformers, and with them, an immense and infinitely rich body of music, from living art.

Performance practice should not represent a concept essentially different from and opposed to modern practices and modern values; some flexibility and a little accommodation is called for. Should we simply dismiss all performers who play Bach or Scarlatti on a Steinway and wait until there is a harpsichord in every front parlor? Shall we lay aside the Boehm flute until everyone can play the recorder and the Baroque flute? Ignore keys and valves that make wind instruments more secure and versatile, and hope that the statutes will be changed so that we can again have castratos? The ideal, "strictly authentic" performances, with the claim to sole validity, threatens to place the "correct" performance with all its appurtenances apart from everyday musical life, surrounding it with an aura of worshipful faith.

Let us take a few examples to demonstrate the fallacy of authenticity claimed by performers for all music they present from the Middle Ages to 1800, and of late well beyond this once sacred *terminus ad quem*. As we look at the songs of the Middle Ages, the landmarks are blurred, yet the scene is engrossing: Crusaders, troubadours, trouvères, Goliards, Minnesingers—all of them happily producing innumerable songs. And in the fifteenth and sixteenth centuries, there were also those malleable humbugs, the Meistersingers, the solid German tradespeople who commendably wanted their own art and whose rules of composition were so strict and farfetched that the minds of the doughty butchers, bakers, and candlestick-makers were completely hedged in. They look engagingly romantic in Wagner's great opera, but their own music—or as much as we can make of it—is not very palatable to us.

Regrettably, we proceed in this maze of medieval song through confusion and false leads, because we have few tangible facts to work with. Reinventing myths may be the only way of preserving them. But performers who are loath to abandon this large and colorful literature are nevertheless against reinventing the myths. To illustrate the situation, consider a historical concert offering troubadour songs, the singer accompanying himself on a rebec or viol or some other "original" instrument; we know such scenes from pictorial sources. The audience is happily persuaded that, after all, this medieval music is not so forbidding and primitive as some books would have it. The only catch is that neither the tune nor the accompaniment can be vouched for. Yes, the pitches of the songs are there, and they are genuine; but we do not know anything about their duration and rhythm. Three distinguished scholars spent a lifetime trying to discover the rhythmic system of these songs, but they arrived at three different hypotheses. They were followed by many others, and the large literature of medieval monophonic songs remains almost as doubtful as the songs the Sirens sang. As to the accompaniments, they are like ill-fitting clip-on ties; nobody knows, or is ever likely to know, what the troubadours and trouvères or jongleurs and minstrels played while they sang. In sum, while the tune is nice and expressive, the accompaniment pleasant, what we are listening to is a new modern composition, "medieval" like Orff's *Carmina Burana*; there can be no question of authenticity. Then there is the uncomfortable diversity of editions. Pérotin's *Sederunt principes*, one of the greatest monuments of Gothic music is available in several modern editions, all of them differing from one another. These editions were not made by amateurs like some earlier volumes of the *Bachgesellschaft*, but by distinguished scholars; yet they could not produce a "definitive" text. Once more we must choose and settle on the version that we consider, if not authentic, the most convincing.

Baroque opera, now being revived with great enthusiasm and professions of authenticity, is another example. In those days, the elapsed time between composition and first performance was usually a few weeks—not years or even months—depending on how much old music was recalled for active service. By the second performance, composer and librettist began to make alterations because both of them had second thoughts gained from the first performance. Then, when new singers joined the cast, all kinds of alterations, transpositions, and re-compositions took place to suit the new singers' capabilities; protocol had to be observed, because the second *donna* or *uomo*, did not rate elaborate music. This in turn necessitated changes in the libretto; but such changes— there were usually many—may not have been entered into the conducting score. There was little time, and the conductor was usually the composer himself, who knew what he was about.

But now the part-books did not agree with the conducting score. When the opera went from theater to theater, it was liberally changed by the resident maestro; indeed, at times it was emasculated. Many of the celebrated traveling singers carried with them their personal repertory, a satchel full of favorite arias from various operas which, more often than not, they forced upon the impresario or conductor to insert into the opera being produced, no matter whether they suited their new environment or not. The consequence of this laissez-faire attitude was that a Baroque opera was seldom performed twice in the same form, and we are dealing with a plethora of arias all belonging to the same work but going in and out of the score. It takes elaborate detective work to establish an "authentic" score from this crazy quilt. Yet there was a certain unity in these manhandled operas. The Italians regarded opera as a plausible unity of text, music, decor, and public as the necessary dramaturgical principle; they wanted a fairly coherent theatrical production. And while they condoned the excesses of the castratos, they always watched the librettos and followed the action, such as it was. Indeed, in most cases, only the libretto was printed. In order to make a revived Baroque opera acceptable and believable, we must consider this aesthetic demand for the theater. To be sure, we must make changes, select from the accumulated arias the ones we judge to be the most likely to serve this end, and then examine and adjust the connecting tissues; hence we are the arbiters for authenticity. The custom of performing nearly all the arias, including the "emergency arias" (*aria di baule*) creates only an inorganic jumble. The critical edition should contain all the music associated with an opera, but performance is another matter.

There is a fascination in exploring a wide-open field in which discoveries can still be made any day. Also, the idea of authenticity derived from historical research appeals to common sense for its logic, directness, and seeming simplicity. Thus the goal is clear and desirable; the implementation and the procedure to be followed, however, are far less so. Uncritical devotion to history and the construction of systems and modes of performances from disparate clues give rise to many unanswerable problems and endless arguments; never have so few reliable historical data yielded such far-ranging conclusions. What we must reject is not historical accuracy or the use of original instruments per se, but the rigid enforcement of incomplete and imperfect historical data and the virtual exclusion of any reasonable and sensible compromise.

History is in us; we are simultaneously bystanders and participants. The past is not behind us; our vitality depends on our ability and willingness to know, to value, and to draw from the past on which we plant our feet. We cannot forget that there were giants on the earth, that we tread the same earth they once trod, that the same sun that shines today is the sun that shone on Lasso and Bach. If we want to be entirely ourselves, we cannot separate ourselves from the past out of which we have come, and to which we are bound; it is always our present we are interpreting, but we are doing so by looking into the past. The question is that of new approaches, not only the solving of old riddles and problems.

There can be no doubt that the believers in the sole validity of historical accuracy in the performance of old music proceed with seriousness and devotion, and it must be acknowledged that this devotion is dangerously convincing, and that they have achieved a great deal. There are many fine musicians among them who realize that absolutely authentic performances are unattainable because, even in this information-laden age, there is no such abundance of facts on performance practice as would ensure absolute authenticity. Considering the inherent ambiguity of "authenticity," perhaps it would be advisable to use a less grandiloquent term and avoid it altogether!

Performance Practice
and the Voice

Singing is one of the primordial acts of man, the direct experience of his body, the immediate expression of his mental states and emotions. With a few exceptions, singing has occupied a central position in rites, pagan or Christian; people sang even without words, for they sang what is difficult to express in words. The human voice is the richest "instrument"; all others try to come as close to it as possible, and for centuries the authors of tracts and tutors urged violists, fiddlers, and wind players to emulate singers. Thus Telemann: "Singing is the fundament of all music. Whoever undertakes to compose must sing in his pieces, and whoever plays on instruments should be well acquainted with singing, hence the super-scription *cantabile* on many a piece of instrumental music." But to attain what Caccini called the *nobile maniera di cantare*, the singer must realize the expressive possibilities of the human voice beyond the acoustical and physi-ological facts; artistic singing must be learned and practiced. This was already recognized in antiquity, a fact corroborated by the Church Fathers, who equated this developed art with the "carnal pleasures" of the heathen and warned against submitting to the sensuous charms of the singing voice. With the Reformation and the "return to simple original Christian life and thought,"

Protestant theologians revived the writings of the Church Fathers and their fear of the sensuality of music. This was especially notable in areas that followed Calvin's teaching.

The history of artistic singing is vague and complicated, because it is closely bound to linguistics—that is, to speech patterns, rhythms, inflections, and verbal articulation in general. And, of course, singing is culturally determined by such institutions as the Church, the court, the theater, and so forth. This is not the place for the discussion of all these aspects in detail; though there are many abstract data available from Homer onward, we will restrict ourselves to singing and its techniques in such areas of Western art music as our performers are called upon to practice.

The new way of singing emerged in the Christian world with the founding in the fifth century of the Roman *schola cantorum,* and by the eighth century there were famous schools for singing in Metz and St. Gallen and subsequently in Paris, Cambrai, and other cathedral and monastic institutions, teaching the correct delivery of the chant. In the German Protestant Latin schools of the sixteenth to eighteenth centuries, participation in choral music was obligatory, and the amount of music taught in Bach's time, in what correspond to our high schools, would make our school boards blanch. Indeed, the cantor, the music teacher, was, next to the rector or principal, the most important and best-known member of the faculty.

The raw human vocal material has to be schooled and polished, made into an instrument that can be manipulated, "played" at will; but the human voice is as individual as its possessor, and universal rules of voice production beyond a few basic facts determined by the physiological construction of the vocal apparatus could never be established. In fact, the teaching of singing is still one of the most problematic subjects of musical pedagogy; yet without it, the finest natural voice could not be employed in the service of higher art. Though the basic elements of voice production were known in the Middle Ages, and a distinction was made between "pectoral," "guttural," and "head" tones, the pedagogy of voice training did not begin in earnest until the fifteenth century. By the middle of the next century, treatises appeared on how to sing "elegantly and suavely" (Hermann Finck, 1556). Then, by Mersenne's time, we begin to read about what today we call the physiology of voice production. In vocal instruction, the art of transforming the visual image of notation into sound is not aided by the sense of touch and by the control of the fingers and arms, as when playing an instrument. Vocal teaching can lead to good control of the "throat," but pitch is controlled by the ear. This ability is innate, though it can be considerably improved by practice.

The vocal cords have a dual role, for they are the organ of both speaking and singing. Most consonants as we enunciate them have a certain "explosive" nature which influences any vowels following them; though we are accustomed to this in speech, the explosion causes difficulties in singing. These facts hide serious impediments to any historical analysis, because language is constantly evolving across the centuries, and with it its pronunciation. We do not know exactly how medieval Latin or French or German were pronounced, and it is futile to train American singers to sing such texts; as a rule, neither they nor their teachers fully understand the words. Since there is no remedy for this situation, we often translate such texts, as for instance Provençal poems. It helps, but we really drop from the frying pan into the fire, for even modern French or German is essentially untranslatable for musical purposes.

All languages are based on certain "musical" inflections that characteristically color the letters and words, and these cannot be shifted from language to language. Modern vocal pedagogy recognizes the essential differences, as well as the connections between the speaking and singing voice, and considers the developing and polishing of speech mandatory before embarking on the training of the singing voice, because poor enunciation and a lack of the natural inflections of the language can ruin dramatic sense.

In Italy, the classic home of singing, teachers did not find it necessary to begin with improving the relationship between vowels and consonants in the spoken language, because Italian has few clusters of consonants. Even the raw Italian singing voice is largely devoid of the problems one encounters in other languages; it is naturally free, flexible, and euphonious, while other voices must acquire this quality by painstaking study and practice. It is for this reason that, in the earliest Italian treatises on singing, we find little analytical examination of the problems of voice production; their authors discuss the hygiene of the voice, and they pay much attention to the equalization of head and chest tones but are more interested in the purely musical aspects of singing.

The particular role and advantages of certain vowels was early recognized. Peri observes in the preface to his *Euridice*: "In our speech some words are so intoned that harmony can be based on them." Caccini is more specific: "The vowel 'u' produces a better effect in the soprano voice than in the tenor; the vowel 'i' makes a better effect in the tenor than the vowel 'u,'" and so forth. The librettists were fully aware of this; notably, Metastasio was remarkably skillful in fashioning his verse with constant regard for the placement of the syllables, which was one of the reasons for his tremendous vogue among composers. The critics, usually men of letters, who reject Metastasio's "frosty and formal" dramas are ignorant of the strict requirements with which Italian opera of the Baroque burdened the librettists. A singing voice developed according to the Italian principles of voice production functions well; but when such a singer is compelled to sing in German or Russian for any length of time, aesthetic values will suffer. Upon hearing a performance of an Italian opera troupe in Vienna, Hegel exclaimed: "Now I understand clearly why Rossini's music is denounced in Germany: that is because it is made for Italian throats."

It is obvious, then, that even though modern vocal training adopted the ideals of ancient Italian vocal culture, it could not adapt it as a direct heritage because of the entirely different phonetic structure of the individual languages which had their own millennial psycho-physiological past and mechanical conditioning. They rise and fall differently, and these qualities are not transferable. It is for this reason that translations of song and opera texts do violence to the original; but even if our artists sing in a language—Russian, for instance— which they do not really know but learn phonetically, they are doing a sort of travesty. The only solution is for singers to learn the language thoroughly and stay in its country for a while, getting their ears tuned to those "secret inflections." Only fast-moving buffo operas should be translated, because otherwise much of their humor and theatrical effect escapes the listener.

Before modern voice culture, which began in the nineteenth century, the old Italian smoothness and euphony of singing, which we somewhat loosely call *bel canto*, was only exceptionally attained by non-Italian singers; and Italian singers singing in other languages had equal difficulties. Whenever Handel used Italian singers in his English oratorios, the critics had a field day making fun of their pronunciation. All this explains the unprecedented hegemony of Italian opera and Italian singers in the seventeenth and eighteenth centuries all over Europe. When the famous singer Madeleine Schmelling was suggested for employment in the Berlin opera of Frederick the Great, the king indignantly rejected the proposition. "A German singer? I would as soon expect pleasure from the neighing of my horse." During the Rossini craze, an author in the *Allgemeine Musikalische Zeitung* was convinced that "Sebastian Bach would have been able to compose better, had he learned something about the art of singing in Italy." Court operas everywhere—except in France—were made up of Italian personnel; even the court poets in Vienna— whose main duty was to compose librettos for operas and oratorios—were Italians, among them the illustrious trio of Zeno, Metastasio, and da Ponte. Both Lully and Purcell, famous for their matchless ability in setting to music their respective languages, studied the problems. It is known that Lully avidly watched the actors' diction in the Comédie Française. And much later, Wagner, also a keen student of both speech and song and disturbed by the conflict between German and Italian singing, decided that the solution was to depart from the Italian bel canto and create a style of singing congenial to the German language.

Modern voice culture, based on scientific principles first propounded by Manual Garcia in his *Traité complet du chant* (1847), managed to reduce considerably the difference between Italian and non-Italian singing; today, well-trained artists can do justice to both, though singers still tend to specialize in Italian, German, or French roles. I might add that, in the seventeenth and eighteenth centuries, the French—unlike the Italians—preferred smaller voices because of their greater ability to carry out the principal requirement which they placed ahead of the singing itself: the clear articulation and declamation of the lyrics and recitatives. This literary requirement is expressed by the very name they gave to their opera: *Tragédie lyrique*. The French had their own difficulties because of their slightly nasal voice and the special care needed to deal with the mute vowels which, in singing, must be enunciated. Musicians accustomed to Italian vocal traditions heartily disliked French singing—Burney is downright nasty about it—and Mozart did not mince words either on this subject.

The pedagogy of singing, in the sense we understand it, goes back to the sixteenth century. About the earlier *scholae* we know too little to form any judgment of their methods; but later the *maîtrises* and *Kantoreien* formed excellent choir schools; and the present-day English cathedral and collegiate choirs have a highly respected choral tradition that goes back to centuries of careful nurturing.

It was the Church which for a long time directed the schooling of singers, but this role was gradually taken over by famous singers and opera maestros. Caccini, in the preface to his *Nuove musiche* (1602), set the new standard of singing instruction, which was greatly admired throughout the century; Praetorius was so taken by this Italian voice teaching that he exhorted German singers to work hard and learn the fine points of the system in order to be able to sing in the Italian manner. Seventeenth-century writers described Italian singing as passionate, affect-laden, and clear, the French as tending to less sonorous and emotional song, while German singing was called "raw, lacking in modulation and finesse." By the turn of the century, singers were trained not only in voice production, but also in expressive delivery and in the thorough knowledge of music and its theory.

Opera created a new type of singer, and virtuoso singing opened a new era. Now, especially in Italy, everyone succumbed to the beauty of the human voice; a body of *maniere* grew to exploit vocal brilliance, and ornamentation became a means to develop the voice. Schools of singing headed by celebrated retired castratos were organized; in 1700 Francisco Antonio Pistocchi founded the first of these in Bologna, where severely methodical vocal training was imparted, mainly to the poor, maimed boys meant to be headed for glamorous castrato careers. Another famous school was that of Nicola Porpora in Milan, among whose pupils were no lesser men than Farinelli and Caffarelli. These singing masters also wrote books on their trade. Some of them, particularly those of Pier Francesco Tosi (ca. 1645–1732) and Giovanni Battista Mancini (1714–1800), can still be studied with profit and make interesting reading.

This scintillating vocal culture seems very impressive, and there can be no question that neither before nor after were singers so well trained and so capable of the most astounding virtuosity; but its world is lost to us, for the essence of solo singing from the middle of the seventeenth century to the latter part of the eighteenth was the maximum exploitation of the vocal material rather than the music itself, a concept difficult for us to understand. Yes, this was the era subsequently called the bel canto period, but also that of the purely material cultivation of the voice. Indeed, the bel canto age's forced brilliance also represents an artistic decline; because of the neglect of the text, the many ornamental insertions and meaningless cadenzas destroyed order and form. In a da capo aria, the listener could scarcely recognize the repetition of the first part: it was so overloaded with improvised ornamentation. To the composer, the poetic values of the words could mean a great deal; but the singer, trained for years with the aid of *textless* vocalises, watched not for poetic interest, but for the syllables most suitable for launching vocal fireworks.

Though much has been written about these phenomenal singers, it is almost impossible for us to imagine, let alone re-create, their art. Take, for instance, the soprano Agujari, praised by Mozart: she could sing an octave higher than our coloratura sopranos. Occasionally we are able to reconstruct the nature of a singer's voice and his or her manner of singing, a good case being that of Faustina Bordoni Hasse. Many operas of Hasse were composed for the beautiful mezzo voice of his wife, and by studying those roles, we learn about her range, her preference for portamento, and the melodic turns that most suited her. The extraordinary art of the Italian singers may puzzle us, but this puzzle is nothing compared to what we face when examining the art of the *voci artificiali*—the castratos. But first let us turn to the intermediary problem of boys versus women, which is one of the most disputed aspects of theories of performance practice.

When the Israelites made Jehovah a monotheistic God, the prototype of the authoritarian male was established. Women were now not only excluded from taking any active part in divine services, but they were sequestered even in the congregation, their mere presence somehow tainting public morals. The Hebrew and Oriental attitude toward women was taken over by the Christian Church with even more severe restrictions. According to the early Christian Church view, women could not attain the moral-ethical status of men because they were thought to be fundamentally lascivious temptresses, deliberately flaunting the attractions of their bodies and thereby representing an evil influence on men which should be suppressed or at least minimized wherever possible. The misogyny of St. Paul and of the Church Fathers went so far that they even doubted whether women could be full-fledged Christians. Luther, too, has some reprehensible things to say in this regard. As a result of these theological views, in church music—which for a long time was the principal field of art music—treble and alto parts were sung by falsettists and later by boys and, in the larger churches, by castratos. It must be emphasized, however, that the exclusion of female singers from participation was not for musical, but solely for moral and theological reasons; Judeo-Christian civilization poisoned Eros, rejecting the mystery of love and all things sexual—"Nature is sin."

The Council of Chalons in 650 C.E. firmly and officially banished women from the sanctuary and the choir loft. The Lord created man in his own image, but that was not always taken to include the female of the species, and St. Paul's dictum *mulier taceat in ecclesia* was obeyed to the letter. In his famous encyclical *Motu proprio* on music in the Church, Pope Pius X declared: "Women, being incapable of exercising a liturgic office, cannot be admitted to the choir." This categorical exclusion was modified for choirs outside the sanctuary, "provided the women are as far as possible apart from the men." It was always the "moral issue" that worried the celibate clergy. Five years after *Motu proprio*, a decree by the Sacred Congregation of Rites reaffirmed the supreme requirement of separating women from men. The commentary of this decree of 1908 is worth quoting for its almost disarming naiveté: "If there were a question of angels, there would have been no harm in mixing men and women choristers, but these men are formed by clay." It is hard to believe, but Tetrazzini, the world-famous diva, tells in her memoirs that it was the greatest sorrow of her life that she could not "thank God for the voice He has given me by singing for Him in church." Pius XII, in his encyclical *Musicae sacra disciplina* (1955), allowed that "where boy singers are not available in sufficient numbers, it is permitted that a choir of men and women may sing the liturgical texts during solemn Mass." However, the austere Pope immediately qualified this relaxation of the moral code by adding that it is permissible only "if the men are entirely separated from the women and girls, and that anything unseemly be avoided."

I am telling this *drama giocoso* to demonstrate that those who will not admit mixed choirs to old music by citing historical authenticity really do not care for the music, only for documented history. But how could persons with common sense advocate practices based on reprehensible and long since discredited ideas? Their attitude is abetted by the great love of tradition that characterizes the English, who, though no longer for moral or theological reasons, maintain excellently trained boys' choirs, especially in their collegiate churches. There is a place for boys in choral music, and they can be very good, especially when they are trained for musical tasks rather than for cherubic charms, as are the present-day commercialized Vienna Choirboys; but there are important areas in music with which boys cannot cope. Boys are uncomfortable in the highest ranges of the choral treble, as well as at the other end of the compass; when they climb above the staff, their voices become glassy, whereas in this very range female singers are in their glory. Similarly, their voices are weak and particularly neutral in the low range where female altos excel. Furthermore, because of the youngsters' limited lung capacity, they have difficulty in precisely articulating long phrases when the tempo is moderate, which often prompts conductors to take faster tempos. For this reason the arias in oratorios and Masses were often assigned to a small group of choirboys, presumably with the thought of safety in numbers.

In 1602, Viadana, in his preface to his *Cento concerti ecclesiastici*, cautioned about using boys who "for the most part sing with little grace . . . no money can pay for a good natural soprano." Of equal importance is the fact that intellectually complex and emotionally powerful texts are outside the grasp of children. No one could expect from little boys a convincing projection of such ideas as "homo factus est" or the ineffable *Stabat mater dolorosa;* they may sing the notes nicely but merely mouth the words without understanding their import. To have the demanding arias in Bach's B Minor Mass or in the Passions sung by boys is almost pitiful.

Mattheson declared that among the most important requirements for a good performance are "the number and selection of singers and instrumentalists, the pure sound of all these, and adequate rehearsals. *Among these persons women are simply indispensable"* (my emphasis). He tells the amusing story of his rather bold act of putting his views into practice by replacing boys with women in the Hamburg Cathedral in 1715, though the opposition was considerable. Not a man to give up easily, he persisted and was grudgingly allowed to proceed with his innovation, provided that "he hides the women in such manner as no one will see them." In the end, however, "one could not hear them enough." Burney also took up the cudgel for the mixed choir: "There is generally a want of sturdiness in such young musicians [as boys] which makes it to be wished that females were permitted in the church to take the soprano part, as the voices of females are more permanent than those of boys."

Curiously, the true mixed chorus was not only known in the late Baroque but distinctly preferred by the musicians—if they could get away with it. Mattheson, reflecting on the desirability of allotting the upper voice parts to women in preference to boys, whom he considered "of little advantage," emphasized that this is particularly true in dramatic music. To sing the St. Matthew Passion or the Mozart Requiem today with boys instead of women in the choir, as is being done especially in historically "correct" recordings, is nothing but dogmatic antiquarianism. How far this misguided desirability of historical authenticity can be carried, despite the demonstrated theological, social, and sexual prejudices, is illustrated by a review I read the other day. The critic found a performance of Kodály's *Missa Brevis* unsatisfactory, recommending that to make the work "liturgically acceptable," boys should replace the women. Obviously this Rip van Winkle knows no history, and his musical judgment is also questionable.

For a long time we have been accustomed to natural singing provided by the four types of voices: soprano, alto, tenor, and bass—that is, vocal ranges determined by physiological facts; but they also correspond to the basic four-part construction of music. The intermediate voices—low soprano (mezzo) and high bass (baritone)—do not alter this pattern, only refine it. These vocal types are inextricably identified and associated with the respective sexes. The Church knew full well that a warm, vibrant soprano or alto is quintessentially feminine, hence their banishment from participation in the liturgy. The first remedy used to cope with the situation caused by the exclusion of women singers, the assignment of the upper parts to tenors singing falsetto, was considered "natural." They were called *alti naturali*, or *tenorini*. Nevertheless, falsetto singing is artificial, a forced tone beyond the natural range of tenors, with greatly limited volume and quality of tone. Objections to falsetto singing were expressed as early as the thirteenth century, when, among others, Roger Bacon protested that falsettists "falsify masculine harmony." In the sixteenth century the critics derided the narrow range of expressiveness of falsettists, as well as the lack of dynamic variety and of color in their voices. With the use of boys and the reign of the castrato, their usefulness gradually diminished to the vanishing point, though the *Männerchor* movement in nineteenth-century Germany revived it.

The alto register is the youngest among the vocal types, and at first it had a purely musico-technical role. It made its first appearance ca. 1450 in the late works of Dufay, when the transition from three-part to four-part singing took place. The contratenor part was split into *contratenor bassus* and *contratenor altus*, hence our "contralto." We notice that it was about this same time that instruments began to be built in "families," to take care of the now-standard four-part division. The new alto part received such instrumental equivalents as, for instance, the alto recorder, alto trombone, and the alto of the viol family. Being originally a musico-technical innovation, for a while the alto did not have any characteristic vocal quality like the three other parts and was sung by falsettists or boys. But history shows that throughout the centuries there was a desire to allow the alto part its natural physiognomy, and eventually it was realized that the female alto has a prominent sonic quality which blends well with the other voices. By the end of the eighteenth century the feminine alto's victory was complete. It is difficult to understand why, given this triumph, we, living at the end of the twentieth century, are now trying to undo this satisfactory development by replacing the natural alto with the artificial voice of the countertenor. Just as the castrato was an almost exclusively Italian institution, so the countertenor was an English specialty. It was popular in England during Purcell's time, when he frequently sang the alto solos in verse anthems; but with the gradual establishment of bel canto in England, it virtually disappeared, to be resurrected only in recent times. Having become fashionable in Britain and the United States, its characterless, hooty, cold voice nevertheless remained unsuitable for dramatic roles. Though some modern countertenors are very fine artists, who articulate and declaim with impeccable taste and musicianship, as Caccini said: "From a feigned voice can come no noble manner of singing, which issues only from a natural voice."

The first castratos, Spaniards, appeared in the papal chapel in the 1560s; but after the turn of the century, the Italians took control of the industry that produced them, and the products dominated singing until the last quarter of the eighteenth century. The title role of Gluck's first "reform" opera, *Orfeo ed*

Euridice, was still written for an alto castrato, the famous Gaetano Guadagni, and both the first and last great operas of Mozart, *Idomeneo* and *La Clemenza di Tito,* had castrato roles. After the rise and great popularity of the opera buffa, which made fun of the opera seria and the castrato, their reign began to topple, and in a remarkably short time they disappeared.

Castration of boys for the sake of creating a special type of singing voice was an ancient Oriental practice. Officially the Church forbade the practice, but it certainly accepted and supported the singers. The Sistine Chapel still had some castratos at the opening of the twentieth century. The castrato voice remained an Italian monopoly; the practice that produced them was not permitted beyond the Alps, but the singers were admired, together with the music they brought with them, as a fashionable exotic importation for the delectation of the sophisticated artistic palates of the aristocracy and the courts which maintained Italian opera troupes. Though Englishmen were appalled by the idea, not so the ruling class which maintained operatic establishments in London solely for the sake of Italian opera. John Gay, in a letter to Swift, complains that "in all polite conversations, Senesino is daily voted to be the greatest man that ever lived." Even the sober Englishmen shouted "one God, one Farinelli." Handel, entirely devoted to Italian opera, accepted the convention and composed for *evirati*. Being a very taciturn man concerning his artistic beliefs, he never let it be known what he really thought of them. But once he abandoned Italian opera and turned exclusively to English oratorio, he seldom employed them. Elsewhere they were spurned. The Germans derisively called them "the Italian capons" and indignantly rejected them, while Raguenet assured his readers that "not one castrato could be found in France."

Benedetto Marcello, in his biting satire *Il teatro alla moda* (1720), denounced the reign of the castrato. "The principal parts should always be entrusted to the castratos, reserving tenors and basses for captains of the guard, shepherds, messengers, etc." Though this was said sarcastically, it was not far from the truth. Vocal ranges themselves changed their identity. Low voices were not considered important, and no delicate singing was expected from "singers of low pitch." Then in the late Baroque the bass became the voice of authority and of high principle—and also of villainy. Handel's magnificent character portrayals of grieving fathers and malevolent tyrants in bass roles illustrate the changing concept. It was also he who began to give the tenor the principal heroic role; in the next century the tenor was to become as dominant as the castrato had been earlier.

Nevertheless, many of the important treatises on singing were, as I have said, written by retired castratos. The first thing that impresses the reader of these treatises is the unanimity of their authors about the planning of a castrato's career. They warn that no one should embark on the profession of a virtuoso singer past his tenth or at most twelfth year. The course of studies was incredibly severe, as can be seen from Giovanni Bontempi's description (1660). The boys got up before sunrise, spent the morning and forenoon practicing difficult vocal exercises: *passaggi*, trills, problems of intonation, and so forth—all this in the presence of their master and standing before a mirror in order to observe the position of the tongue, facial muscles, and their mouths, so as to avoid grimacing while singing. There was more singing in the afternoon, but also lessons in music theory, composition, and harpsichord playing. They were forbidden to sing in public until the long course of studies (eight to ten years) was completed. Because of this comprehensive training, not a few of them also became competent composers and instrumentalists. One of the cardinal rules of the instruction was that for several years the pupil was not permitted to sing any music with a text. The teachers did not want him to be distracted by emotions from his primary task of faultless singing. The textless *messa di voce*, the gradual swelling and decreasing of the voice on one note on one breath, and the seamless binding of consecutive notes—the portamento— were the touchstones of the singer's art. This, of course, brought with it an attitude, acquired in boyhood, at the most impressionable age, that the virtuoso singer's first and principal task is impeccable voice production, smoothness of delivery, rather than emotional communication. Obviously the castrato was considered a sort of virtuoso instrumentalist of the larynx, rather than a singer in the sense we understand the term; he was an infallible singing machine. To do justice to the castratos, I should add that there were also a few—Farinelli, Guadagni, Caffarelli come to mind—whose delivery was sensitive and moving; but they were the exception.

It is significant that whenever a castrato was praised, it was the marvelous flexibility and accuracy of his voice that were held up for admiration—that is, his extraordinary technique; the sensuous beauty of the voice and the power of emotional communication that we expect from a singer were seldom mentioned. The castrato was in fact an *outré* countertenor; thus his voice had a quality fundamentally different from those of the women who are substituted for him today. The cold neutrality and lack of color of his voice were intensified by the demand, expressed by Tartini and among others, that he sing without vibrato.

All this is borne out by my own observation when, about 1912, I heard two castratos—soprano and alto—who toured Europe with the Sistine Chapel

Choir. They were billed as victims of accidents (an old subterfuge ever since the seventeenth century), but there they were, middle-aged and no longer at the peak of their power, relics from another age. Though I was young, just about the age when a castrato would have his "accident," I vividly remember their voices because of the shock of hearing grown men sing in the stratosphere. Their voices were white, clear, and powerful and had absolutely no resemblance to a woman's voice.

The question arises: What are we resurrecting? We are faced with a concept totally and irrevocably alien to us and impossible to re-create; even the greatest singing artists alive could not approximate the demands once placed on the castrato, and of course the quality of his voice, even if it could be conjured up, might not be acceptable to us. The castrato earned his fame not because he faithfully sang what was in the score, but for what was *not* in the score and not even indicated: the *fioriture*, the trills, the *roulades*, the cadenzas, and the long chains of ornaments. No one could (nor, I believe, would want to) reinstall this exaggerated tampering with the composers' fine melodies; the miserable vocal sallies that some of our conductors and vocal coaches today splice into the scores for their singers who no longer know the art of improvisation bear no resemblance to the castrato's art. Time and again we read in contemporaneous records that the da capo of an aria, ornamented by a castrato, did not even faintly resemble that which he was supposed to be repeating.

The Baroque cultivated a third, neutral gender with an artificial range. The high voice, because it is the most maneuverable, became the ideal, and, as we have seen, the low voices were considered mere supporting members of the cast, and not infrequently they are altogether missing. In many a Baroque opera there are only high parts, and entire opera troupes were made up of women and castratos. Echoes of this cult are still present in the nineteenth century, and even today, in the adulation of the tenor—the highest male voice—with his high C usually eliciting an ovation that effectively disrupts the performance. It is an idle pursuit to try to recapture the castrato's world. It has disappeared forever.

I must return to the cardinal truth in the art of music. The singer is the only musician who carries his instrument in his body; his voice is *himself*, because it projects the whole person and is thus the immediate expression of the human in music. When Mattheson bravely defied his church's exclusion of women from church choirs, his example was immediately followed by others, as if they had only been waiting for the chance to have their visions realized. Needless to say, I am not advocating the kind of reconstructions that took place at the Göttingen Handel revivals in the 1920s. These performances were prepared and directed by well-meaning amateurs, enthusiastic, but insufficiently acquainted with musicology and the theater.

But it will not be enough to invoke historical authenticity. We must examine the reasons for the peculiar ideas and practices followed by Baroque opera, and these reasons may ultimately become untenable in the eyes of posterity.

Period Instruments

New tools are usually experimental
and are gradually improved as their users learn how to handle them. Musical
instruments similarly go through many improvements until they arrive at their
stage of greatest utility. Our heritage of these musical tools is extremely rich,
and a special branch of musicology, called organology, was created to investigate their history and nature. As we follow their development, we find that
many have disappeared; some at a certain point in their evolution were sup-
planted by kindred instruments more capable of further development, and
some, like the flutes, guitars, and horns, have survived millennia to serve us
today, with changes, yet still retaining their basic characteristics. The shapes,
measurements, and purposes of musical instruments are always dependent on
the varying tonal and tuning systems (for instance, equal temperament, which
gave idiomatic instrumental writing a tremendous boost), but also on sociocultural and economic factors. We see startling metamorphoses as the instruments wander from East to West, from beggars' hands to those of courtiers—
and vice versa—and from small rooms to great halls.

Such social changes usually demand corresponding changes in the instruments' construction and use. Take, for instance, the history of plucked

instruments. In the Mediterranean basin they were the great favorites of all classes, but in the Germanic North they were the instruments of beggars and wandering minstrels. When they were beginning to be widely appreciated in the North of Europe they were at first equipped with a bow, creating such hybrid instruments as the "bowed lute." Another curious mixed breed was the hurdy-gurdy (*vielle à roue*), shaped like a lute, with a wheel for a bow that was cranked by one hand while the other hand played on a miniature keyboard. Other stringed instruments had a set of extra strings, not played on but resonating "in sympathy" with those actually bowed. Throughout the Middle Ages the hurdy-gurdy was popular, but Praetorius indignantly calls it good only "for peasants and itinerant wenches." With the coming of the French infatuation with the *champêtre*, when the aristocracy dressed in Arcadian garments as shepherds and shepherdesses, the hurdy-gurdy, though a typical rustic instrument, became the favorite of the ladies in their salons. Similarly, the bagpipe, originally a folk instrument, reappeared for a brief artistic existence in high society under the name of *musette*. Needless to say, all such instruments, including even the violin's predecessor, the rebec, though picturesque in lecture recitals, lend themselves only to specific reconstructions of certain kinds of medieval secular music. The gradual growth of public concerts, especially in the nineteenth century, led to larger halls for larger audiences, until in our time they reached the dimensions of four thousand-seat auditoriums. The new rooms' acoustics compelled many revisions in the choice and construction of instruments and also excluded a large variety of music as unsuitable for public performance under the changed conditions; this in turn occasioned preposterous transcriptions and arrangements, in vogue until a few decades ago, delicate chorale preludes blown up to "Death and Transfiguration" proportions.

The movement of returning to original instruments and ensemble proportions started in the late nineteenth century with a few knowledgeable scholars and musicians, but was little heeded. More recently it received a great impetus from specialists and amateurs who wanted to use authentic instruments in their gatherings. The enthusiastic zeal of these cultivated instrumentalists eventually found a larger response in professional circles, and the tentative beginnings at the opening of our century developed into a widespread movement. At first the pioneers went a bit overboard in their search for authenticity, a typical example being the flurry caused by the alleged reconstruction of the "Bach bow," taken up by good violinists, who recorded Bach's sonatas and partitas for unaccompanied violin with this "authentic" bow. With the disposal of such engaging fantasies, a much more serious and well-founded use of period instruments began. The manufacture of replicas of old instruments became a respectable business; the new harpsichords in particular turned out to be excellent, with certain advantages over the old ones because of the use of such stable materials as plastics and pressure-treated lumber impervious to swelling in humid weather. However, performances on old and reconstructed instruments have proved to be more generally successful in phonograph recordings than in live concerts, because performance in small auditoriums, where the original instruments sound well, seldom pays for expenses, and the small ensembles sound puny in larger, even middle-sized theaters or concert halls.

The sister arts are of great importance to us in approaching the duplication of old instruments, the bas-reliefs on cathedrals, illustrated manuscripts, tapestries, and paintings showing musical scenes effectively supplementing the treatises. The latter, like Praetorius's *De organographica* (1619) also contain many good drawings. Usually, though not always, even in the most imaginative and fantastic "Annunciation," "Wedding in Cana," or angelic concerts, the musical instruments are portrayed with persuasive accuracy of detail; but we must remain alert to the instances in which instruments are pictured in a symbolic and imaginary way. And, of course, we possess magnificent collections of instruments in museums all over the world. Yet, despite this wealth of material, there is a very long road from the physical and pictorial existence of an old instrument to its actual playing, especially to what is considered "historically authentic" playing.

Those instruments under glass in a museum are separated from us by a whole world more effectively than by the glass panes. What sound can be elicited, how were they played—even what was played on them—are all grave questions. When we do succeed in restoring and reactivating an old instrument, new psychological inhibitions may assert themselves. Take, for instance, the harpsichord, which is not a primitive predecessor of the modern piano, but a fully and superbly developed instrument with pronounced characteristics of its own. Some twentieth-century composers, beginning with de Falla, have actually used it, yet it is difficult to delete from our mind a strong period bias, for to us the harpsichord is wedded to sixteenth- to eighteenth-century music. The same is true to some degree of the organ. When listening to the color fantasies of Tournemire or Messiaen, one feels that an orchestra would suit this kind of music better.

The history of musical instruments is incredibly complicated, because many types are encountered in nearly all civilizations, and each type has different sounds, uses, functions, and many offspring. The study of this history is very important, because instruments are one of the bridges to the understanding of old music and to the techniques of musical composition. But unless we keep constantly in mind the craftsmen who make them, the composers who write for them, and the performers who play on them, we may arrive at biased or even untenable conclusions. There are many aspects to this history, especially relating to the use of original instruments in our present-day performances, that are either insufficiently explained or misinterpreted. The literary sources are often unreliable. Virdung's *Musica getutscht* (1511), the earliest printed work to deal with musical instruments and one of the earliest treatises in the vernacular, though for a long time a respected documentary source, has been proved inaccurate and unreliable by recent scholarship. A more egregious example is a famous letter attributed to St. Jerome in which the instruments mentioned in the Bible are described. From the ninth century onward this letter was quoted by many theologians and musicographers, and Johann Gottfried Walther, in his *Musicalisches Lexicon* (1732), still carried the old story; yet the letter turned out to be spurious, the instruments described largely nonexistent.

When reading the fascinating modern scholarly works on organology, we notice a Darwinian touch in the selective development of the various species of musical instruments, and we find to our amazement that, as in the animal kingdom, crossbreeds are sterile. The same is true of instruments deliberately constructed as extensions or combinations of old and still gloriously living instruments. In the first category are bowed instruments fitted with tiny reeds or even pipes, like the *claviorganum* (fifteenth century), the *viola pomposa* (whose invention is attributed, perhaps erroneously, to Bach), and, to mention a more recent freak, Wagner's bass trumpet, which sounds like a foghorn and is a contradiction in terms, the trumpet being a treble instrument par excellence. (Today its part is usually given to a trombone.) It is interesting to note the use of these latter-day deliberate hybrids. A typical case is furnished by the saxophone. Though immensely popular in jazz, pop, school and military bands, it has never made it into the modern symphony orchestra. It is also interesting to observe that while many instruments are totally forgotten, those that reached full maturity and development in their own time could not be eclipsed; when recorders, the harpsichord, and the tracker organ were revived, they triumphantly repossessed their erstwhile respect and position in the musical world.

The one continuing feature of the millennial history of musical instruments is the desire for progress. Instrument makers at all times sought to improve their wares in order to provide better and fuller sound for the composers and to meet the demands of the performers for improved playing mechanisms. They did so by altering the boxes of wind instruments, adding keys and valves, and seating the reeds in better positions. Above all, the improvements in the quality of the sound of the instruments belonging to the violin family were spectacular. We must repeat that the changes made by these hardy and inventive builders were *in response* to the desire of composers and performers to realize their artistic imaginations more fully. The composer always wants optimum usability and euphony and never ceases to search for it. Even though the early composers knew the limitations of the instruments at their disposal, they always heard in their mind's ear the ideal, the perfect instrument, and they often seemed to write for it, causing their contemporaries to call such music "unperformable." It was because of this prophetic reach of the composers that the development of musical instruments shows a steady tendency toward more euphonious, sonorous, rounded, and flexible tone. Technical improvements led to the oblivion of entire families of instruments and to the creation of new or radically changed ones.

There was another weighty reason for the improvements, seldom realized by composers and old instrument specialists but well expressed by Carl Almenräder in his treatise on the bassoon (1817): "Composers cannot possibly know the technical side of every instrument, so there remains to the instrument makers the task to enable these most difficult passages to be played through improved construction." The process of such technical changes was accomplished by a changed concept of sound which, as we have remarked, was also affected by sociocultural factors. Even at the height of the Baroque, the new music room at Fishamble Street in Dublin, where Handel first performed *Messiah*, seated about 600—if the ladies left home their hoops and the gentlemen their dress swords—and was considered a very large hall in 1742. Only some of the Continental opera houses had really large auditoriums (comparable to the space of the large cathedrals). In the music rooms, given the eighteenth-century conditions, concepts, and ideals, both the small ensembles and the sound they produced were adequate; but ours is a different world, and we have vastly enlarged audiences.

Let us now examine the quality of the sound that must have emanated from the original instruments in their heyday. This is really the crux of the whole authenticity movement and the core of many of the disagreements. Jean Rousseau, the great master of the viol, in his treatise of 1689, makes it the first condition of string playing "to imitate all that a beautiful voice can do." We hear this comparison with the human voice as a sort of *ostinato* throughout the centuries. Geminiani, in his violin method (1751), furnishes incontrovertible evidence that a large, rounded, and well-modulated tone was desired by all musicians, and since his work was a codification of long-standing practices (as was his study of vibrato), the nonresonant, vibrato-free playing we often hear at concerts and in historical recordings is plainly contradicted. Quantz, in his *Versuch* (1752), states that "each sound must be made as beautiful as it is possible to produce . . . you must carefully avoid all stiffness . . . and good execution must be full of variety"—and so forth.

Though the strings could easily fulfill the demand for a full and warm tone (the correct pitch is, of course, the player's responsibility), the wind instruments had to struggle until post-Beethovenian times to join the strings on even terms. They were inaccurate in intonation; some of their registers were weaker than others; and they differed in practical ways from instrument to instrument. When Quantz was introduced by Hasse to Alessandro Scarlatti, the aged composer told him: "My son, you know I hate wind instruments, they are never in tune." The principal reason for the unreliability of the woodwinds was that the fingerholes were drilled not exactly at the acoustically necessary spots but with slight modifications at places where the average players' fingers could reach them. This resulted in ill tuning, which the players had to counteract by using a clumsy and complicated fingering, covering some of the holes partially ("half" and "three-quarter" holes), the awkward, so-called fork positions, as well as using different lip pressure. Even in moderately animated passages the "half holes" would never be covered to the same extent every time, hence the faulty intonation. I know this from personal experience, having learned to play the bassoon on an instrument from the 1860s that had seen long service in the conservatory (it was loaned to beginners) but was still in excellent condition. My teacher, almost as ancient as the instrument, was perfectly familiar with the old system and taught me the complicated fingering. When, later, I acquired a fine modern Heckel bassoon and a new, younger teacher, I had to start all over again to learn an almost new technique. The gains in accuracy of pitch and fluency in playing were remarkable. The keys, devices that permit the holes to be closed and opened by making them accessible with the aid of levers, enabled the instrument makers to locate the holes at the acoustically proper places, because the connecting rods of the levers, of various lengths, were so arranged as to be within comfortable range of the fingers. At first keys appeared singly, but ever since the flutist Theobald Boehm invented his system of covering *all* the holes of the flute with keys (ca. 1830), his system, which was extended to the other wind instruments (except the recorders), made all other systems of construction and fingering obsolete; we now have instruments with reliable tuning and greatly improved ease of playing.

Burney, in his travel diary, speaks with admiration of the "Mannheim band" but laments an "imperfection" common to all orchestras he has heard, "the want of truth [i.e. correct pitch] in their wind instruments." It is interesting to see how Burney, an experienced and knowledgeable observer, approaches this problem. He accepts it as natural for these instruments to be out of tune but wonders why "the art and diligence which these great instrument makers and performers have manifested in vanquishing difficulties of other kinds" are not employed in overcoming these shortcomings. Having made these observations, he relents: "Since this imperfection is so common in orchestras, the censure will not be severe upon it." No one seems to point out the contradictions implied in these statements. The instruments were flawed, and the ill-tuned orchestras must have annoyed not only Alessandro Scarlatti but every person with a musical ear; therefore the "authenticity" we are striving for actually conjures up conditions that never existed—no one today would listen to instruments consistently out of tune.

Our improved instruments avoid the flaws and more closely approach the *ideal* the composer sought, yet it is exactly the improvements that are decried by the dyed-in-the-wool authenticists. There was an additional reason, however, for the frequently poor intonation. As late as in Mozart's time, flutes, oboes, and clarinets were still interchangeable and frequently played by the same musician. Also, if there are both trumpets and horns in an eighteenth-century score and they are alternating, one movement having horns, the other trumpets, we may be assured that they were played by the same instrumentalists (hence they could not have trumpets and horns together). After a while the insufficiency of this practice was recognized. Burney reports a conversation with Quantz in which the latter, who used to play both the oboe and the flute, said that he abandoned the oboe "supposing it hurtful to the *embouchure* on the flute." Curiously—and this is another example of the rather selective treatment of history—Beethoven is more rarely forced back to his own times, though in his orchestra he also used "old" and "original" instruments—that is, woodwinds with uncovered fingerholes, valveless horns and trumpets, as well as gut strings. Nevertheless, there is no widespread demand to confiscate the modern instruments now used when playing his symphonies. Unfortunately, however, Beethoven—even Schubert and the earlier Romantics—are gradually being added to the "old masters" as the limits of early music begin to be extended beyond the official date of 1800. I believe, though, that it will remain difficult to accept the *Eroica* and her sisters played with a small orchestra in a collegium musicum type of performance as satisfactory, either to musicians or to the public.

A few further remarks concerning the historical justification for exchanging various instruments are in order. We are not speaking of the ad hoc ensembles of the Middle Ages and the Renaissance but of seventeenth- and eighteenth-century practices, these centuries furnishing the bulk of old music performed and recorded today. It used to be common for musicians literally to "double in brass." Some of the upper-echelon servants were often hired because of their ability to sing or play an instrument, then were pressed into the house orchestra of a prince or bishop and often ordered to learn to play an additional instrument. This must have reduced their proficiency, already limited by their household duties; there were, of course, some exceptions. The composers did not take such limitations into consideration, however, and when the creative act was finished, they often had to make compromises. To quote an example, Rameau's *Pièces de clavecin en concert* are written for harpsichord, violin, and viola da gamba, but the composer advises that a cornett (the ancient medieval instrument that is still alive, not the modern cornet) can replace the violin and a second violin the gamba.

In the use of those instruments that do not offer an uninterrupted tradition of performance practice, we must either avail ourselves of modern replacements or invent a tradition, which is what some performing organizations do in the name of authenticity. The baryton, for which Haydn wrote close to two hundred pieces, mostly trios, comes to mind. This instrument was a cross between the viola d'amore and the viola da gamba and, like the former, had a set of sympathetic strings arranged on the awkward body of the instrument so that they could be plucked with the left thumb. The baryton was a favorite of Prince Nicholas Esterházy, prompting Haydn to compose the trios for his master. Since the instrument, without any other literature to speak of, being ungainly and difficult to play, became extinct, if we want to hear Haydn's music, we must substitute something for the departed inglorious hybrid. I heard Haydn's trios performed with a harpsichord taking the place of the baryton; they sounded fine. Many other instruments were bastardized—and so-called—*vide* the *viola bastarda*—and some of them strike one almost as sideshow freaks. There was, for instance, the *arpeggione*, the offspring of mating a cello with a guitar, and the *lira organizzata*, which was a hurdy-gurdy equipped with a few tiny organ pipes, the bellows for the latter being inside the instrument and pumped by the cranked wheel.

The use of original instruments within certain limits is entirely justified; they can be both delightful and enlightening, but they cannot be used indiscriminately in all old music. They have different timbres from those we are used to, but in many instances their more delicate and transparent sound shows up part writing more clearly than is possible to achieve with modern instruments. The proponents of their exclusive use, however, tend to stress these advantages but seldom deal with the disadvantages. We can readily state the issue of limits opposed to optimality, but how shall we make our choice in view of the historical, artistic, and sociocultural conditions? Whichever way we make our decision, it will be contested.

During the Middle Ages there were few professional instrument makers except for organ builders and bell makers, who were usually supported by the Church; but by the Renaissance, instrument makers formed guilds which established and observed high standards. Their output shows a bewildering variety, because each of the guilds, as well as many of their individual members, jealously guarded their shop secrets. In addition, many teachers and performing musicians continued to make their own instruments. Burney, in his travel diaries, mentions that "Mr. Quantz finding a great scarcity of German flutes, undertook to bore them himself for the use of his students; an enterprise which afterwards he found to be very lucrative."

All this resulted in a confusion of shapes, tuning, timbres, and number and quantity of strings used. Instruments differed, often considerably, not only from country to country but from maker to maker in the same country. Italian harpsichords could not match the more robust Dutch instruments, and very few others could even approach the products of the Italian luthiers. To this day, French double reeds differ slightly in sound from German and American oboes and bassoons, while Russian horns do not fit at all into Western orchestras. It is seldom that we have the luck to discover very old instruments still intact and in playing condition, but if we do, we may be sure that they have been rebuilt, often more than once. Even the magnificent instruments of the Cremonese masters are no longer the same as they were when they left their builders' shops centuries ago. While their design is intact and inimitable, the bass bars are now larger, neck and fingerboard a little longer; but all this only enhances their inherent qualities. Unfortunately, if we want a really authentic Baroque fiddle, we must eviscerate and amputate these glorious works of art. Excellent copies of Baroque violins, however, are now being made, and most performers acquire a Baroque violin instead of jeopardizing their "conventional" instrument. Since well-preserved instruments are rare—and inordinately expensive—we must content ourselves with copies, or with less expensive but good violins and other instruments rebuilt to Baroque specifications. The newly built instruments are made to follow two different ground rules, one stipulating that the copy should be exact to the millimeter, the other permitting the incorporation of some later improvements. Whether the first type of reconstruction is best today for the performance of old music is questionable, since considerably changed conditions call for some compromises. We may mention here an example of the right move to achieve this compromise. On the sleeve of a recording of clarinet concertos by Hummel and Crusell we read the following: "The clarinet used for this recording is similar to James Wood's patented design of 1800 but four more keys were added to the original instrument *to make certain passages purer in execution*" (my emphasis). The record annotator is a little embarrassed by this violation of authenticity and sheepish in his defense—he did not realize that he had hit on the only sensible solution. The clarinet under discussion is of course not an "original" instrument but one quite close to our modern kind. It is possible to reconstruct old instruments with at least a few of the excellent and useful improvements of recent times without losing their personality and with very little "damage" to their original tonal characteristics; yet some of our Baroque ensembles will not permit the use of even such innocent but very useful devices as the chin rests for the violin. It is absurd to insist on such asceticism; or would the chin rest destroy authenticity by making the playing on the violin easier? Does authenticity mean that performers must be condemned to be permanently uncomfortable?

The statements appearing in program notes and on the sleeves of recordings announcing that the performers are playing on original instruments often do not weather close scrutiny. For example, the notes to a recent recording say that the soloist plays on "a Grancino violin of 1722." Now this sounds pretty precise, and the statement no doubt satisfies the bylaws of the fraternity. But there was a whole family of instrument makers by that name, working in Mantua, Milan, and Cremona, and at least three of its members became famous for their violins and cellos; therefore the attribution is vague. Even less trustworthy is the date given. If 1722 stands for the year when the instrument left the luthier's shop, it was certainly no longer the *same* violin when the present owner acquired it; he may be playing on a fine instrument rebuilt in 1822, or for that matter in 1922, as it wandered from dealer to dealer.

The situation is actually the same when one of our good little bands of specialists gives a concert or makes a recording playing on what are called original instruments. Even though the stringed instruments almost surely are either rebuilt or copied, let us accept the claim that the fiddles, violas, and cellos are close to the historical truth. Now the ensemble plays a varied program which includes pieces by Rosenmüller and a mid-career Haydn symphony. Both of them are certified old music composers, but they are from entirely different style periods, each of which had its own instruments, aesthetics, and ideals of sound. If the Baroque instruments fit Rosenmüller's music, they certainly do not fit Haydn's. Haydn, and the instruments his players used, had left the Baroque far behind; the rising Classical style preferred a crisper sound, a typical example of which is provided by the oboes, the pitch-giving instruments of the orchestra. By the 1780s the oboe had twice as many keys as its Baroque predecessor, the bore was a little narrower, the bell smaller, and the double reed was cut slimmer, all adding to the bright, "optimistic" tone that so well suits the style. This late eighteenth-century oboe was already nearly identical in tone to our modern oboes, as the somewhat nasal twang of the Baroque oboe had gone out of fashion. Unfortunately, to many aficionados of the performance practice movement, anything old is acceptable, provided it does not remind us of our modern instruments. We must reiterate that changes and improvements in the manufacture of instruments *follow* the growing demands of the composers and the new ideals and concepts of sound. One of the most convincing examples of this is the growth of the great Italian schools of luthiers in the wake of the prolific output of Italian music for the violin family. For a time the new instruments were decried by the conservatives; there is the pathetic protest of Hubert le Blanc in 1790 against "the encroachment" of the cello upon the viola da gamba, but the changes were inevitable.

Considering all the foregoing, it is fair to conclude that old instruments and the playing on them do not necessarily represent real authenticity, for there is a significant gap between the ideal and the possible; we must temper what may be historically desirable by what is practically and aesthetically reasonable in order to realize the composer's aims and intentions, even those he could not always carry out with the means available to him. When in good hands free of antiquarian chicanery, and applied to appropriate music, period instruments can contribute a great deal to enjoyment and to the appreciation of old music. Nevertheless, the use of period instruments is only one aspect and not the sole criterion for performing old music faithfully; indeed, their use is not always, or primarily, the proper way to resurrect such music satisfactorily.

Ornamentation and
Improvisation

The "long lost, late won, and yet half regained" art of ornamentation, as it has been called, figures prominently in the theories of performance practice, because improvised ornamentation in music used to be the completion of the written score. The practice is as old as music itself, though its modern terminology comes in good measure from the visual arts, with the attendant confusion when applied to music. Embellishments, diminution, division, *passaggi, gorgia, broderie, agréments,* Ver-*zierung,* and whatever else they were called, these additions to existing compositions were improvised or written down, indicated by special signs or simply by small notes, but they could also be fully integrated into the composition. It seems that the embellishments illuminate the music in an almost magical way; they become glowing, even mystical, against the body upon which they are lavished. One of the motivations for ornamentation may be the ancient *horror vacui,* the "horror of empty spaces," which many feel should be filled; but while this is no doubt true, the artistic reasons are stronger, for one of the basic human instincts is decoration, "an irresistible and even consuming impulse" (Ada Huxtable). Fritz Winckel thought that there must be a certain neurophysiological necessity for some sort of ornamentation. At any rate, an ornament is *added* to preexisting music, therefore it can also be dispensable. Then again, in earlier times (and in modern performance practice doctrine) embellishments are more often added not by the composer but by the performer. All musicians considered the art of ornamentation and improvisation an important and integral part of their profession, which is acknowledged by the many treatises on the subject from Conrad Paumann's *Fundamentum organisandi* (1452) onward. Borrowed from the fine arts as well as from rhetoric—that is, from extramusical fields—however, the concept was not always well adapted or even well suited to musical needs. While as early as 1552 Adrian Petit Coclico in his *Compendium musices* declared that "a singer who sings the music not only as written but with embellishments, transforms something simple, common, plain, and crude into something elegant and ornate, like a tasteless piece of meat properly salted and seasoned," he adds that if the composer wants the music sung as written, "he should take the precaution of making his wish known."

Ornamentation can be latent or manifest, structural or expressive, without recognizable lines of differentiation, or obviously trivial surface decoration. Misapplied ornamentation can minimize the force of converging lines and completely hide the construction when constantly and aimlessly used. In such cases we do not have a body of music, only numerous arms and legs dangling. But ornamentation stands for much more than its first meaning. It can fruitfully interact with the works to which it is applied; it has a wide range, from little grace notes to great decorative concepts; and it is capable of heightening beauty. It is a form of ornamentation when Bernini surrounds the severe front of St. Peter's with an immense colonnade that organizes space and enhances the entire architectural vision.

Such examples represent the summit of the eternal artistic instinct for decoration. Ornamentation is not only aesthetically valid; under certain circumstances it is a necessity, as, for instance, with instruments that produce an evanescent sound, like the lute or the clavichord. It is equally true that the proliferation of embellishments as it is practiced today is neither justified nor desirable. Of the main aspects of ornamentation, form and function, only the first-named received considerable attention, while the latter is still in need of elaborate study, though Frederick Neumann's fine books and articles on the subject have closed many of the gaps. Ornamentation, originally and essentially, is the breaking up of large note values into smaller ones; the long notes can also be circumnavigated, which produces the same effect. At any rate, it is part of the various styles, and we cannot ignore it. Once the improvised music is notated, the impromptu character is lessened or even disappears altogether.

Nevertheless, the instinct for it remains strong, and until the demise of the basso continuo, a degree of improvisation was an essential ingredient of any style and the undisputed bailiwick of the performer. Opposed to this are the works which the composer finished and committed to paper with written instructions to make sure that the performer would be fully aware of his intentions. It is beyond question that ornamentation, which can be profound, highly expressive, or genially playful, can also be abstract, artificial, forced, and free of any sentiment. It can have a purely irrational decorative significance, and it can be purely aesthetic or constructive, and it can even be the actual carrier of the style. Unfortunately, it can also be completely extraneous to the composition itself. We must distinguish between mere decorative ornaments and expressive ones; the two extremes are the unconscionable excesses of the castratos and the severe restrictions imposed by Gluck and Spontini. We must also consider the fact that the embellishments of one era may be changed, abandoned, even proscribed, by the next one. In the various treatises we often encounter remarks that this or that embellishment "is no longer used in that form" or that it is now "old-fashioned." Juan Bermudo, in his important treatise *Declaración de instrumentos* (1555) remarks: "The embellishments the reader will learn from a good teacher, therefore they do not have to be discussed in detail." He adds: "They change almost from day to day." This same idea is expressed by many writers.

I had better follow Bermudo's advice and forego discussing the various ornaments in detail; they are readily available in the large literature on the subject, as many of the composers and theorists drew up tables of them. But I wish to discuss the aesthetic background and the ever recurring problem with old music: whether authenticity and historical correctness can be relied upon in this field and whether such authenticity is even welcome.

Ornamentation and improvisation are a tentative and chaotic field in which composition, *ex tempore* invention, oral tradition, paleography, folk music, organology, monophony, homophony, polyphony, motor urge, and the elemental desire to "play" cross one another; for there are no fixed boundaries—the whole complex is constantly involved in the contradictory problem of what is spontaneous versus what is premeditated. In older music it can lead to impressive large forms such as the fantasia or the toccata, though in these the metier of composition has large claims. For a long time, and far into the recorded past, improvisation was the only form of music making; thus we must consider it the basic feature of all ancient music. The entire field of monophonic music, from the Greek *nomoi* on, Gregorian chant and the various forms of cantillation and psalmody, as well as (genuine) folk song, must be understood as based on improvisation which, in the *jubilus* of the Alleluia, could reach considerable proportions. Improvisation descending from such ancient sources was gradually absorbed by "learned" music, which established rules that could be taught and learned. Early polyphony arose from this spirit, and henceforth we can speak of compositionally oriented improvisation. In the case of polyphony the rules for "putting music together" were rigidly enforced; the theoretical fiats determined to a considerable degree both procedure and the results, though history proves that the composer gradually gained more independence in manipulating these elements, while the performing improviser remained far more bound to formulas. The question of how and when musical composition in our sense really began has not yet been determined, but there must have been a long transition period between primitive improvisation and the first attempts at deliberately constructed music.

The next important step in composition and ornamentation ensued when the vividly melismatic clausulae of the organa were given texts, *mots*, which necessitated a form of organization. This was the motet, the principal musical art form of medieval music. Diminution and coloration still prevailed in most genres, though less so in the Mass, which was to wrest primacy from the motet in the fifteenth century. There were also weighty sociocultural changes which exerted a profound influence on music.

The more or less exclusive monastic culture admits two new strains: one knightly-aristocratic, the other the art of the educated cleric who now also takes his learning into the secular sphere while still composing motets. In the French and Flemish cities there arose a decidedly middle-class culture which drew its materials from the various schools, old and new. Now we see an entirely new phenomenon: poetic-musical genres with highly artistic aims that require a form of performance different from what we are accustomed to. We shall not tarry here, because a modern choir and its master are too busy with transcribed mensural music to be worrying about embellishments in the medieval world of music. Nevertheless, we should say a word about the *musica reservata* mentioned by Coclico in connection with the work of his (alleged) teacher Josquin. Though we cannot be sure about the various interpretations of the term and practice, what is certain is that this was a kind of highly distilled system of ornamentation—by exceptionally trained singers—about the nature of which, however, we know little. Nor should the reader be concerned about how these embellishments can be reproduced for the delectation of the authenticists: they cannot be conjured up. We should follow the fine performances of Josquin's music on the occasion of the impressive 1971 New York commemoration of the Josquin anniversary: the participating international vocal groups used a minimum of ornamentation or none at all. We do have some authoritative documents about choral ornamentation going back to the sixteenth century, but we should be very careful in following their precepts, because almost all the examples and counsels are stereotyped formulas. The field remained wide open, and finally the ornamentation was either written out, thus compelling the performer to follow the composer's wishes, or totally integrated within the works.

These chansons, madrigals, and (Renaissance) motets that we are trying to embellish with the aid of contemporaneous theoretical writings are beautiful, finished compositions, which absolutely stand on their own without any cosmetic additions. If we are hanging Spanish moss on them, we are simply meddling with great music by great composers. While to the twentieth-century mind Renaissance part songs are very attractive as they are, *composing* embellishments in that style is anachronistic antiquarianism that may be embarrassing. Yet many did not yet get the word. Perhaps the best description of their efforts was made by Yvonne Rockseth, a fine scholar who was a classmate of mine at the Sorbonne: "Ornamentation without architecture."

As instrumental music gained its independence, it borrowed from vocal music many of the latter's decorative figures and formulas. The important deduction that should be made is that here was the real beginning of a changing relationship between composer and performer, as gradually the relative freedom of the improviser to manipulate the composer's original text gives way to "fixed melodies."

Unfortunately, this changing relationship between composer and performer suffered several setbacks to our very own day. Some of the late Renaissance improvisations survived in the earlier Baroque, but the older forms became obsolete and were replaced by new ones. With the great stylistic change around 1600, a latent but never dead form of embellishment, popular in the Middle Ages, the free improvisation in the discantus over a bass, reappeared in a form we call monody. Perhaps it was the result of disaffection with the admirable, smooth, delicate part-writing of Renaissance polyphony, which demanded long study and application and gave the performers little scope in manipulating the individual parts. As a matter of fact, the Florentine objections were directed against the *gorgia* also, because they made the text unintelligible. The humanist reformers pleaded for simple and brief embellishments that would be expressive without conflicting with the requirements of the words set to music.

Essentially it was this question of the intelligibility of the sacred texts that was the cause of the Tridentine reforms. The great stylistic difference was not that the bass was no longer an active linear participant in the polyphony, but that it became a harmonic support, the harmonies being indicated by figures or written out. In the art of the Camerata we see a great deal of formula music, which, especially on account of the constant cadencing, soon causes *ennui*; no wonder the composers rebelled, denouncing the "tedium of the recitatives." Yet quite a few of the formulas survived throughout the Baroque—Burney constantly complains about the "stereotyped fugue themes."

The floodgates open to a new stage of improvisation as we enter the long thoroughbass era, in which the *maestro al cembalo* and the virtuoso singer take charge and again limit the composer's authority. The phenomenal virtuosity of the castratos and the rapid advances in instrumental composition and playing created a new art of improvisation and ornamentation that exceeded everything hitherto known. The violin and viola da gamba soloists of the Baroque indulged in excesses that rivaled those of the castratos; many of them—Simpson, Playford, Geminiani, and others—also wrote their improvisations down, and it can readily be seen that the results are a destruction of the original melody.

As the Baroque era waned, the ornaments went beyond melodic figures, extending the improvisational practice to harmony and rhythm and using free dissonances, while the composers, in self-defense, began to write out what was formerly left to the performers' discretion. In the slow movement of his Italian Concerto Bach wrote out the ornamentation in full. This is obviously a violinistic piece (though it is not a transcription), and the harpsichord with its evanescent tones can barely cope with the sustained melody. Aware that, because of this, the players would embellish every measure, Bach prevented them from going far afield by composing and fixing the ornamentation himself. I might add here that most ornamentation took place in slow movements; very little is said in the treatises about how to decorate fast movements. This is understandable when one considers that Baroque textures, notably Bach's, in fast fugal movements are dense, with lots of black notes and little daylight showing between them; if they are ornamented beyond a few fast trills, we are only adding dumplings to the minestrone. Indeed, in playing such movements, the performer's task is to minimize the density by clearly rendering the part-writing. Among many others, Domenico Scarlatti also preferred to write out the ornamentation. The wishes of such composers should be respected, because they have already taken care of the decorations—yet occasionally the opposite is true.

As we look at the vocal and instrumental ornamentation of Bassani, Bovicelli, and, even later, at the embellished examples of Geminiani, we wonder how a melody was recognized by the listener. The singers especially demanded opportunities for freely improvised outré passages and other embellishments, trills, and cadenzas to be inserted wherever possible, as something that was their rightful privilege; and if the composer did not provide them, they were always ready to produce the fireworks which the public, then as now, loved. Such unbridled liberties continued far into the nineteenth century. Angelica Catalani, the world-famous coloratura soprano, would overload her arias in Mozart's *Le Nozze di Figaro* with so much bunting of her invention that the critics spoke of "Mozart's Countess with music by Madame Catalani." (Incidentally, she had such a phenomenal technique that in her Paris concerts she would sing Rode's elaborate violin études without missing a note.) The luxuriant embellishments of the castratos, as has been mentioned above, had a nefarious influence on music for a long time to come. I must add, though, that most of the *evirati* were thoroughly trained musicians, versed in theory and composition, a quality demanded by the great singing teachers, and not a few of them were established and respected composers. Pier Francesco Tosi went so far as to declare that singers who did not belong to this highly trained upper echelon "have no right to improvise." This proviso surely applies to the majority of our singers today.

Now we come to French music, the ornamented style par excellence, that captured all Europe. Though practically forgotten in the nineteenth century, even in France, it is again highly appreciated today—the favorite at harpsichord recitals. Harpsichordists virtually live on it, as it is the most suitable medium for displaying the resurrected art of ornamentation. The origins of this style are instrumental and quite natural. One can observe in the early lute and keyboard transcriptions of vocal music how the instruments' particular idiom, ornamentation, and playing techniques are closely related, in that some of the figurations resulted from the physical possibilities of the use of the fingers. The genius of the instruments gradually asserts itself as instrumental music makes great advances; and the vocal elements are transformed to suit manual dexterity, just as the dance pieces changed rhythm and tempo. There are few styles in which idiom and tone are so uniform as in clavecin music; here the performer must really step in quite actively. Despite its elegance, the *style galant* (with significant exceptions, of course) is cold and hollow, thus in need of ornaments to cover the paucity of ideas; hence scarcely a note is permitted to remain naked. However, many of our harpsichordists carry this too far and overload the scant melodies with so many embellishments that they shine with the perpetual fluorescence of the shopping center. And if we examine the lute and keyboard compositions and intabulations of the late sixteenth and early seventeenth centuries, whether German organ music, French clavecin music, or English virginals pieces, we will see that the ornamental turns and runs soon became stereotyped and simply tacked on, not infrequently without any musical meaning.

Nevertheless, this represents a valiant groping for genuine instrumental writing, and we must accept the ornaments as a historical necessity; an intelligent and literate performer will always know how to stay within the natural needs of the music. The lute, a charming and delicate instrument, has a fugitive tone, and the gaps between intervals and chords had to be filled to maintain continuity; therefore an elaborate system of ornamentation was devised. The subsequent clavecin school took over many of the embellishments of the lute literature, adding to it a number of new ones of its own creation. This highly and incessantly ornamented keyboard style, carried everywhere by the popular French dance forms, induced the keyboard players of our day to redouble their attention to the art of ornamentation. The embellishments flow into one another like the bleeding colors of Madras cloth, while the melody drifts eccentrically in and out of focus. This *coquillage* is a skill that can be pocketed like a bunch of keys. Every keyboard composer all over Europe studied and used the tables of the agréments, the greatest of the age, Sebastian Bach not exempted. But Bach, as not a few other German composers, used the French systems of ornamentation when he turned to French dance forms, but not elsewhere This ornamentation of the clavecinists was genuinely "pianistic" and owes very little to the violinistic and vocal embellishments of the Italians; the French formulas are precisely stated, while the Italians preferred a freedom in selecting the jewels. Regrettably, Tosi, who in one way or another was the source of all writing on this subject, did not use musical illustrations in his original work of 1723. It was the editors and translators of the numerous editions of this basic work who furnished them, naturally with a good deal of bias favoring their national musical views, and therefore they cannot be used as documentation; one must make one's own translations. The Germans accepted both the French and the Italian systems and used them almost interchangeably, which can be very disconcerting occasionally. Also, they used the French abbreviations but often either misunderstood or misapplied them.

At the height of the style galant, ornamentation became the chief concern of composers and especially of performers; it virtually determined melody and harmony, and it was almost the sole means of expression. Every interval was bridged; trills and arpeggios were inserted in every nook and cranny; and a "sitting" note was seen as an abomination. At times we even notice that it is not a matter of the embellishment figures being superimposed on the musical stock, but that the line itself is designed from the outset so as to invite and accommodate the ornaments. The three principal essays of the age—those of Emanuel Bach, Quantz, and Leopold Mozart—combine this body with their own additions. We must read them carefully and critically, because they stand somewhere between the old and the new generation, and it is a mistake to accept their ideas and counsel as valid for the entire long span of the eighteenth century. They are very important sources but must be used with discretion.

In the meantime the growing popularity of the fortepiano, with its longer-lived sound which could be dynamically manipulated and the new accents that could not be produced on the harpsichord or the organ, compelled changes in ornamentation. Often these went back to older sources and do not apply to the post-1770 era; they are concerned mainly with the by then nearly forgotten ornamentation of earlier days, which makes some of them ambiguous. But they also deal with such subtleties as the *degree* of accentuation on the beat. They like to break up the harmonies into arpeggios, and the vibrato on the strings is used in our sense; there is also a manifest preference for short dissonant appoggiaturas. But every author warns about preserving the clarity of the part-writing; though, judging by their own compositions, they did not always practice what they preached.

Elaborate embellishments under French influence ruled unchallenged until the advent of the Classic era; in the second half of the eighteenth century there is a noticeable decrease in both the form and the purpose of ornamentation. The directness of the Classic style, as opposed to the style galant does not permit ornamentation without cause; any additions to the score must be subordinate to the whole. In this music every ornament is telling, even if on its own it has no meaning or importance. The composers began to integrate the embellishments into the running texture of the composition, and soon there was little leeway left to the performer; he was no longer a quasi-coauthor, because scores were meant to be performed as written. The decline in improvised ornamentation was especially noticeable in the reprise forms in instrumental music, which prompted Emanuel Bach to compose six sonatas "with changed [i.e. ornamented] reprises" as a model for those who lacked the skill to improvise. Still, improvisation in the form of fantasias remained alive, if somewhat standardized, and many such were performed as creations of the moment, though sketches were made in advance, even by the greatest composers. Here again Emanuel Bach was the flag-bearer.

Two new forms of improvised alterations of the written musical text which have recently acquired considerable attention, even popularity, with early music groups have evolved into a veritable battlefield of opinions, causing many sharp personal clashes. They were so widely known and practiced that the writers did not find it necessary to pay much attention to them. Not so today, and since they are deemed to be of extraordinary importance, perhaps we should single them out and examine them a little more closely.

The first of these, *notes inégales*, uneven notes, is a form of rhythmic ornamentation that was the product of the French Baroque. Given the great influence of French music, the practice reached other countries, notably England and Germany, both of which had able musicians studying in Paris and observing Lully, the dictator of French music, at close range. The device is not indicated in notation or by verbal instructions; it was so well known that composers indicated when they *did not* want it applied. Obviously, we are dealing here with a murky situation, because agogic accents, rubato, and notes inégales are really in the same camp and are interchangeable, used in, and valid for, all ages, because they are concerned with the most intimate manifestations of musicianship and taste. The practice of rhythmic alterations must have been ancient and ubiquitous, but we cannot make it a requirement, for it has always been variable and often has not been observed. We know, for instance, that Frescobaldi already demanded abundant use of rubato. The aim of all these practices was—and still is—to liberate the performer from "the rigors of the measure" for the sake of freedom of interpretation. Like agogic accents, notes inégales are expressive means, but their role is not mandatory, nor should the device be used with monotonous regularity throughout a whole work or movement. And in vocal music, it must be carefully watched whether its application accords with speech rhythm. Outside France the use of *inégalité* was by no means as widespread as in its country of origin. It is interesting to compare Lully's and Purcell's use of the device, which Purcell often wrote out in his scores. One soon realizes that while the principle is the same, the cadence of the English language demands subtle deviations from that of the French model. The modern performer should simply follow his own feelings and instincts when using notes inégales and not worry about historical considerations; but these feelings and instincts must be educated.

The second current ornamental fad is double dotting (*recte* over-dotting). Before the advanced Baroque style, it was undetermined, and though much research has gone into it, and even more fierce discussion, no uniform use can be established; nor do we know how far beyond the French frontiers over-dotting penetrated. To the committed fraternity each extra dot appears to be a major problem to which there is only one solution, and these solutions fill the critical reports of the new *Gesamtausgaben* and the musicological journals. There could not be precise time values in dotting any more than in rubato playing, because they depend on the rhythmic sense of the performer, who has every right to act according to his wishes. The execution of over-dotting was left to the performer's discretion; therefore we too are at liberty to use our own musical imagination. The composers used dotting freely and with no binding consistency, and they were not nearly so exercised by its problems as are many of our musicologists and performers. Dotting should mean *slight* increase, which lends liveliness to the pompous bass in the French overture; but the extension of over-dotting to all Baroque music is an egregious mistake. To quote a regrettable example of the extent to which some musicians go in applying over-dotting, even in styles that no longer admit the practice, a recent recording of *Don Giovanni* adds an extra dot to the bass notes in the overture at the passage which is an anticipation of the dramatic denouement in the second finale. Mozart deliberately used a heavy sluggish rhythm in the bass to indicate the doom-laden atmosphere and the ponderous gait of the Commendatore. The double dotting radically changes everything, and the "stone guest" seems to be hopping and skipping.

It is difficult to understand the fuss made about over-dotting, especially since the arguments started long after composers ceased to leave the performers in the dark about the rhythmic values in their manuscripts. The writers agreed that the French overture should be majestic, but how does a highly pointed rhythm make it so? On the contrary. Consider the overture to *Messiah*, which opens with flowing vaulted melodic gestures patently involving dotting; but if the dotting is overdone, the piece loses the flow and becomes jerky. Surely the rhythmic figures of old cannot be enforced and will be interpreted differently by different persons. Also, most of the theorists maintain—and rightly so— that the sharpness of dotted rhythm depends on the texture of the music, and frequently the written-out repetitions of such spots clearly indicate the situation.

The same is true of the appoggiaturas marked by small notes. They could be short or long, but the length cannot be determined from the notation; the player must watch the general texture and decide on his own. Appoggiaturas in vocal music, especially in recitatives were, in fact, not necessarily indicated in the score; they were so well understood, said Tosi, that the student "would laugh at those who mark them." Unfortunately, their use is still not understood by the average singing teacher and pupil. Endless chains of appoggiaturas in arias and recitatives contradict their intended effect. The singer must at all times take into consideration tempo, phrasing, and above all, the text, and must save the appoggiaturas for important words and phrase endings, but avoid any at all on unimportant words and at punctuation within phrases. There is nothing more annoying and musically and dramatically upsetting than a profusion of unmotivated appoggiaturas delivered with the same resigned groan, no matter what sentiment the words express. Indeed, there could not be any consistent or standardized use of them, for they depend on the performers' feelings and empathy with the composer's unexpressed thoughts. They should be shunned for the same reason that translations of the texts of vocal music from one language to another should, generally speaking, be avoided. Finally, I would like to show the tremendous sentimental and dramatic force even the shortest appoggiatura can have.

In the delightful duet "La ci darem le mano" in *Don Giovanni,* where the Don suavely tries to entice Zerlina to come and see his etchings, the peasant girl, disarmed by the dashing nobleman's entreaties, finally whispers her consent—*"andiamo"* ("let us go"). Mozart, with his uncanny dramatic sense and timing, saved the appoggiatura for the moment of decision, where surrender, eagerness, but also vague doubts, are expressed miraculously in three notes of a simple appoggiatura with unparalleled poignancy and feeling.

By reading the old theorists, students of performance practice would have come to accept the fact that the vibrato was one of a large body of ornaments and not a basic requirement of expressive music making. It has long since lost its character as an embellishment and has become a means of *normal* sound production. But we must touch upon it here because the question of its use was actually made into the Eleventh Commandment by the authenticists. We must protest not only because their proscription of the vibrato is not valid—there is no evidence to support the theory of its banishment—but we must quickly push through the thicket of terminology. Vibrato was also called *verre cassé* (in lute music), tremolo, *battement, Zittern* (trembling), *flattement,* close shake, *Bebung,* and so forth. All these terms, while they may cause confusion, obviously signify a desire to make the tone warmer and livelier. One would think that this aim is a fundamental requirement, a birthright; yet today's performance practice doctrine considers vibrato well-nigh reprehensible. We should rightfully denounce the tone of violinists of the old persuasion (many are still among us), but that does not negate the principle itself. Though almost all theorists used the many terms loosely, they did know the vibrato's essential role. Silvestro Ganassi, in his viola da gamba tutor (1543), allows that it is used "freely," while Mersenne in 1636 mentions *tremblement* as a powerful effect "to sweeten the sound." But the first and most important description and discussion of it appears in Geminiani's *The Art of Playing on the Violin* (1740 and 1751). He states that "the vibrato contributes materially to make the sound agreeable, and for this reason it *should be made use of as often as possible*" (my emphasis). Clearly, Geminiani does not speak of some new-fangled ornamental trick, but of an ancient device which, even when it was only "a very Neat and Pretty Grace" (Mace), was always used for expressive purposes.

A few years ago I heard a performance of Mozart's "Dissonance" Quartet by a well-established group of old music ascetics. The magnificent slow introduction was played with a total absence of vibrato and hence warmth and expressivity; the effect of the bold yet subtle dissonances caused by the gradual entry of the four instruments was lost as the glassy, uncommunicative, and noncommittal tone cast a deathly pallor over the eagerly converging texture toward a triumphal consonance. Incidentally, the quartet played on their Baroque instruments a work composed in 1785, not only long after the expiration of the Baroque, but at a time when the "modernization" of Baroque string instruments had already begun, to reach full swing in another decade. It must have been such a performance that made Ernest Newman, a highly literate critic, disgrace himself by declaring this wondrous gem of a piece as a "bad mistake and a poor example of composition" (*A Musical Critic's Holiday*, 1925). If the authenticists want to be consistent, they should play the clavichord without Bebung—a form of vibrato obtained by gently changing the pressure on the keys. This permitted expressive playing cherished by all keyboard players and produced what Bach and all the others wanted: expressivity and freely modulated sound.

I have already mentioned that the decline of excessive ornamentation did not take place in vocal and instrumental music at the same time, because the singers remained incorrigible; well into the Verdian era they routinely double-crossed the composer. The liberties taken by performers during the seventeenth and the better part of the eighteenth centuries would be inconceivable today. Yet there were always some strong-willed maestros who enforced the composer's rights—Lully, Handel, Gluck, Spontini, and Weber come to mind—and who knew how to keep the singers within bounds; but they were the exceptions. Conversely, there were also some who, lacking historical insight, refused to accept even a minimal form of ornamentation. Mahler permitted no appoggiaturas in Mozart's operas because "the score does not indicate any."

The elaboration of the da capo repeat in arias, which was the old singers' favorite spot for vocal acrobatics, caught the fancy of those who insist on authenticity, and the revived practice became *de rigueur* with them. To be sure, historically they are well within their rights, but it was this very reveling in passaggi, trills, and cadenzas which destroyed design, melody, and dramatic verisimilitude and which was among the main reasons for the demise of the opera seria. Now that we eagerly want to resurrect Baroque opera, shall we also resurrect the practice that killed it? How can we, living as we do in the final years of the twentieth century and lacking the extraordinary vocal prowess of the old singers, invent vocal ornaments in the spirit of those times? The patron saint of ornamentation, Emanuel Bach, earnestly imposes an obligation on the performer: he must be as well trained in composition and all that it implies as a professional composer. Surely very few of our singers and their ghost composers of ornamentation and improvisation can fulfill these specifications; they cannot, because for a long time this sort of thing was not expected of their profession. The da capo we hear today is usually bedecked with anachronistic musical platitudes grafted on great music, embellishments derived from heterogeneous sources optimistically gathered and applied. It is beyond question that these "historically correct" ornaments are bereft of any real value and sentiment.

Ornamentation is one of the most prominent aspects of performance practice; it is also the most intemperately discussed, as perfectly able, decent, and hard-working scholars and performers get into one another's hair with a vengeance. For this reason I should like to give a little selective historical aperçu of statements by distinguished musicians and writers whose warnings and admonitions for caution and reserve are seldom quoted.

Objections to excessive ornamentation were frequent in every epoch. Bernhard Schmid the elder, a Strasbourg organist and composer, published a book in 1577 on the "new and artistic arrangements played on the organ and other instruments," in which he recommends that "the art of the composer should be left unchanged, profusion of ornaments, especially when singing a solo above an instrument, can result in a situation whereby not a word is being understood." He adds that it is the *vulgari* who make such singers famous. Peri, in the preface to his *Euridice* (1601)—speaking of the great diva Vittoria Archilei, famous for her virtuoso embellishments—remarks that she used her "lively talent" to invent decorations "more to comply with the customs of our times than because she considered the beauty and force of singing to reside in them." In 1601 Viadana recommends "understandable accents" and "sparing use of embellishments," while in Marco da Gagliano's *Dafne* the author cautions against the constant application of ornaments and indicates the places where ornamentation is proper and where it should be avoided.

Proceeding to the next century, we find Mattheson warning that "too many embellishments should be avoided," and even Tosi, the arch-embellisher, advising restraint. François Couperin, the paragon of French composers, a truly great master before whose icon every harpsichordist burns a candle, sternly enjoins the performer neither to disregard his instructions for ornamentation nor to add to or alter the composer's original text. Similarly, Corelli demands in one of his concertos that the performer "play sostenuto and as it stands in the score." Jean Marie Leclair, in the preface to his Op. 9 Violin Sonatas (1743) is quite explicit on this subject: "An important thing, and one on which we cannot insist too much, is to avoid that confusion of notes which people add to melodic and expressive pieces." Most interesting and perceptive advice comes from Emperor Charles VI of Austria, one of those Habsburgs who were inept rulers but excellent and knowledgeable musicians. He gently admonished the great castrato Farinelli who, in the fashion of the times, indulged in elaborate embellishments and cadenzas: "Those wandering notes and passages only *surprise*, it is now time for you to *please*; you must take a more plain and simple road." Gluck, repelled by the embellishments used by his French predecessors, said: "Their operas are full of trills, runs and other inappropriate devices."

Emanuel Bach time and again warns against "lost clarity," especially when the accompanist goes as far as to engage in thematic imitation, insisting that ornamentation should never interfere with the logic of part-writing. Quantz also warns about meddling with melodies: "One should avoid embellishing melodic ideas of which one does not easily tire; similarly, brilliant passages which have a sufficiently pleasing melody in themselves should be left alone." Daniel Gottlob Türk, in his *Klavierschule* (1789), is full of protestations; he evidently witnessed too many shoddy improvisations and ornamentations and quotes some sorry examples. Francesco Algarotti, one of the most cultivated writers on music—a sort of Italian *philosophe*—protests in his *Saggio sopra l'opera* (1755) that "the brilliant *passaggi* improvised by the singers are so many impertinent interruptions of the musical scene." Christoph Nichelmann, one of Sebastian Bach's pupils and later one of Quantz's, in his treatise on melody (1755), again condemns the "unnecessary adornments" in vocal music. Charles Burney, the peripatetic historian, upon hearing a work by Lotti performed in Venice, remarks that "all was clear and distinct, no confusion or unnecessary notes." He also tells us about the Potsdam court where Frederick the Great had his royal house concerts for invited guests. "The King playing the transverse flute, always stands behind the *maestro di cappella*, in sight of the score which he frequently looks at, and if any of the Italian troops dare to deviate from strict discipline by adding or diminishing simple passages in his part, an order is sent to him next day *de par le roi* to deviate from the written notes at his peril." Elsewhere he reports that "the love of *gracing* is carried to such a pitch as frequently to change the passages from good to bad and from bad to worse. A little paint may embellish an ordinary face, though a great deal would render it hideous. True beauty is surely best in a natural state."

Finally, to round out the century, here is an observation by Mozart as critic of a fashionable violinist named Esser: "He plays well, but adds too many notes; he should play music as it is written." Beethoven once took Czerny to task for ornamenting his sonatas. Czerny, loyal to and fearful of the master, never forgot the tongue-lashing, and when his turn came to teach, held his pupils to the letter of the scores. Yet a hundred years later, Wanda Landowska, the grand old lady of "musique ancienne," recorded a Mozart concerto loaded with embellishments of another age.

Let us now turn to the larger aspects of improvisation. A precondition for any form of improvisation is the existence of a common musical language or dialect; but how are we going to recapture this common language hundreds of years later? Yes, we can recapture its spirit for performance, but no musician who is a product of the twentieth century can recapture it for *creative* purposes—we cannot think in an ancient "patois." Those compositions with a deliberately archaic tone and form called "Suite in the olden style" or "Tribute to Bach" are carrying their death sentence in their titles.

Musicians of the High Renaissance called improvisation *déchant sur le livre* (in English simply "descant") and *contrappunto alla mente* (mental, i.e., unwritten, counterpoint)—improvised parts placed against a given part. The theorists always considered this kind of counterpoint one of the mainstays of the art of composition, and in its most advanced form it could lead to substantial creations. But there are also innumerable documents to prove that, rather than being entirely invented on the spot, such improvisations were more or less planned. They may follow a very simple plan or pattern or delight with all kinds of "unexpected" turns or modulations, but their composers usually knew the outlines.

The simplest forms were the little cadenzas inserted at phrase endings and—as the term implies—especially at cadences. This is where present-day singers often fail. The Bellinian ornamentations and cadenzas used in the da capo arias of Baroque operas and even in those of Mozart are entirely out of place and style, and such grand opera tricks as shouting the notes in the final cadence an octave higher than written are not only silly but vulgar and offensive.

In instrumental music improvisation was extensively practiced on a larger scale, leading to some substantial forms. To satisfy the ever growing middle-class consumers of music, there grew up a theoretical literature in the form of practical manuals, of which I should mention two by Bach's student Johann Philipp Kirnberger, not only because of their explicit and amusing titles, but because they illustrate the temper and the social ambitions of the times. The first one is called *The Ever Ready Minuet and Polonaise Composer*, the other *Method of Tossing off Sonatas from One's Sleeve*. The system was a curious one, and we encounter it repeatedly, even with great composers. In a nutshell this is the procedure: Take the bass part of a composition and construct a melody over it. When done, remove the bass and compose a new one to suit the melody just obtained. The result is obviously an entirely new composition. (By the way, the sample piece Kirnberger composed for illustration is a very good one.) Now this may strike the reader as entertaining, which it certainly is, but it does hide a serious—though seemingly innocent—stylistic truth. However, we must be careful with epithets like "innocent" or "naive," because they may hide profound psychological issues as yet unexplored. The following example will illustrate this.

One afternoon the strolling Prince Esterházy dropped in at Haydn's tidy little house and told his favorite composer, "Make me a new symphony because I will have a dinner party the day after tomorrow." "Yes, your Grace," said the composer, and as soon as the prince left, he sat down to work on the new symphony. It was composed, delivered, and performed in two days. Now, one wonders how Haydn turned on the creative flow—more precisely, *what* turned it on for him? The proper answer would disclose how the great Classical composers approached their task, but for two hundred years musicographers have carefully avoided the question—except for Kirnberger. But his answer was so simple that no one took it seriously: "One chooses a few tones from different harmonies and, after having composed a few measures by this means, gets inspired." This is exactly the procedure followed by the Classical composers. They took a motif from the public domain and started to compose. In a few measures the lightning struck, and the everyday cliché blossomed into something entirely personal. The vast majority of the great sonatas, quartets, and symphonies composed between 1770 and 1830, which we treasure so much, are based on such snippets. The question is only how soon the *coup de foudre* sets in. With Haydn or Mozart, even two measures sufficed, though usually it happened at the first repeat of the motif, while with others it never came. Although these interesting musical byways are worth knowing, they are immaterial to our performers' immediate needs; but as we consider the larger species of improvisation, using for instance Handel's organ concertos or Mozart's piano concertos, our own performers are very much involved.

The solo parts of Handel's organ concertos are skeletal; the master played them himself in the intermissions at oratorio performances, and he knew what he was about. To a much lesser degree but for the same reason, Mozart's piano concertos contain occasional passages that are merely sketched in the solo part. Replenishing in Handel's concertos is patently more necessary than in Mozart's, because in his genial way Handel threw in anything that came to his mind; here we hear a little aria, there a dance piece, and one can never tell what unorthodoxy comes next, though many of the organ concertos are transcriptions of known original pieces. Here the caprice must be matched by imagination, which can be assisted by referring to the original compositions. Much more reticence is in order when it comes to Mozart's occasional lapses, because while the solo part in a concerto may be barely drafted in one line, the orchestra is always fully part of the game. All that the performer can do is to write in the bass line for the left hand, add a few harmonies—Mozart does not leave any doubts about the missing measures—but nothing more. People are always ready to help out genius in distress. The "completion" of Schubert's "Unfinished" Symphony or Mahler's Tenth is either a case of incredible arrogance or real naiveté; how can anyone believe that he can rise to the creative level of the great composers? At this writing, no one has attempted to "complete" the Venus de Milo by fastening new arms to her torso; we are glad to have her as she is and would not insult the memory of the great sculptor by practicing orthopedic surgery on his transcendent creation.

I have left for last a form of extensive improvisation: the free cadenza in the solo concertos. The idea of the cadenza is of vocal origin, once more the legacy of the castrato's art of virtuosity; it was taken over by instrumental music with the birth and rapidly growing popularity of the solo concerto. The practice of bringing the cadenza into a closer relationship with the composition itself, mainly by the use of thematic material taken from the body of the movement, started with Tartini. The six–four chord and the fermata indicated the place where the soloist can take off on his own. The idea of heightening the denouement by delaying it is a good one and worked well while the composer was his own interpreter, but with the advent of the traveling virtuoso, who was only a composer *malgré lui*, the cadenza became mere exhibitionism. Mozart would still improvise beautifully, but there are many cadenzas he explicitly composed, dating from years later—that is, when he realized that cadenzas by amateur composers just would not do. Some of the great concertos like the D Minor Piano Concerto have no original cadenzas from his hand and have had to be served by others. Many have been composed—among them those by Hummel, Beethoven, Clara Schumann, Reinecke, and Busoni. It would seem that the best choice would be Beethoven's cadenza; he was close enough to Mozart in time, and his is an interesting piece. But the Beethoven cadenza is not an improvisation; it is, rather, a commentary or exegesis already considerably removed in style and sound from Mozart. When the composers are gone forever, it is usually the pedagogues and virtuosos who move in, and only now and then a distinguished composer, who, however, is generations removed from the original master. Whether the performer tries to do something original or only imitates the original composer's style, we are invariably jarred by the interpolation of his own mind. It is not unlike the stylistic discrepancy in the architecture of a Baroque edifice which has received an extension in the nineteenth century. The great cadenza in Bach's Fifth Brandenburg Concerto may be the first written-out large cadenza, but then it was by the composer himself, and it organically completes the movement. Composers' distrust of cadenzas added by other hands to their works was manifest quite early. Tartini speaks of "natural" and "artificial" cadenzas, as well as of "erudite peregrinations."

There were also special compositions written for the purpose of inserting them into concertos as cadenzas, which of course had no connection whatever with the compositions into which they were planted but served only the performers' purposes. Locatelli's Opus 3, a dozen violin concertos (1733), included a collection of capriccios for this very purpose. Yet the composers became more and more restive about the alien cadenzas which clashed with their concepts, and they began to withdraw the license formerly granted to the performers. In his G Major Piano Concerto Beethoven wrote over the fermata "the cadenza should be brief." In his last concerto, the Piano Concerto in E-flat, he did not permit the addition of any cadenzas, making brief ones himself which are integral parts of the composition. To make sure that his intentions would be well understood and to prevent the performer from having different ideas, he brusquely admonishes the performer: "Make no cadenza here but attack instantly what follows." After Beethoven, composers generally preferred to *compose*, not improvise, their cadenzas, or let others improvise them. The ideal models are Mendelssohn's cadenza for his violin concerto, and Schumann's for his piano concerto.

Nevertheless, we are left with many fine concertos without cadenzas, so we must take care of what has become a traditional formal and stylistic fact. This can be done tactfully and tastefully if we follow such models as Bach's written-out cadenza in his E Major Violin Concerto. It is very brief, yet it admirably fulfills its role. Since it is unreasonable to expect a modern musician to write a period piece which would accord with the long-departed composer's wishes and fit his personal style, a few simple passages—just enough to appease the six-four chord and the fermata—are sufficient; the sooner the composer of the cadenza yields to the creator of the concerto, the better it is for all concerned. It is high time that all nineteenth- and twentieth-century cadenzas by Joachim, Reinecke, Auer, Busoni, and others were abandoned. Our younger pianists and violinists should have the courage to disregard these anachronistic relics and substitute their own cadenzas. The modern cadenza should be short, and particular attention should be paid to its beginning and end, so that it starts organically and leads naturally to the final tutti. The eighteenth-century concerto is not a monologue; the orchestra, notably in Mozart's works, is an equal partner. An extended cadenza will disturb this equal partnership which is an essential formal and compositional factor.

But what about the few chords between the first and second movements of the third Brandenburg Concerto or those in Handel's Opus 7? Do they call for improvised slow movements? They probably did. But if so, who would dare to provide such a thing today? Any self-respecting and well-trained artist would simply leave them undisturbed, or at most extend them to a mini-cadenza.

"The trouble with ornamentation is not that there is too little information available but that there is too much," wrote Thurston Dart. Indeed, the tables and instructions left by many theorists and composers have been raked over by innumerable modern writers and performers, but this large literature requires skeptical scrutiny. Take the "big five": Couperin, Tosi, Emanuel Bach, Quantz, and Tartini. After studying their statements thoroughly, we become aware of many discrepancies and contradictions; it is impossible to bear in mind all the instructions and distinguish between the various exceptions, prohibitions, and recommendations. If performers were to take an unmarked *Urtext* and enter all the embellishments found in these treatises, they would realize that they cannot play the piece for want of room left for the composition itself.

We are constantly referring to the "creative" contributions to the written score, but in truth what we are doing is repeating and varying well-established and standardized figures and patterns. The system of ornamentation was already well stereotyped in the first Attaingnant prints of keyboard music, as it was in the Fitzwilliam Virginal Book; and as for the agréments of the clavecinists, they were not only standardized but predictable: any musician could apply them almost mechanically. The old composers and performers had the *Zeitstil* in their bones and showed versatility in manipulating common materials with originality. Present-day performers are largely dependent on what the musicologists hand down to them, and they can use their imaginations only within certain limits. They are in double jeopardy, for if they are docile partisans and accept and carry out all the embellishments strictly according to the "book," they may earn only the plaudits of their coreligionists; if they assert their own musicality and clip and choose, they may be denounced as nonconformist. Their problem is how to survive without surrendering their musical souls. It is a sad irony if performers yield to amateur historians without asserting their rights: they make the music they want to resurrect die for a second time—"It dies of ennui," says the great historian of violin music, Marc Pincherle. Fortunately, there are more and more intelligent and judicious artists who know that their allegiance must be *to the composition* alone.

Our studies show us that in any given period there was more than one way of performing music, more than one musical dialect and idiom, and that styles overlap and can feed on one another. After all, Palestrina and Marenzio lived and worked in the same city of Rome, and Pergolesi died before Sebastian Bach reached the zenith of his art. Modern performers should be aware of this and question such ornaments as have disappeared long ago and if revived may strike us as nonsense. Take, for instance, the *trillo*, which refers not only to what we ordinarily take the term to mean, but also to a particular vocal ornament that became fashionable around 1600: the repetition of a single note, beginning slowly and gradually becoming faster. It never sounds natural, and it was characterized in its own time as "more a goat's bleating than singing." I have heard it a couple of times at concerts when the singer wanted to be very authentic, but struck me as a person in distress and about to give up his dinner.

Those, like Locke or Avison, who decried the "fantasticall and unnecessary extravagances of performers," considered unrelieved "gracing" the denial of the meaning and purpose of ornamentation, which is to relieve monotony, assist phrasing and articulation, and preserve vitality when the continuity slackens. If we sprinkle jewels on every bald note, we create a new monotony, and what we see is the glitter that conceals the music. We cannot approach the art of ornamentation purely via historical facts, for the artist is God's mouthpiece and the guardian of his mysteries. Performing artists must transliterate atavistic formulas into their own language, so that their living music will accept them as its own property. Above all, they must not permit interpretation to degenerate into routine, or ideas to freeze into doctrinal techniques and obscure the radiation of the composer's imagination. Ornamentation can— and must—be expressive; it has a wide range of moods and colors and should not be a hothouse where artificial heat warms pale flowers. We do not have to fill in the gaps everywhere and round off all corners, leaving no single note untouched. The indications for embellishments were never seen as being compulsory; we should not be afraid to dispense with them if we feel that they are not needed. It is incumbent on performers to use their freedom to prevent loosening of the construction and to guard against embellishing music already ornate in character. They must serve as architectural aides to the composer, protect the purity of the form by not permitting the frame to overwhelm the picture, hone away all superficial trimmings, prevent giving the impression of a mosaic the individual pieces of which do not quite touch—the edges must always be clean. In this spirit they will escape truculent elegance—indolent gracefulness in which the ornaments are like fallen petals.

Allegory and Symbolism in Music

Because music is not verbally accountable, a special language of metaphors and symbols had to be created to carry its messages. Now we have arrived at the most esoteric and arcane part of the aesthetics of music, and one which is of particular importance to critics and performers.

Everything we utter, even simple sounds, is expressive of something; the question is how these expressions are understood by other persons. All manner of forces, energies, tensions, and relaxations emanate from music, but they can be apprehended only symbolically.

We are well acquainted with such symbols as, for instance, the cross for Christianity, the sword for the military, or the flag for the nation; these and many others are used by all of us, and their meaning is clear to everyone. But a symbol in music is an arbitrary coupling of two disparate elements, a more or less concrete idea with objectless music, the aim being that music will absorb and convert the idea. However, unless grossly and forcibly imitative in a pictorial fashion, the idea remains idea, and the music remains music. An idea is an idea only when it can be formulated in words, but musical ideas can be formulated only in tones. "Symbol" is a term applied to a visible object representing to the mind the semblance of something that is not shown but realized by association with it. The symbol is an indispensable tool of thinking, and a knowledge of theories concerning symbolism and its conveyance is of essential value to the performer. These theories went far beyond mere imitation and descriptiveness, influencing design, texture, and sound.

A musical symbol is the result of a correlation between an idea expressed in the text or the title of a work and the technique of composition. It can be graphic, at times perceptible only in the notation, or it can be a musical substance, a melodic or rhythmic pattern, an *idée fixe*, a leitmotiv, or a cantus firmus whose original text is known, as in a chorale prelude. Symbolism is a mode of substitution, of figurative expression; things are not represented directly but by means of expressive signs that are in themselves something other than what they mean. The problem is obviously the relationship of sign and meaning, as these two diverge. Music, especially what is considered "old" music, is often steeped in allegory, symbolism, and "text interpretation," all of which require a mental act by the performer and the listener. Such symbolism can be understood, misunderstood, not understood, or missed altogether, yet the music does not become senseless when we miss the symbols. We are dealing here with the transference of a concrete idea or notion to a musical constellation following music's own nonconceptual, autonomous laws. The more extensive such symbolism, the more it lends itself to varying interpretation, and distant symbols are understandable only after much study.

It is for this reason that old and unfamiliar music is difficult to experience even to those who can decipher the symbols. Symbolism in music can be visual or aural or a combination of the two. It can palpably reveal feelings and moods, but it can also be totally abstract, not detectable to the naked ear, and thus wasted on the uninitiated listener. In this connection the most important thing is that a musical symbol does not define its object unequivocally, because music lacks the capacity for representation; the idea no longer lives for itself. It is dissolved in music, though perhaps it can suggest a mood. If concrete meaning is to be conveyed, extramusical glosses must be added. As a matter of fact, even if no symbolism was intended, the listener can still attribute symbolic meanings to the music he hears. Although vocal music can be innocent of expression of feelings, and instrumental music can be no more than a play of muscles and fingers, nevertheless, in both instances the performer, the listener, and even the historian can invest it with various symbolic meanings. On the other hand, what has symbolic meaning to the composer may not appear so either to the performer who interprets the music or to his audience. Melody is usually able to create the feeling of an experience even if no object of reference is indicated. The types and degrees of symbolism change with the times, but it appears that symbols are never entirely absent in music; they belong to music's nature and essence, as do style and form, and thus constitute a genuine category of understanding that cannot be ignored by the performer; nor can it be peremptorily dismissed, as it was by the Neoclassicists.

The types of musical symbols can be established and distinguished when we combine symbol, effect, and object of reference. The idea of motion lends itself most easily to musical representation both visually and aurally; and of course the arrangement of pitches on the staff can convey motion. In Bach's chorale prelude "Out of the depth I cry unto Thee," the melody soars in rising intervals. In Handel's oratorio, Joshua bids sun and moon to stand still; the magnificent scene is represented almost graphically as all voices and instruments stop for a moment in their tracks; yet the impression is also purely musical. However, notational symbols can turn into what is aptly called "eye music," for only by *looking* at the graphic image of the notes can we perceive the intended meaning. Black notes can stand for death or mourning, the sharp sign (in German *Kreuz*, 'cross') can represent the Crucifixion, and long-held notes or chords can symbolize sleep or eternity, and so forth. Persons unacquainted with music history may not realize why Christ's recitatives in the Bach Passions are accompanied by quiet, stationary string chords, but Bach knew that the *ombra* (shadow) scenes of the old Venetian opera used this device in accompanied recitatives and arias whenever the text depicted death, or passing, the nether world, ghosts, or impending catastrophe. These scenes were popular from Cavalli to Gluck (*Orfeo*) and Mozart (*Idomeneo*), and contemporaries were well aware of the references.

In the fifteenth and sixteenth centuries, especially in the riddle canons of the Netherlands composers, graphic symbolism was carried to extremes, though some of the Franco-Flemish composers' graphic tricks, like the so-called cordiform chansons, whose notation was arranged so as to outline the shape of a heart, are engaging. Then there is a variety of symbolism which we may call demographic, when a known form or rhythm is extended to encompass the people of a whole region or nation, like the Venetian barcarole, the Polonaise, the hornpipe of the English, or the Viennese waltz. And there is naturalistic imitation of birdcalls, of thunder, of a rippling brook, and so forth. These symbol types have their own history: some survive, others disappear, some survive with altogether different connotations, some characterize an entire epoch, others the style of a particular composer only. Even when symbols are universally understood, they can soon be forgotten, for the symbols of one era can easily become strange with changing cultural currents. At times the symbols cf one style period can be taken over by another, and when the tradition is strong, symbols can have a remarkably long life. Chromaticism, especially the falling chromatic line within the compass of a fourth, which expresses sorrow or pain, survived from the sixteenth to the twentieth century. But we must also bear in mind that history tends to level symbols to conventions, with all associative meaning lost. Indeed, all symbols are the result of convention, of a general agreement, a form of intellectualization, which makes it very difficult for the performer and listener distant from the time when the convention was common knowledge to receive and experience these *fables convenients*. Finally, several caveats must be mentioned. When Mattheson speaks of "depicting the affections," he does not mean a musical rendering of them, but figurative analogies which are produced by the intellect. "It is necessary to realize," says Manfred Bukofzer, "that the affections which Baroque theoreticians discuss are not identical with our feelings, they are rather to be described as a group of typified and fairly static attitudes of mind represented by corresponding figures." And these figures have been stereotyped to such an extent and have become so remote to us that all we see are certain musical configurations that occur again and again.

As we have seen, the musical tone can become the basis for an allegorical type of symbolism and thus acquire meaning by way of nonsounding subjects. This type of symbolism is easily apprehended once its meaning is made clear by visual illustration or verbal hints, as in program music; but now we come to a form of symbolism that goes far beyond these simple images: the wholly abstract symbolism of numbers.

By the term "numerology" we understand the musical exploitation of symbolic—usually biblical—numbers and any kind of arithmetic patterning. The repetition of a tone or motif can symbolize a corresponding number of ideas or persons, examples being the representation of the Trinity by a motif consisting of three notes or the Ten Commandments by ten notes. The correspondence and connections between tones and numbers have intrigued all high civilizations, and they were connected since ancient times with the concept of the order of the universe, and of course numbers are eminently suitable for rational organization. Several questions intrude here: To what extent were musicians acquainted with the doctrines of numerology? Did they understand, for instance, Bach's admittedly ultra-abstract and sophisticated use of it? And, especially, how does the application of numerology affect perception, design, performance, and plain musical sense and enjoyment? The first of these questions can readily be answered. The use of biblical numerology was not only known and practiced by Flemish and German composers, clumsily by journeyman musicians, with ingenuity and mastery by the great composers; it was systematically taught, and there was a considerable literature on the subject, because numerology was also used in the other arts. Among many others I cite the widely used textbook by J. J. Schmidt entitled *The Biblical Mathematician* (1736). Werckmeister, the famous acoustician, was also an influential authority on the application of biblical numbers to music. Unfortunately, the composers' intended symbolism may be lost on the listener, interpreted differently by the performer, and still differently by the scholar. The subtleties are often not manifest to the listener and are discovered only by painstaking study of the score and the text, because the symbolism is intrinsic, unconcerned with physical likeness; its imported material brings its meaning with it but does so not by any resemblance between symbol and object, rather solely by prior association, which may be totally private, at times not even detectable unless in some way we stumble on it. Still, while it is difficult to do so, some of these things can be unraveled.

In cabalistic numerology the letters of the alphabet are given serial numbers: 1 for A, 2 for B, and so forth, with the aid of which words, names, ideas, even sequences of them, can be expressed in music by using a corresponding number of notes or measures, points of imitation, entries of themes, and other ways. Bach used a signature B-A-C-H at times in notes (the German H is our B natural) but more often in cabalistic numbers: B is 2, A is 1, C is 3, H is 8 in the alphabet, which adds up to a group of 14 notes. To use his initials J.S.B., he needed 41 notes. What matters, and what the examples quoted illustrate, is that by means of a carefully constructed network of numerical references and allusions, Bach was able to use numbers in a manner in which they express his "signature," his personal profession of faith (Credo = 43), and his purpose in writing a work. If the composer accepted the ancient belief that the Almighty created the world according to a numerical pattern, then the composer's use of such patterns in his own creative work becomes an *imitatio Dei*; he too strives to create order out of chaos. Ever since antiquity and the earliest Christian universities, music was taught as one of the mathematical sciences, and the universe was considered structurally identical with music. The astronomers usually explained the cosmos in musical terms, and Rudolf Wittkower, in his great work on Renaissance architecture (1969), proved that, beginning with the fifteenth century, the mathematical theory of music became the source for architectural proportions. But—and this is a difficult thing for us to swallow—all this mathematical theorizing concerned the *idea* of music divorced from its sound; it was Christian musical mysticism that endeavored to combine idea with sound.

We have come to realize that numerical proportions play an important part in this music, which makes the understanding—though not necessarily the enjoyment—of many works of the past very difficult. Ever since the discovery of this secret art, scholars have been trying to penetrate the minds of these composers, notably that of Bach, who said little about his art. The questions raised are inevitable and have not yet been fully answered. To what extent was Christian symbolism in conflict with natural, commonsense musicianship? Was it a pious rationalism, a deliberate endeavor to represent articles of faith, the word of God, in such hidden meanings?

Noticing that in order to buttress their theories, Baroque writers invoked and applied the rules of poetic and rhetoric to music, the better to render the meaning of the affections, modern music scholars hit upon the idea of harnessing similar procedures for the purpose of analysis and interpretation. Around the turn of the nineteenth century they borrowed from theology a kind of exegesis called *hermeneutics,* which they applied to musical analysis, thus creating a new approach to aesthetics and criticism. The writings of Albert Schweitzer, André Pirro, and Hermann Kretzschmar were enthusiastically received, Schweitzer even winning popular success. The scholars were justified in their quest for a workable system of analysis that would carry them past the prevailing mode of scholastic harmonic and formal analysis, and they appreciated the older philosophical, rational, and symbolic approach. The aim was to endow music, down to single intervals, with concrete affective meaning. They also remembered what Heinichen, one of the ablest eighteenth-century writers, declared, that "the expression of the affections is the *finis musices."* Indeed, all writers emphasized the desirability of translating the feelings and passions into organized sound. In the hands of responsible scholars, the new hermeneutics should be a legitimate form of interpretation. Regrettably, when associating ideas with music, there is an obvious temptation to find parallels a little too readily and to allow more weight to imagery than it deserves, leading to almost unbelievable excesses as even reputable scholars presented with grave seriousness and with an actuary's respect for minutiae the most farfetched spiritual interpretations of innocent musical passages. No wonder popular musicography found this kind of analysis, in which anything goes, a powerful—and lamentable—incentive. Hermeneutics turned the symbolic into a system of cognitive interpretation, seeing behind every melodic or rhythmic figure and every modulation some deep hidden truth.

Against this we must oppose the many instances in which the composer ignores his own hermeneutical intentions or indications and does so deliberately in order to safeguard common musical sense. When Handel did not like the lyrics in an aria, he went ahead by picking out single words or lines, shifting the musical emphasis to them with exquisite inappropriateness, thus literally double-crossing his librettist's poetry and images. Close examination of the music and texts will, in many instances, show that the whole process of associations is rather trifling, while in others the reputed hermeneutical contents are to a considerable extent artificial reconstructions after the event. Finally, when we consider an immensely complicated work that is the incarnation of "absolute" music—*The Art of Fugue* or the *Grosse Fuge* come to mind—we get nowhere with hermeneutics; to represent something that is ideally indistinct is a contradiction in terms.

Anton Schindler, Beethoven's amanuensis, relates that when Beethoven was asked the meaning of his D Minor and E Minor Sonatas, he answered: "Read Shakespeare's *Tempest.*" A number of able scholars reread *The Tempest* with much attention to any possible clues but could find none; yet Arnold Schering, the distinguished pioneer investigator of the history of the oratorio and the concerto, built an entire book on the interpretation of this anecdote and on the titles of books found in Beethoven's library. Even this *ne plus ultra* was later surpassed by Ilmary Krohn's work on Bruckner, in which literally every measure in the symphonies was given a lengthy exegesis.

Once we enter the field of musical symbolism and hermeneutics, we are on uncertain ground and may lose our sense of what is possible and what is not. As we have seen, some distinguished scholars and musicians carried their interpretations to absurd lengths, while others, from Hanslick to Stravinsky, summarily rejected the whole thing as being foisted on music. Yet the arguments directed for and against hermeneutics are hard to contradict, and the questions are difficult to answer. Indeed, what mental associations, if any, does the so-called parody Mass of the Renaissance evoke in us? Constructed from materials taken from another polyphonic composition, the parody Mass is an incredible *tour de force*, yet many of Palestrina's and Lasso's greatest masterpieces are parody Masses—how can they be interpreted hermeneutically? Or, to quote another example, surely the *chanson fricassé*, a popular version of the French Renaissance chanson put together from a multitude of snippets culled from dozens of sources, could not even evoke associations, because the loaned bits of music alternate too rapidly to register on the mind as alien goods; it takes strenuous detective work to discover the sources. Then there is the case of the *contrafacta*, the "counterfeit" pieces, in which the original text is replaced by new and entirely different words without altering the music. The famous medieval farce *Festum asinorum*, the "Donkey Mass," has a fine melody to the text "Out of the Orient there came the Donkey," which in the nineteenth century was turned into a Protestant hymn; Bach, in the *Christmas Oratorio*, gives the Blessed Virgin a song with which previously Pleasure had lulled Hercules to sleep; and the magnificent chorus "For unto us a child is born" (in *Messiah*) was originally a delightful and slightly erotic Italian love-duet. Such transfers are numerous and are still practiced, but then what happens to the original meaning of the symbols? How can we explain such extreme cases as that of the graduals for the nuptial Mass, *Uxor tua sicut vitis abundans*, and the Mass for the dead, *Requiem aeternam dona eis Domine*—both have the same melody!

Interpretations of the textures and designs of the layers of symbolic suggestions often prove to be mere plot synopses of imaginary events. Then again we may notice a vacillation between figuration and abstraction, a deliberate obscurity, and the elements of imagery are seen no longer as unequivocal signs but drift as floating metaphors to a symbolic generality applicable anywhere. The affections and humors cannot be conjured up, converted into a musical configuration, and then conveyed to the listener; but by establishing conventions, as was done in the Baroque, a conscious recognition can be achieved, even in textless compositions. However, these conventions are not stable: they are passing, their significance changes, all of which vindicates Hanslick.

Well, we may smile at much of this, but make no mistake, it is a serious matter, for we must not forget that at one time these fantasies were honest attempts to make the essence of music understandable. We cannot summarily dismiss them, despite their being highly speculative, pronouncedly individual, though romantically warm, and at times endearingly or annoyingly silly; but caution, moderation, and good common sense and taste must govern their use. (The old movie house pianist, whom those of us old enough may remember vividly, was an expert practitioner of musical symbolism.) We must also realize that most of this symbolism is lost forever; but above all we must realize that while it is incontestably true that all symbolism was conceived intellectually, its aesthetic impact is the prominent reaction evoked in the listener—that even explicitly programmatic music can and should be "more the expression of feelings than painting." In the end it is always the listener's response and imagination that gives meaning to musical symbols.

Scholars and performers are puzzled no end by one seemingly inexplicable phenomenon: this music, whether parody, contrafactum, or loaded with borrowed materials and extramusical symbolism, is nonetheless naturally flowing and euphonious, without the slightest hint of its heterogeneous sources and extramusical connotations. It never loses its poise and equilibrium, its purposefulness, its ironclad discipline, its concentration, and its severe organization; yet at the same time it is pure and enjoyable. How should it be performed to do justice to it with respect to music and convey its extremely complicated background and ideas? To increase the puzzlement, this kind of music not only falls pleasantly on the ear but is not lost even on the lay listener because our innate musical sense catches its integrity: we hear the solemn pomp of the smoothly gliding parody Mass; the multifaceted chanson fricassé strikes us like freshly poured champagne; while the Credo of the B Minor Mass is imposingly majestic despite its heavy ballast of numerology. Our experience has taught us that music inevitably has psychological and affective radiations, whether intended or not, and though the Enlightenment wanted to place music under the aegis of reason, it could not stifle its affective power and the priority of purely musical processes even in the most "cerebral" compositions. I still owe the reader an answer, an explanation of how this incredible mastery and perfection is achieved—at least I will try to provide one.

Advocates of historical authenticity and accuracy in performance practice seem to believe that by reviving old instruments, inserting ornaments and cadenzas wherever possible, inegalizing the egals and dotting the dots, they have accounted for everything necessary to consummate authenticity. They take pains to track down the history of every instrument used in their performance and print the list in their program notes as vital information for the listener. But they seldom deal with problems of aesthetics. Thus the miracle of the palingenesis of old music escapes them, and ignorance thereof affects their performances. The answer to the puzzle is the sovereignty of the métier. I am not speaking of the basic Fachlehre that every musician must learn in order to be able to put music together and how to acquire a reasonable technique of composition, as indeed very good technique can be acquired by able musicians in this fashion; but this technique of "setting" is always conditioned by socioeconomic and cultural trends. What I am speaking of may perhaps be called a "meta-technique" that transcends ethical, social, and pedagogical parameters. This is the organic union of spirit, style, idiom, and form with the unfathomable creative force in which everything from the outside world is filtered out. The technique, the craft of composition itself, becomes a symbol that transcends the world of appearances. Philipp Spitta has already observed that time and again the scholar reaches a point in his study of Bach's works beyond which he is unable to proceed. Robert Lewis Marshall, in his remarkable work entitled *The Compositional Process of J. S. Bach* (1972), touches upon this inability to penetrate fully into the last recesses of a genius's mind with these honest and insightful words: "Scholars are reticent to be drawn into the seemingly metaphysical realms of genius, inspiration, fantasy, and so on, which seem to belong more properly in the domain of the psychologist if not that of the poet and philosopher." The incredible mastery of those Renaissance musicians who composed parody Masses, the *ouvrier* perfection, raised the craft of composition to the status of high art by itself. The composers admired and respected one another, expressing their appreciation in dedications, eulogies, funeral motets and cantatas like Ockeghem's motet on the death of Binchois or Couperin's *L'Apothéose de Lully*. Another sign of homage was expressed when a composer borrowed materials from his brethren. This sanctification of the métier crossed the centuries, which once more leads us to Sebastian Bach, always the focal point when we ponder "old" music. There were few in the history of arts and letters more profoundly, more constitutionally steeped in the métier and its symbolic use—and with greater consequence—than Bach—except perhaps Dante. I cite the great Italian poet for comparison because both he and Bach lived in the world of symbolism, and they themselves became symbols.

When a philosopher talked volubly about the celestial bodies to Diogenes, the latter asked him, "When did you come back from heaven?" The performing artist may ask similar questions of the hermeneuticists when confronted with the task of making this symbol-saturated music part of our living heritage. He knows that the impinging of the performer's personality on the *sounding* music creates an entirely new situation. The conclusion is inescapable that symbolic representation in music is valid and vital, but that it is successful only when it *coincides* with the logic of the musical process. How this coincidence is achieved is one of the secrets of the creative process to which Marshall alludes. How do Bach's tremendous visions and profound experiences, the arching Baroque pathos, the blaring trumpets and rolling drums, accord with the cabalistic numerology of the Christian mystic? Bach was certainly not in a trance when he composed the Credo of the B Minor Mass; he was always on top of the situation, and his awesome mastery of the métier and musical intelligence never slept. Did he shuffle the notes until the required number for Credo (43) was reached? No, because the ever present and vigilant possession of his meta-technique, a technique beyond the purely technical domain, took care of it. One might contradict this by saying that he certainly must have made preliminary sketches. Granted that all composers make sketches—Beethoven made enough of them to fill a number of volumes—but there are some who did not rely on many sketches, they composed "in their head." Bach and Mozart were of this kind. (The many little unfinished pieces in Köchel's catalogue are not sketches but torsos; when Mozart realized that his plan would not materialize the way he expected, he simply abandoned the piece and started anew or on something else.) Whenever Bach reached the stage of committing to paper what he had worked out in his head, there was no hesitation and little need for corrections. (It was of course another matter when he revived an old piece or arranged a Vivaldi concerto; then the full weight of his critical faculties was exerted.)

Whenever a musician is called upon to perform one of these symbol-laden works, he must realize that the minute the symbols are converted into actual musical sounds and thus become audible musical reality, totally different from the allegories they were supposed to represent, they become his property, for it is he who carries out the metamorphosis. He must be aware of the composer's intention as expressed in the symbols, because they will influence him in a subtle and unconscious way; but he must direct his total attention to the musical *results* created by the symbolism; *he cannot play or sing the symbols themselves*. Indeed, when he tries to indicate or clarify the symbols or their sources, as for instance by playing the chorale tune in a chorale prelude with neon-light registration, he will fail artistically, because he will destroy the music's equilibrium. But if he places all his abilities at the service of the music, when he divines that a certain pattern of so many notes is Bach's very personal confession and is not intended to be conveyed in some fashion by the performer to the listener, he will achieve that indefinable blend of the performer with the spirit of the composer of which Wordsworth said

> There is a dark
> Inscrutable workmanship that reconciles
> Discordant elements, making
> them cling together.

Postscript

The long career reflected in these essays offers the critical observer a picture that is complex yet equally clear and impressive. To the question once asked by a neophyte, "What is Professor Lang's speciality?," there could be only one answer: "Comprehensiveness." His interest combined far-flung aspects of the musicological spectrum, and he was devoted to safeguarding flawless professionalism as much as to addressing a vast readership.

The German editor who invited the opening article of this volume—written originally as a contribution to a Festschrift for the president of Bären-reiter Verlag, Kassel—received it with both delight and surprise. Lang, one of the most sought-after authors for the planned volume, had long refused but finally given in (with a congenial "You win"). Yet the nature of the text he sent was in no way expected. Characteristic was the editor's comment: "He seems to say, people should write more books like his"—books addressed to the general public as well as to the specialist. In a way, that impression was quite right. Lang, true to his role as supreme critic, though with unvarying tact, had availed himself of the occasion to educate even the most distinguished publisher representing the discipline of musicology.

The graduate student who entered Lang's seminar was apt to be as surprised as the German editor. Instead of the expected atmosphere of rigid discipline, what developed seemed to resemble, rather, a casual conversation. Topics of pressing importance were everywhere to be found—in yesterday's performance as much as in an issue of a supposedly strict curricular nature; Lang distrusted the discipline as it was practiced. On the way to the first session of an introductory seminar, he picked up from a new display of textbooks in the university bookstore one entitled *Music*. To the students ready to learn from its pages, he explained that this was to be considered not a text but a pretext. They were indeed meant to study its contents, but as critics rather than disciples. His concern for musicology became as comprehensive as his choice of inquiries. In the 1930s the word, still largely attached only to his name, had to be defined and defended. Fifty years later it had to be rescued from threats of dilettante abuse.

The need to deal in this volume with the several orientations of Lang's work precluded a chronological arrangement of selections, as it did an entirely categorical division of approaches. The latter would have violated the very comprehensiveness of Lang's scholarly nature, the element that necessarily had to remain a guiding thought in the presentation of his writings. Nor did the choices made from his writings lend themselves to the nature of editorial commentary that one might expect in a book of scholarly studies.

Yet a progression from early to middle and late years can be generally recognized. Lang's activity underwent a decisive change when he added his work for the daily press to his academic duties. Covering a period from 1954 to 1963, it did not, in fact, end then. It merely shifted from concert to record reviews, less frequent but more extensive. Nevertheless, it was here—especially in view of the remarkably widened market which developed with innovations in record production—that he realized the need for the scholar's judgment. It continued even when his interest turned to what, as he realized, would be his last book, a project that occupied him for a long time, beclouded by the gradual loss of his sight. As the project grew beyond his direct control, its insecure state became the reason for his—quite clearly—perceived plan for this collection.

Throughout his career, he was invariably ready to illuminate any subject with fresh insight. In the anniversary years 1956 and 1970, he was the author who presented to the readers of *The Musical Quarterly* a novel summary of greatest artistic personalities in history. But with the same ease with which he presented the pictures of Mozart and Beethoven, he liked to speak of current issues. The story of Bartók's only formal appointment in this country was entirely founded in his personal intervention. His was the voice of warning in the popular storm over *Amadeus*. He offered critical comment to the fumbling small-town scholar as well as to the White House. Yet it was never to be forgotten that the critical comment came from the knowledge of a writer who had placed the history of music into the framework of Western civilization and the history of Handel's work into the framework of the entire culture of the composer's time. And it was a point of great pride with him that *Music in Western Civilization* was in as great a demand by colleagues in the field as it was by those in other faculties.

Lang was not infrequently criticized for his dual role, but though he spoke, with his ever-ready critical judgment, of "steam-shovel musicology," he remained the scholar who could cut to the core of the most minute detail. His comprehensiveness made him both the revolutionary avant-garde spokesman and the conservative moderator. In taking on the task of his Handel biography, he realized that he had to deal with two deep-seated prejudices: one German, the other English. The reader, who might have expected new, particular items of information, was instead presented with a new basis from which to view the entire artistic personality. With a few strokes, Lang explained to the scholars assembled during the 1979 New York meeting of the American Musicological Society, at a first American panel devoted to Handel scholarship, that only a totally fresh appraisal could do justice to the subject.

When *Die Musik in Geschichte und Gegenwart* was completed, it proved, after careful search, that no one but this scholar could say the last word, could summarize the challenge of what was an encyclopedia rather than a dictionary. And his final turn to the subject of musicology as well as to that of performance practice was guided by the conscience of unique authority, by that of the guardian who saw that both were threatened from two sides. Just as he had had to stem the dangers of ignorance in his early years, so he later had to deal with those inherent in the proliferation of musicological studies; and when he entered, at a late date, the discussion of historically informed performance, it was the threat of the amateur musicologist of which he became once more fully aware. Musicology and performance practice had become "popular," and what seemed needed was the voice of the scholar who had been their advocate in the first place.

The heterogeneous sources of this book tell their own story, offering a documentation of the author's rare many-sidedness. This becomes all the more enlightening because throughout he remains the scholar of shining distinction, a mentor to whose influence his century remains in debt.

Index

Index